# CALHOUN AND POPULAR RULE

# Calhoun
## AND POPULAR RULE

The Political Theory
of the
*Disquisition* and *Discourse*

H. Lee Cheek, Jr.

UNIVERSITY OF MISSOURI PRESS    COLUMBIA AND LONDON

Copyright © 2001 by
The Curators of the University of Missouri
University of Missouri Press, Columbia, Missouri 65201
Printed and bound in the United States of America
First paperback printing, 2004
All rights reserved
5 4 3 2 1   08 07 06 05 04

Library of Congress Cataloging-in-Publication Data

Cheek, H. Lee.
  Calhoun and popular rule : the political theory of the Disquisition
and Discourse / H. Lee Cheek, Jr.
      p.   cm.
  Includes bibliographical references and index.
  ISBN 0-8262-1548-3 (alk. paper)
  1. Calhoun, John C. (John Caldwell), 1782–1850. Disquisition on
government.   2. United States—Politics and government—Philosophy.
3. Political science—United States—History—19th century. I. Title.
JK216.C16 C48 2001
320.01'1—dc21                                        2001027422

®™ This paper meets the requirements of the
American National Standard for Permanence of Paper
for Printed Library Materials, Z39.48, 1984.

Designer: Stephanie Foley
Typesetter: BOOKCOMP, Inc.
Printer and binder: Thomson-Shore, Inc.
Typefaces: GillSans, Palation, and Sabon

The University of Missouri Press offers its grateful acknowledgment for a generous contribution from the Earhart Foundation in support of the publication of this volume.

*For Howard "Red" and*
*Ann Clinch Cheek*

*Kathy Braun Cheek*

# CONTENTS

# PREFACE

John Caldwell Calhoun is usually recognized as one of the main figures in American political thought, but most observers attempt to minimize the philosophical significance of his work by arguing that Calhoun was merely a champion of sectional interests or that his ideas were antiquated even during his lifetime. This book will suggest that Calhoun was in fact a seminal political thinker who spoke not only to his own time and place, but also to the modern world. We will show that he had a coherent, systematic view of human nature and society and made a lasting contribution to constitutional and democratic theory. He also made a notable attempt to reconcile the need for popular rule with the ethical preconditions for its survival.

Calhoun's critique of majoritarian democracy forms part of a philosophy of humankind and politics that has relevance beyond the American experience. Calhoun's idea of popular rule was original, but was related to earlier attempts in America and elsewhere to limit the power of the majority and to protect minority interests. As we shall see, Calhoun stood in the American political tradition and attempted to rearticulate some of its central elements for coming generations. In the ensuing pages, we will explicate Calhoun's idea of the concurrent majority and examine how it has been presented both by his critics and by his supporters. We will compare Calhoun's ideas to those of Jefferson and Madison, as well as to the more legalistic and unitary constitutionalism of other nineteenth-century political thinkers. We will also relate Calhoun's thinking to current theories of popular rule.

This book will attempt to examine Calhoun's views of popular rule as part of an integrated philosophical whole. It will bring together for the first time the political theory of the *Disquisition* and *Discourse*

ix

and will show that Calhoun offers a theoretically vital rearticulation and extension of the American constitutional tradition. Calhoun's theory of constitutionalism and popular government makes explicit and further develops elements that were already prominent in the U.S. Constitution of 1787. Calhoun was not a political or philosophical aberration, but an authentic exponent of American constitutionalism.

Calhoun's understanding of the need for ethical-political restraint and for institutional means for obtaining concurrence is especially relevant to the present situation in the Western world, marked as it is by growing ethnic and cultural conflict and social fragmentation.

*Cleveland, Tennessee*
*All Saints, 2000*

# ACKNOWLEDGMENTS

This book was made possible through the assistance of many kind souls. For years Professors Claes G. Ryn, David Walsh, and Steve Schneck have served as my guides and mentors. Professor Ryn assumed a major role in my maturation as a student of political theory and American politics.

My initial interest in American political thought was encouraged by my professors at Western Carolina University—Al Gilman, Gordon Mercer, Bill Latimer, Cliff Lovin, Steve Ealy, and Max Williams. While I was a student at Duke Divinity School, Stanley Hauerwas and Will Willimon were helpful in many ways. The advice of the late Russell Kirk was critical in my decision to pursue a study of Calhoun's political thought. George Carey and Jim McClellan have been more like older siblings than mentors to me during the last decade, and I am forever indebted to them for their support.

In the course of researching and writing this book, I was blessed with the kind assistance of phenomenal friends—Tim Goodman, Tim Sifert, David Hockett, Constantine Gutzman, Clyde Ellis, Clyde Wilson, Larry Toll, Mark Farnsworth, Don Pace, Jerry Ray, Doug Weaver, Harry Bayne, Brad Frazier, and Ruth Ediger.

Clyde Wilson, Constantine Gutzman, Harry Bayne, and Tim Goodman are due special thanks. As the longtime editor of *The Papers of John C. Calhoun* and the world's leading authority on the Carolinian, Clyde was an inspiration by example. This project would have been impossible without his friendship, tutelage, and encouragement. Conversations with my dear friend Constantine Gutzman were invaluable—and his criticisms aided every aspect of this book. My pal and former colleague Harry Bayne offered much sage advice about the South and answered my countless questions on a variety of subjects. Tim Goodman has been a model friend and colleague for two decades, and he never let me neglect my academic chores.

My students at Western Carolina University, Brewton-Parker College, and Lee University also deserve a special note of appreciation. They helped me develop the themes of the "effort" in many ways. Casey Cater of Brewton-Parker College assisted in the preparation of the bibliography, and I am most grateful to him for his kind labors and philosophical acumen.

Richard Spencer Cheek deserves an expression of gratitude for encouraging his older brother to undertake a study of Calhoun. Grants from the Wilbur Foundation, the Institute for Humane Studies, and the Earhart Foundation provided me with the opportunity to prepare the manuscript for publication. I must also express my indebtedness to Bev Jarrett of the University of Missouri Press for her diligent labors on my behalf; her associates, Michelle Niemeyer, Jane Lago, Gloria Thomas Beckfield, and Karen Caplinger, were also very helpful.

I owe my greatest debt to my parents, Howard "Red" and Ann Clinch Cheek, and to my loving and indefatigable wife, Kathy Braun Cheek. Had it not been for their love, support, and toleration of my neglectfulness in many regards, this book could never have been completed. It is a great honor and pleasure to dedicate this work to my parents and my wife.

# CALHOUN AND POPULAR RULE

# Calhoun and the American Political Tradition

In her 1990 presidential address to the American Political Science Association, the late Judith Shklar urged the redemption of American political theory from its "petty intellectual squabbles" and "ideological combat" of recent decades, while encouraging a rekindled emphasis on the imaginative study of the American tradition of theorizing about political life.[1] Such an invitation begs the revisiting of neglected and maligned sources of the "tradition" by arguing for a departure from the norms of recent scholarship, as well as a new willingness to encounter the richness of American political theory undeterred by previous models of textual, historical, and philosophical exposition.

One means of overcoming the various academic barriers to authentic historical and philosophical reflection in the field of American political theory can be found by exploring the self-understanding of the citizenry. The process of self-interpretation is the result of a quest for ultimate meaning, and the search usually ends with a turn to the divine, transcendent basis of history and a shared experience. Throughout American history, this quest for explaining and explicating the historical and philosophical foundations of American political thought has continued to unfold.

The place of American self-understanding and its progression towards a greater complexity and completeness belies a simplistic explanation. In addition to the pioneering work of Willmoore Kendall and George Carey, several important recent studies have also succeeded in applying this approach to American political

---

1. Judith Shklar, "Redeeming American Political Theory," 3.

thought.[2] These studies by Gregory Butler and Jürgen Gebhardt assume a related and coherent framework for expressing the growth of
the American political self-understanding, albeit from a point of view
that suggests that a unitary model of interpretation is adequate for
explaining the complex and multifaceted world of early national and
nineteenth-century political thought in America.

This book offers the possibility for the presentation of a greater
philosophical depth of field within the corpus of American political
thought, as well as a more complex framework for understanding the
regime than previously acknowledged or articulated. The purpose
of this work is to probe the tensions of existence manifested in the
political thought of a representative of the generation of Americans
who attempted to translate the Founders' worldview to the nineteenth
century. The tensions of the new century would bring this articulation
of the political order under increased scrutiny and would encourage
aberrant interpretations of the republic's political existence.[3] Accordingly, the task of defining and elucidating the salient contributions
of the period is always subject to lapsing into a deformative manifestation of the tradition, distracting and ultimately undermining
the project at hand; however, this work attempts to avoid such a
pitfall by stressing the persistence of a particular vision throughout
the Founding, Early National, and Jacksonian periods of American
political thought, as expressed in the works of John Caldwell Calhoun.
We also contend that Calhoun was one of the preeminent leaders in
the extension of the political tradition of the Founding in the first
half of the nineteenth century, which should enhance the existing
understanding of this worldview, as well as the emerging diversity
and continuity of the tradition itself. In American political thought,
however, the foundational search and presentation of this vision continue to assume a distinctly New England flavor.

The significance of New England, and more specifically the Massachusetts Bay settlement and subsequent political developments, in
American political thought is not being disputed here. Moreover,
the understanding of political authority that arose from this early
colony forces the theorist to search for other experiences to approach

2. Willmoore Kendall and George W. Carey, *The Basic Symbols of the American
Political Tradition;* Gregory S. Butler, *In Search of the American Spirit;* Jürgen Gebhardt,
*Americanism.*
    3. Irving H. Bartlett, *The American Mind in the Mid-Nineteenth Century;* Charles M.
Wiltse, *The New Nation, 1800–1845;* Eugene D. Genovese, *The Slaveholders' Dilemma,*
46–75; and Charles Seller, *The Market Revolution.*

a wholeness of understanding regarding the sources of the country's political authority. The New England "experiment" provides students of American political theory with a useful application inherited from a number of sources, but nurtured by their particular variety of Christian doctrine and polity. All aspects of the American political, religious, and social experience, as well as the resulting vision for politics, are usually attributed to Puritan New England. The historian Sydney Ahlstrom argues that the "Puritan ethic" of legalistic moral strictures, and a doctrine of labor as serving and pleasing God, became the American ethic.[4] And in the hands of the Puritan divines, the "ethic" became incorporated into their understanding of politics, nourishing New England political thought and influencing the Founding generation by providing a way of understanding the unique nature of the American political experience. The contribution of John Winthrop and Roger Williams, among others, remains important in the development, even though the early interpreters were supplanted by others who offered the prospect of refinement.

The consummation of the New England experience was the development of a civil theology based upon the special status of the American regime. America was regarded as the "New Israel," an expression of similarity with the biblical and historical narrative modes of expression. America's situation in the pantheon of world political history was understood as unequaled. The regime was special, a providential gift offered to the world, a city on a hill, a light amidst the darkness of political despotism. The transcendent aspects of American civil theology served a rememorative purpose, providing a basis for appreciating the generosity of the Divine while also looking to the future. The increasing importance of the "Jeremiad," a New England theological and political sermon based upon a recollection of bygone blessings and with strategies detailing how a recovery of the past might come about, became the basis for a recapitulation of the earlier vision, albeit with some dramatic changes in emphasis, including the support of revolutionary actions that were more properly understood as acts of reclamation.[5] Kendall and Carey present the New England political self-illumination as originating in the Mayflower Compact (1620), the

---

4. Sydney Ahlstrom, *A Religious History of the American People*, 1090. Mark A. Noll's *History of Christianity in the United States and Canada* offers an important new presentation of American religious history, emphasizing the role of Catholics, Baptists, and Methodists during the Founding and Early National periods.

5. See Friedrich Gentz, *The French and American Revolutions Compared*.

Orders of Connecticut (1639), and the Massachusetts Body of Liberties (1641). Donald Lutz augments this initial survey by demonstrating the contributions of early covenants and state charters, and those of later manifestations of the development, including the Connecticut Charter of 1662 and the Rhode Island Charter of 1662, as these interpretative models developed into state constitutions of one variety or another. Such important contributions as these advance our approach of stressing the continuity of experiences underlying a developing understanding of popular rule.[6] In an attempt to depict the continued elaboration of theories of popular rule, most scholars portray the Declaration, the Constitutional Period, and the Bill of Rights as the successors of the early manifestations of the American understanding of the concept. Presenting the American political tradition in such a manner boasts many merits, but it is not without its limitations. The minimization of significant portions of the evolving political tradition must follow, if such an approach is taken. This book charts a different course, namely, to explore an aspect of the richness of American political experience usually excluded from the "canon" of established texts, and suggests that the entirety of American contributions cannot be appreciated without the inclusion of all its parts, even those considered outside the normative collections.

The understanding of popular rule, exhibited in the colonial documents to the early charters, provides fertile material for this book, although our concern is primarily with the transference of experience from the settlement and Founding periods to the mid-nineteenth century. From the earliest movement of American political thought, an important bifurcation in the conceptualization of popular rule can be observed and is of great importance to the transmittal of understanding. Alongside the development of the self-interpretation of New England, there arose a less dogmatic and more explicitly pastoral presentation associated with the other great colonial settlement, Jamestown. The Virginia colony, nearly simultaneous in date of origin with the Puritan Massachusetts Bay colony, shared a related history and many related aspects of political development, while also exhibiting distinctiveness. This book appropriates the developing understanding within the South Atlantic colonies as mirroring New England in possessing a revelatory component of central importance. These colonies also offered many persistent particularities of interpretation that influenced

6. Kendall and Carey, *Basic Symbols*, 30–60; Donald S. Lutz, *The Origins of American Constitutionalism*.

the self-understanding of political order within the South Atlantic political tradition, and that continue to inform contemporary politics in the United States.

The English and South Atlantic tradition produced a political understanding different from the New England version.[7] Instead of the tendency to endorse a theocratic and unitary form of political order, the South Atlantic experience accommodated divergent theological and political understandings of order and sought to nurture an ecumenism grounded in the acceptance of dissent and a diffusion of political power. With an application of religious tolerance both related and dissimilar to John Locke's formulation, the South Atlantic colonies tended to accept a diversity of views within a Hebraic-Christian worldview, without providing a great advancement in development from earlier sources.[8] Due more to the spirit of a rising tide of evangelism deeply influenced by Arminian theological precepts than a pure application of Lockean notions, the South Atlantic colonies tended to question the role of the civil magistrate as moral arbiter. As Locke argued, "[T]he care of souls cannot belong to the civil magistrate"—the perfection of virtue and godliness were "inward" quests that could not be forced upon an individual, but were dependent upon a deeper, spiritual transformation. The absolute division between secular and religious authority was not the issue, although it would increase in volatility during the Founding period and the early nineteenth century.[9] Liberty was conceived in terms of its corporateness, a *societas*, combining the family and larger units of an interconnected citizenry with each other to form associations. Instead of using the rigorous moral codes found in New England, the South Atlantic colonies were more dependent upon the English model of ecclesiastic and civil subsidiarity, relying on representatives nearest the situation to provide order and preside over the settlement of disputes. As this book suggests, the political and social developments within the South replicated an English cast founded upon a spirit of

7. Fletcher Green, *Constitutional Development in the South Atlantic States, 1776–1860.*

8. See Francis Butler Simkins, *A History of the South*, 13–27; Wesley F. Craven, *The Southern Colonies in the Seventeenth Century*; Donald G. Mathews, *Religion in the Old South*; and Robert M. Calhoon, *Evangelicals and Conservatives in the Early South, 1740–1861.*

9. John Locke, *A Letter Concerning Toleration*, 18. As an example of localism within a worldview imbued with Christian symbolization, one could find in the Virginia House of Delegates in 1784 many representatives who supported Jefferson's disestablishment efforts while also affirming a "general assessment" tax for spreading the Christian faith. See Thomas E. Buckley, *Church and State in Revolutionary Virginia.*

localism in theory and practice. For example, the movement towards "establishing" state-sponsored churches met with great success in New England, while in the South a decentralized theory of control and the habit of localism in matters of church and state insured a greater autonomy and forbearance among the associations of the faithful and governing authorities.[10]

The New England and South Atlantic communities shared a political worldview that encouraged a community of a sort that remains unappreciated by many interpreters of American political thought.[11] However, the Southern colonies had already begun a different and equally important development of popular rule before the introduction of slavery at Jamestown in 1619. The political quest commenced in earnest during the early period of colonization, as the emerging planter and yeoman classes looked to the past as a means of understanding the future, incorporating a preexisting political worldview and adapting it to a new and difficult environment. Instead of refining a teleology that identified the promised land as the final goal of a self-understanding, the South Atlantic colonies participated in an understanding guided by an appreciation of the transcendent working within history—and the need for the continued, prudential development of society. As M. E. Bradford posits, the South Atlantic "spirit" looked to Eden after the Fall as a model, with "the best of the gifts of this life," and anticipated that a fruitful social and political existence was possible only when "pursued with prudence, energy, honor, and regard for a wise prescription." The implantation of the "garden" as a metaphor for explaining how the Southern understanding differed from the New England version deserves our attention. Contrary to the New England understanding of precision in all social and political arrangements, the Southern worldview identified the ancient imperfections of a civilization with the need for an enduring pattern of improvement and refinement within human nature.[12] A society grounded upon the rock of such a prescriptive development of political thinking was less likely to be consumed by ideological deformations of its understanding; conversely, it was also more reluctant to submit to a reformation of defects in the preexisting worldview

10. Mathews, *Religion in the Old South,* 1–38.

11. For a useful exception to depicting "individualism" as the great impetus for the development of American political thought, see Barry Alan Shain, *The Myth of American Individualism,* 22–47.

12. M. E. Bradford, *A Better Guide Than Reason,* 174; Eric Voegelin, *Anamnesis,* trans. Gerhart Niemeyer, 136–40.

inherited from previous generations. Distant and overbearing sources of political authority were not easily accepted and were viewed with skepticism. In the long struggle within the development of the South Atlantic worldview, a distinct version of the regime was articulated that was incompatible with the New England presentation, but shared its original design for the diffusion of political authority. From the colonial period we can witness the beginning of two divergent understandings of the reality of politics and popular rule, prompting historian Nathan Hatch to suggest that at some point in the development of the two great regions one "could draw upon precious few common traditions in defining their Americanness." John Randolph, cousin of Thomas Jefferson and an influential model of statesmanship for Calhoun, could defend the extraordinary position of an inherited Southern worldview in response to a confidant's query about his attendance at a religious gathering:

> I was born and baptized in the Church of England. If I attend the Convention at Charlottesville, which I rather doubt, I shall oppose myself then and always at every attempt at encroachment on the part of the church, the clergy especially, on the rights of conscience. I attribute, in a very great degree, my long estrangement from God to my abhorrence of prelatical pride and puritanical preciseness; to ecclesiastical tyranny. . . . Should I fail to attend, it will arise from a repugnance to submit the religion, or church, any more than the liberty of my country, to foreign influence. When I speak of my country, I mean the Commonwealth of Virginia. I was born in allegiance to George III; the bishop of London (Terrick!) was my diocesan. My ancestors threw off the oppressive yoke of the mother country, but they never made me subject to *New* England in matters spiritual or temporal; neither do I mean to become so, voluntarily.[13]

Within the South Atlantic region even as eccentric (and brilliant) a representative as Randolph could be appreciated as the defender of the verities of a mode of understanding that relied upon the reclaiming of a preexisting order while recognizing the need for imparting

---

13. Mark A. Noll, Nathan Hatch, and George Marsden, *The Search for Christian America,* 110 (also see Nathan Hatch, *The Democratization of American Christianity*); *The Papers of John C. Calhoun,* ed. Clyde N. Wilson et al., 14:88 (hereafter cited as *Papers*); John Randolph to John Brockenbrough, September 25, 1818, in *Collected Letters of John Randolph of Roanoke to Dr. John Brockenbrough, 1812–1833,* ed. Kenneth Shorey, 21.

this understanding with particular attention to a rapidly expanding republic.[14]

Randolph affirmed, as would Calhoun more elaborately two decades later, the vision of a moral regime focused upon the idea of
subsidiarity (or localism) in political and religious concerns. Subsidiarity as a means of dividing public authority and political power
and perpetuating the republic was dependent on the virtue of the
citizenry within the states. Contrary to criticisms offered regarding the
philosophical progenitors of Calhoun (especially those of an Antifederalist cast), virtue was of great importance to their understanding of
political order. It required a sustained effort to inculcate virtue and to
allow each generation to hear the "voice of tradition," Patrick Henry
urged. If the witnesses expired without fulfilling the need to "inform
posterity," social and political life might suffer the consequences of
such a collective loss of memory and purpose. Although Calhoun
did not define himself explicitly as an Antifederalist, he imbibed
Antifederalist political theory from his father, Patrick Calhoun. As
a member of the South Carolina House of Representatives, Patrick
Calhoun opposed the work of the Philadelphia Convention on the
grounds that it had sacrificed liberty to protect the regime. The elder
Calhoun would also impart his concern regarding the prevention of
revolutionary changes to democratic mechanisms to his son, who
would come to champion the older constitutional limitations upon
popular rule.[15]

As Michael Lienesch suggests, the Antifederalists urged a spirit
of inhibition or prudence towards accepting too quickly any radical innovation that deserved comparison with the Federalist plea
for immediate action to maintain the regime. Antifederalists were
neither a monolithic response against the prospects for ratification
of the Constitution nor a remnant of irredentist elements from the
earlier conflict with England. Instead, the Antifederalists accepted
the imperfections of the Articles of Confederation concerning governmental authority while advocating many impediments to the dangers
resulting from what George Mason decried as "the natural lust of

14. See Robert Dawidoff, *The Education of John Randolph;* and Russell Kirk, *John
Randolph of Roanoke: A Study in American Politics.*
15. Patrick Henry, "Speech Before the Virginia State Ratifying Convention, 5 June
1788," in *The Anti-Federalist,* ed. Herbert J. Storing, 309; see Rachel N. Klein, *Unification
of a Slave State.*

power so inherent in man."[16] As members of a political movement, the Antifederalists shared a similar problem with the representatives of the South Atlantic tradition who came to exert political influence a generation after the ratification of the Constitution: "[T]hey spoke in too many voices." The advances of recent scholarship force a reconsideration of the Antifederalist critique of the Constitution and encourage a reaffirmation of the enduring value of their criticism of popular rule. Instead of being portrayed as hapless liberal theorists who failed in their effort to defeat the Constitution, the Antifederalists should more appropriately be understood as offering a profound and enduring criticism of the Constitution and American politics. The Federalists won the ratification battle, but not necessarily the war for the soul of American politics. Herbert Storing, encyclopedist of the Antifederalists, aptly suggested that they represent a consistent "echo" throughout American history, and that the dialogue between the Federalists and the Antifederalists is where "the country's principles are to be discovered."[17] Even though the Antifederalists were an assortment of representatives with many theoretical and geographical differences, they were united by an unwillingness to accept consolidationist measures, regardless of the form, and an insistence upon protecting a decentralized, group-oriented society, as defined in a variety of ways. But neither the Antifederalists nor Calhoun can be adequately fathomed simply by noting their negative response to particular issues; on the contrary, both the Antifederalists and Calhoun were part of a clear republican understanding of the nature of the American regime. Quite distinct from the "puritanical" republicanism of New England, this second comprehensible "stream" of interpretation assumes an "agrarian" character. Forrest McDonald describes the similarities between the two republicanisms as resting primarily upon a defense of the moral nature of the republic. While the New England version stressed purely moral solutions to the problems of maintaining civic virtue, the South Atlantic or agrarian persuasion

16. Michael Lienesch, *New Order of the Ages*, 141; George Mason, quoted in *Federalists and Antifederalists*, ed. John P. Kaminski and Richard Leffler, 43.
17. The "too many voices" quotation is from Joshua Miller, *The Rise and Fall of Democracy in Early America, 1630–1789*, 83. Herbert J. Storing, *What the Anti-Federalists Were For*, 72. Storing's praise should be understood within the context of his general skepticism of the Antifederalists. He believed that the Antifederalists' failure was the result of their "weaker argument" (71). Storing's analysis tends to agree with the earlier, problematic criticisms of Max Farrand, Cecilia Kenyon, and Gordon Wood.

offered institutional means of providing for a virtuous republic.[18] This presentation of two clearly demarcated strands of republicanism within the American political tradition allows for a fuller delineation of the tradition that Calhoun would come to represent in American politics a generation after the Founding. An account of the flowering of two patterns of republican political thought also distinguishes itself from the normative presentation of a seamless republicanism at the heart of the Founding and ensuing political thinking, although most commentators ascribe radically different origins to their respective republican genealogies.[19] The collapse of the influential "Republican synthesis," commonly associated with the scholarship of Bernard Bailyn, Gordon Wood, and J. G. A. Pocock, suggests the need to explore the importance of a South Atlantic republicanism separate from the larger movement. On the other hand, the demise of a unitary theory of republicanism should not lead to the devaluation of the concept. Republicanism properly understood as a means of codifying the complex political theory of the Founding remains integral to the development and explication of popular rule. Although beyond the scope of this study, the problem of discerning the foci of the two strains of republican thought remains an important field for scholarly investigation.

This study attempts to understand Calhoun as a representative of South Atlantic republicanism, as well as an original political thinker whose thought challenges the "mechanistic" epistemology usually ascribed to the agrarian tradition. As chapter 2 will indicate, a world-view was bestowed upon Calhoun's generation by many influences, and Calhoun understood himself as participating within this mode of interpretation. For Calhoun the recovery of a proper mode of popular rule was dependent upon a return to the self-understanding of the older regime; such a goal could not be accomplished without revisiting and expounding the "primitive principles" and experiences of the Founding generation for a new day.[20] Calhoun devoted his life to this task, and the *Disquisition* and *Discourse* are the most profound examples of his attempt at recovery and self-understanding, reframed for a nineteenth-century America that was consumed by new challenges.

18. Forrest McDonald, *Novus Ordo Seclorum*, 76–78, 71.
19. Compare Robert E. Shalhope's "Toward a Republican Synthesis" with his later essay "Republicanism and Early American Historiography" for an account of the demise of a composite republicanism.
20. *Papers*, 10:407.

For Calhoun and South Atlantic republicanism the overwhelming practical and theoretical inheritance was established upon an appreciation of the necessary limitations of social and political life. Primary among the means of limitation was the need for societal and personal restraint when faced with the possibility of radical transformation.[21] While change and social mobility were not the most commonly acknowledged aspects of Southern society, neither were such considerations beyond the pale of possibility. As an articulate representative of agrarian republicanism during the first half of the nineteenth century, Calhoun could present an Aristotelian mean as the basis for installing an element of restraint in the operation of government. If government could not be restricted, the regime would necessarily lose a sense of liberty and the populace's role in governing would be greatly diminished. Government, with its use and abuse of power, must become more moderate, or suffer its eventual demise:

> . . . we must hold it as a fundamental maxim, that the action of Government should, with our growth, gradually become more moderate, instead of more intense, a maxim resting on principles deep and irreversible; and which cannot be violated without inevitable destruction.[22]

The quality of restraint was instilled and encouraged by a vast number of sources, including the works of antiquity, the treatises of Christian authors, and the genius of the Founding generation. Living within a society aware of its constraints, Calhoun also appreciated the limits of human experience, acknowledging the shortcomings of his own perspectives and holding utopian schemes in disdain. The necessary balance between the need for popular participation in the government and the need to avoid the potential excesses of popular rule guided Calhoun's philosophical mission. In this regard, Calhoun's political theory should be understood as a reflective journey towards recovering genuine popular rule amidst the national crises that occurred during his career as a statesman and political philosopher.

21. Calhoun's complex understanding of the role of slavery as a "political institution" within Southern society cannot be separated from his defense of communal life (Calhoun to Richard Packenham, *Papers*, 18:278).
22. "Report of the Select Committee on the Extent of the Executive Patronage," February 9, 1835, *Papers*, 12:424.

Due to the complexity of Calhoun's experiences and inherited worldview, and his own psyche, discernible policy formulations were not always the result of his theoretical labors. Consequently, Calhoun has often been criticized for his "metaphysical" approach to politics. Instead of dismissing Calhoun on the grounds that he at some junctures did not conform to the mold of a "practical" political thinker, this book seeks to appreciate and explicate his principled disavowal of efforts to diminish the Western tradition's attachment to individual and social responsibility in an effort to seek the deeper truths regarding political life as a means of preserving the republic. Calhoun and the South Atlantic experience present a political theory girded by a doctrine of restraint that would develop into a collective self-understanding that was grounded in a moral obligation to restore the regime to its original principles. In a letter to his friend and erstwhile political supporter James Hammond, Calhoun reflected, "I have been actuated and sustained solely by a sense of duty."[23] Today, the centrality of Calhoun's devotion to the preservation of an inherited worldview and its explication for a new generation of Americans serve as the hallmarks of his thought. To appreciate Calhoun the political theorist one must first attempt to examine the several currents of criticism of his political theory, and to distinguish the contribution of this book from the tangled web of Calhoun's critics and admirers.

## A TENOR OF DISCONTENT: CALHOUN AND HIS CRITICS

The legacy of Calhoun as a political theorist remains an issue of great debate. Unlike normal patterns of criticism in which one encounters early formative critiques disputed by subsequent revisionist efforts buttressed by new research, assessments of Calhoun's position as a political thinker have not benefited from a systematic advancement of scholarly knowledge. For example, the original disputes over Calhoun's political theory during his lifetime continue, although with greater complexity and without consensus, among contemporary theorists. Calhoun's incisive commentary on American politics raised the most important issues and concerns within the American historical experience to the forefront of national concern, as well as provided new insight on many counts. Many of the implications of his thought

---

23. Calhoun to James Hammond, November 27, 1842, *Papers*, 16:555.

for contemporary politics are neglected today, but the philosophical and historical questions Calhoun pondered are of perennial interest to Americans and the world. Liberty, freedom, equality, sovereignty, popular rule—it is difficult to contemplate the major theoretical concerns that have preoccupied Americans without considering Calhoun's contribution. While many studies of Calhoun's political theory have appeared, almost all of these works neglect his interpretation of the proper mode of popular rule, and his connection with the political theory of the Founding generation. What is of greatest importance here and to the legacy of Calhoun as a political theorist is the evolving self-understanding of the Carolinian as he faced the exigencies of political life. As we examine his political thought as contained in the *Disquisition* and *Discourse*, we will argue that Calhoun made a lasting contribution to American political theory in many ways. Most important, his rearticulation of the South Atlantic republican worldview for a mid-nineteenth-century generation removed from the experiences and insight of the country's primary actors facilitated an advancement in political life and the survival of the republic. It is precisely Calhoun's understanding of the nature of political experience that figures most prominently in his worldview and distinguishes his political theory during the Age of Jackson. His principles serve as the philosophical foundation for a theory of politics, one that is of importance to a larger audience because it frames a notion of personal and societal restraint as an alternative to imprudent modification and dissension. And Calhoun's conception of restraint within political existence was more important to his own understanding than to the perpetuation of any particular regime.[24] When such an understanding is presented, Calhoun can be appreciated as a political philosopher of great importance for the modern world.

In rediscovering Calhoun, we shall overview some of the most important appraisals of his political theory. The direction of most academic work has been to portray Calhoun as a source of a derailment of rather than as an important contributor to the American political tradition. Many of these authors have relied on previous scholarship without examining Calhoun in his totality as a political thinker. Some resourceful scholars attempt from time to time to place Calhoun studies in groupings based on the critics' theses. Most commonly, critics label Calhoun as a conservative, a pluralist, a radical, a class

24. "I would do any thing for Union, except to surrender my principles," Calhoun wrote in a letter to B[olling] Hall, February 13, 1831, *Papers*, 11:553.

theorist, or a classical republican. Classification of Calhoun's political theory, especially on the basis of original sources, countermands this placement of Calhoun within rigid "paradigms" or interpretative models. Clyde Wilson, editor of Calhoun's *Papers*, has summarized the predicament in this way: "The literature does not so much progress as go round in circles, and large gaps remain in our knowledge. Nor can it be assumed that recent literature is in any sense more reliable than older writings."[25] This study attempts to place Calhoun's contribution in a new light by examining and concentrating upon his two major treatises, supplemented by his most important speeches and letters. To accomplish this task we shall examine the pitfalls of previous scholarship and move towards understanding Calhoun as a political thinker within a definite historical and political reality. Further, this book marks an effort to appreciate and chronicle Calhoun's self-understanding within a larger quest for "republican simplicity and virtue" in American politics.[26] Our pursuit commences with an overview of the most influential criticisms of Calhoun's political theory.

In assessing the major critiques of Calhoun, this study seeks not to offer either new "paradigms" or classes of criticisms, but to recover Calhoun's concept of popular rule. In accord with such a process of refinement, we shall attempt to avoid the temptation to succumb to a purely conventionalist mold, preventing a fuller mining of Calhoun's rich philosophical and political contribution, while also not being consumed by various modes of ideological interpretation that abound in modern scholarship. When convention is overvalued, Calhoun is often represented as a deeply flawed participant within a larger, more resilient pattern of American political thought. While this work certainly urges consideration of Calhoun as a figure within the larger republican model of statecraft, it will show his special contribution and significance. The opposing tendency of designating an ideological "box" for a thinker and then placing the person permanently in it simply cannot contain the genius and enduring influence of John C. Calhoun. Calhoun's understanding of the American republic's vision presented an adequate rebuttal to an ideological typecasting of his political philosophy. Most ideological interpretations aspire to

25. Clyde N. Wilson, *John C. Calhoun: A Bibliography*, 2–3. For a complementary depiction of the "categories," see Carson Wilson, "John C. Calhoun and the American Political Tradition."

26. "Remarks on the Bill to Authorize an Issue of Treasury Notes," May 18, 1838, *Papers*, 14:302.

control the conversation between generations, forming hegemonies of discourse that disrupt the sharing of political understanding to which Calhoun devoted his life and political career. In politics, such forces seek to dominate the political process by staging elections and extending patronage. Perhaps more than any figure in the first half of the nineteenth century, Calhoun was cognizant of these true sources of derailment within American politics and sought to ameliorate their influence. This effort assumed both a philosophical and a historical dimension, and neither could be neglected without damaging the overall effort. For Calhoun the South Atlantic understanding of the original design was to be perpetuated and interpreted as one also confronted the political realities of the day. The philosophical and the practical were not inimical, and, as his political thought makes clear, to separate the two would lead both to a loss of prudence in the affairs of state and to eventual tyranny. Calhoun often lamented the movement of political life towards the extremes of the theoretical or the pragmatic, away from the need for thoughtful statecraft. His concern assumed the form of a plea for a combination of the two great qualities, and he often bemoaned the subordination of one element to the other; all too frequently the practical assumed priority over the theoretical, as Calhoun noted on occasion: "It was much to be regretted that the all absorbing question among the people was, not whether great fundamental principles should be established or overthrown, but who should be President."[27] Consequently, Calhoun the political philosopher was also one of the most prominent figures in American political history. The many and varied appellations used to describe the man—from the "young Hercules" of the War of 1812 to the "cast iron man" of later life—distract us from a rigorous appreciation of his contribution to political thought.[28]

We shall now begin our effort to understand Calhoun's most enduring offering of insight to American political thought, his critique of popular rule, by surveying some representative commentaries on his political theory. Three schools or currents of interpretation connect these disparate and often conflicting views of Calhoun as a political thinker. The first and predominant current connects a large assemblage of critics who see Calhoun as a strange, deviant force in American political thought. Calhoun, in the view of most criticisms united by this current, marks a departure from the "normative" and

27. Calhoun, "Remarks at Montgomery, Alabama," May 8, 1841, Papers, 15:536.
28. See Margaret L. Coit, ed., Great Lives Observed: John C. Calhoun, 68–84.

serves as a harbinger of the destructive forces prevailing within American politics during the sectional crisis as well as in modern political thought. We suggest that much of this scholarship emanates from within particular traditions of interpretation that benefit in a political sense from disparaging Calhoun's political theory, and in many cases such critiques deserve more skeptical scrutiny, if an appreciation of Calhoun as an original thinker is to be attempted.

## Calhoun the Aberration

The plethora of books and articles on Calhoun remains overshadowed by the influence of Richard Hofstadter's essay on Calhoun in *The American Political Tradition* and Louis Hartz's treatment of Calhoun in *The Liberal Tradition in America*, arguably the two most widely read works in American political thought during the postwar era. These article-length studies are the most familiar considerations of Calhoun as a political theorist. Both Hofstadter and Hartz are working within a framework of thought that Michael Sandel has aptly described as "deontological liberalism," reaching back to Kant for inspiration and emphasizing the rights of the individual over the good of society.[29] Another manner of looking at the mode of interpretation employed in these works by Hofstadter and Hartz is to consider them as authentic modern liberal responses to the work of an earlier generation of deterministic and egalitarian assessments of American political thought, namely, the writings of Vernon Parrington, Charles Beard, and Charles Merriam. Hofstadter and Hartz present John Locke as the progenitor of American liberalism, which has provoked a revolution in the understanding of the American political tradition. Neither author particularly adores Locke, with Hofstadter rejecting Locke's materialism and Hartz loathing the ideological "tyranny" of Locke as the destructive force behind all of America's current problems. By bringing the influence of Locke to the forefront of academic discussions regarding American political thought, both authors set the stage for later scholars, who would take their work too seriously and promote Locke as a Solon for America. The tension between Hofstadter's desire to recover a lost liberalism uncorrupted by the cast of characters he offers and Hartz's desire to move beyond Locke to a statist "Americanism" actually promotes the invention of a Lockean

29. Michael J. Sandel, *Liberalism and the Limits of Justice*, 1, 15–18.

founding of American political theory.[30] In one sense, the similarity between the individualism and radical majoritarianism of Lockean liberalism decried by Hofstadter and Hartz becomes the inspiration for the modern liberalism; instead of providing a critique of Locke, we are treated in these works to studies of a "Manchesterian" liberal America examined through the lens of contemporary liberalism, without the presentation of convincing alternatives.

At least two problems complicate these authors' treatment of Calhoun. The first is an inability to assess Locke's true influence on American political theory, and a preference instead for presenting Locke as the fountainhead for the maladies of liberal society. In this pursuit, both Hofstadter and Hartz could have benefited from a closer reading of Calhoun, who acknowledged Locke's influence upon American political theory throughout his life, as well as its limitations. For example, Locke presented the idea of an unburdened and egalitarian humankind in a state of nature as a "hypothetical" possibility, but Calhoun argued that a society founded upon such a premise would be "opposed to the constitution of man."[31] The political order required a deeper and richer ground for its existence. The second problem is the antipathy both scholars evince for the development of organic political community—for Calhoun the cradle of social and political life, even with all its foibles and dissimilarities—as well as their failure to appreciate Calhoun's attachment to such a natural order; these weaknesses also clearly indicate Hofstadter's and Hartz's inability to apprehend the foundation of the worldview that nurtured the political theory of John Calhoun. Instead, Hofstadter focuses on Calhoun's penchant for isolation and independent study throughout his career; Hartz, following a very different path, offers a plea of sorts for a unitary communitarianism as a means of overcoming the ambivalences and complexities of organic social life. Both seek a social and political structure to be imposed upon society from without, while Calhoun saw the community and society as preceding the state. For Calhoun, the South (and the North to some degree) was a collection

---

30. Hartz, *Liberal Tradition*, 8, 62, 260.

31. For a useful correction to Hofstadter and Hartz, albeit from a perspective that seeks to identify Locke as the authoritative source of a practical liberalism, see Ruth Grant, *John Locke's Liberalism*, 198–205. We will examine these limitations more thoroughly in chapter 3. On Calhoun's acknowledgment of Locke's influence, see *Papers*, 13:353 (on revolution); *Papers*, 17:285; and *The Works of John C. Calhoun*, ed. Richard K. Crallé, 4:509 (hereafter cited as *Works*). The Calhoun quotation on "the constitution of man" is from "Speech on the Oregon Bill," June 27, 1848, in *Works*, 4:509–10.

of communities, constituted and defined by the people of these states, which he argued allowed for a great deal of autonomy and liberty: "The Southern states are an aggregate, in fact, of communities, not of individuals. Every plantation is a little community, with the master at its head, who concentrates in himself the united interests of capital and labor, of which he is the common representative."[32] There really was no life outside of community. The possessive individualism of modern liberalism was not even contemplated by Calhoun, except in a few nascent pockets of industrialism in the North. With the emerging conflicts between labor and capital in America, Calhoun found solace in the harmony so prominent in Southern society. The disputes that would come to dominate the industrial revolution might be reduced, Calhoun saw, if the community was preserved as the basis of society.[33] It is the failure of Hofstadter and Hartz to observe the centrality of community and its importance for Calhoun's political theory that hinders their overall appreciation of his contribution. Some specific comparisons will further elucidate the problem.

For Hofstadter, Calhoun's political theory was a precursor to a Marxist, class-based theory of economic and political life, and he portrays Calhoun as one choosing to promote the upper strata of society, the planter-capitalist class, against the peasantry, the workers and slaves. He extends the critique so far as to argue that Calhoun's only concern was for "class" without an interest in the protection of slaves or the less fortunate. While accepting Charles Wiltse's outmoded description of Calhoun's evolving political theory as a progression from an early nationalism to a midlife promotion of regional interests and finally to his role as sectional defender, Hofstadter understands Calhoun as a "brilliant if narrow dialectician" who did not understand the implications for greater movements within American society.[34] According to this view, Calhoun's central failure was his inability to appreciate the success of Northern industrialism and wage labor. To the degree that Calhoun accepted the merits of economic growth, he sought to manipulate this expansion of the economy as a means of aligning Northern capitalists with the agrarian leadership of the South. Calhoun could see the future, but he could not appreciate the ramifications of such a vision for his homeland. In actuality, Calhoun

---

32. Hofstadter, *American Political Tradition*, 94; Hartz, *Liberal Tradition*, 56; Calhoun, "Further Remarks in Debate on His Fifth Resolution," *Papers*, 14:84.
33. *Works*, 4:360.
34. Hofstadter, *American Political Tradition*, 116.

praised improvements in limiting the control that government exerted over commerce, as he believed the economic success of America hinged upon "a free exchange of our products with the rest of the world." Tariffs of one variety or another, a staple of American politics during his political career, were the most dangerous by-product of government's involvement in the economic sphere. The increase in revenue from the tariffs was quickly consumed by a growing rank of career politicians, who became leeches upon the body politic and whose lifeblood was the burgeoning patronage system. Calhoun's political theory was based upon a recognition of the value of a free exchange of goods, a republican notion of political liberty, and the need for social restraint. All of these elements could come to fulfillment only within the setting of the organic community. As we have suggested, the community served as the basis for preventing the degradation of the lower classes, functioning as an all-encompassing safety net for the larger society. The Whig "American system," with all its accoutrements, was the embodiment of government-sponsored economic activity that was antithetical to the deeper needs of the community and the promotion of the virtuous civic culture Calhoun cherished. Hofstadter's image of Calhoun as the "Marx of the Master Class" falters when compared with the statesman who, amidst the great battle over the tariff and other issues during the special congressional session of 1841, would lead the effort against the "great overruling moneyed power" that he said was seeking to "reduce the rest of the community to servitude."[35] The oligarchic revolution Hofstadter envisions as the fulfillment of Calhoun's political theory was in reality opposed, not promoted, by the Carolinian.

If Hofstadter's conception of Calhoun lacks an appreciation of the essential organic and systematic nature of Calhoun's theoretical work, Hartz contends that Calhoun inherited a self-contradictory worldview. Combining the wisdom of Locke with the romanticism of Sir Walter Scott must result in a "profoundly disintegrated political theorist," he suggests. For Hartz, Calhoun was a disjointed Burkean defender of an organic society, colored by Lockean notions about the rights of individuals, and further complicated by the requirement to defend a slave society. He concludes that Calhoun suffered from an "intellectual madness."[36] But Hartz's Calhoun never existed. In all

35. *Papers*, 13:272; "Remarks on the Goochland County Resolutions," August 20, 1841, *Papers*, 15:703.
36. Hartz, *Liberal Tradition*, 158–59, 166.

of American political thought, no major thinker was less inclined to the excesses of European romanticism than Calhoun, with the possible exception of John Adams. Calhoun was, according to Hartz, a second-generation *philosophe* who provided "a scheme of man-made instruments which the French Enlightenment in its palmiest days never dared to develop."[37] And as a political theorist, Hartz argued, Calhoun was closer to the anarchism popularized by the novels of William Godwin than to the republicanism of the Founding generation. The placement of Calhoun within a revolutionary heritage must be viewed as dubious. As a student of history, he was aware that revolutions were usually carried out in an attempt to return to an earlier political existence. Throughout his life Calhoun was a proponent of the federal union, albeit as outlined in the original design. Disruptions of the social order were to be avoided, if possible, and the concept of revolution was defined as an effort directed towards recovering a lost or neglected aspect of popular government. Foremost among the historical influences upon Calhoun was the English model of popular rule, and he often affirmed the primary importance of that tradition: "[T]o them we are indebted for nearly all that has been gained for liberty in modern times."[38] This study will elaborate upon Calhoun's use of England, especially in the *Disquisition*, as the model for his theory and practice of popular rule as it evolves within a community and a political tradition. And, as chapter 2 will show, Calhoun utilized the particular American contributions—with an emphasis upon the Founding, the ratification debates, the Virginia and Kentucky Resolutions, and Madison's Report—as the primary sources of the South Atlantic tradition. Calhoun's idea of revolution corresponded to the English and American examples so well known to his generation, but his remarkable exegesis of the texts and his participation in the translation of the theoretical and philosophical heritage encourage consideration of Calhoun as a seminal thinker.

When Calhoun made use of revolutionary language on several occasions, as in the case of the debate over removing the Senate's censure of President Jackson in 1835, he argued for a restoration of a damaged or lost notion of political order. The alternatives for a flawed regime were usually framed in terms of a revolution, signifying a recouping of sorts, or a reformation, a pragmatic emendation of the

37. Calhoun, *Papers*, 11:468; on romanticism, see Irving Babbitt, *Rousseau and Romanticism*; Hartz, *Liberal Tradition*, 161.
38. *Papers*, 13:98.

existing structure of political participation or governing. Neither the *Disquisition* nor the *Discourse* resembled a radical new approach; in fact, Calhoun's defense of the older idea of revolution supports the assessment of Calhoun as one of the last proponents of an ancient understanding of the corrigibility of regimes.[39] Rich in metaphor and association, Hartz's portrayal of Calhoun lacks an adequate comprehension of the statesman's attachment to community and, ultimately, to liberty.

If Hofstadter and Hartz are the most prominent examples of a philosophical current that represents Calhoun as a digression among the rich sources of American political thought—a radical amidst a liberal mainstream, or the leader of the Southern "reaction" against the "Jeffersonian" center who temporarily retarded the movement toward greater individual freedom and a more complete utilization of democratic processes—a cadre of more recent scholars has continued and elaborated upon their work. Among the successors to Hofstadter and Hartz, Richard Current emerges as perhaps the most acerbic. Current's importance lies not in his contribution to an advancement of understanding, but in his remarkable attachment to the shibboleths of previous scholarship. In an influential article published early in his career, followed by a book-length expansion upon the themes contained in the article, Current suggests that Calhoun's "ghost" influences all aspects of Southern political thought. He observes that Calhoun was the central problem for Southern political thought because he departed from Jefferson's understanding of the relationship between the federal government and the states. Most of Current's arguments simply replicate Hofstadter's, although Current also explicates Calhoun's political works at some length. According to Current, Calhoun actually reduced the design of the regime to one purpose: the protection of slavery.[40] While Calhoun offered a moderate defense of slavery, viewing the slavery situation as part of a larger discussion of the evolving nature of Southern society, it was neither the most important nor the most consuming aspect of his political thought.

---

39. Calhoun, "Remarks on the Alabama Expunging Resolutions," January 28, 1835, *Papers,* 12:406 ("I say boldly things are now come to such a crisis that no alternative is left but reformation or revolution"). The modern revolution is usually understood as a progression toward a new stage of understanding not hitherto imagined. A prominent representative of such an approach is Mao Tse-tung: "Do not stop half way and do not ever go backward" (as quoted in Frederic Wakeman, Jr., *History and Will,* 275).

40. Richard Current, "John C. Calhoun, Philosopher of Reaction," 223–34, and *John C. Calhoun,* 83.

In most of the great debates of his lifetime, covering a myriad of concerns from nullification to slavery, Calhoun should be understood as a source of moderation amid seas of extremism. Current, among others, attempts to use slavery as a means of distracting students of Calhoun's political thought from a more complete examination of his work and its continuing importance to American politics. Defending slavery was not the touchstone of Calhoun's political thought. Calhoun believed that the slavery problem would resolve itself over time, but the need to preserve the republic and to improve the citizenry's understanding of the regime's foundational elements was of greater importance.[41] The proper constitution of popular rule, "the elementary principles of our Government, of which the right of self-government is the first; the right of every people to form their own government, and to determine their political condition . . . for the cause of liberty," was the predominant theme of Calhoun's life and work. Consequently, Current's unusual presentation of Calhoun as an obstacle to world peace and the rights of minorities in our own day shows a reluctance to consider the diversity and depth of Calhoun's political thought.[42] In actuality, Calhoun's political theory, with its emphasis upon consensual rule, is of great importance to regions where increasing social and political conflict has hitherto prevented the establishment of a governing authority.[43] Contrary to Current's notion that minorities cannot benefit from Calhoun's insight, the persistence of Calhoun as a defender of minority elements remains an evocative if misunderstood aspect of his work. The use of Calhoun's political theory by minority groups continues, and has experienced a revival in recent years, encouraging the need for a thorough presentation of Calhoun's thought, especially the *Disquisition* and *Discourse*. For example, an American professor of political science who studied in Washington during the 1960s once came upon "black power" theorist Stokely Carmichael reading a copy of the *Disquisition* "and exhibiting great interest in Calhoun's thought."[44] Obviously, the inspiration for Carmichael's labors

41. "Speech on the Treaty of Washington," *Papers,* 16:406. The diminishing market for slaves and the declining profitability of the institution were the most telling indicators of the need for the eventual transition to another relationship.

42. Calhoun, "Second Speech on the Bill for the Admission of Michigan," January 5, 1837, *Papers,* 13:342; Current, "John C. Calhoun," 234; Current, *Calhoun,* 147.

43. Arend Lijphart, "Majority Rule versus Democracy in Deeply Divided Societies"; Ronnie W. Faulkner, "Taking John C. Calhoun to the United Nations."

44. Interview with Donald S. Lutz, November 6, 1993, Houston, Tex.; for another version, see Lutz, *A Preface to American Political Theory,* 11.

regarding minority political participation did not come directly from Calhoun's work; however, this encounter provides some additional evidence for the persistence of Calhoun's influence. The durability and complexity of Calhoun's political theory suggest its importance as well as the potential for misunderstanding and falsely applying it.

For Current and many others who share an attachment to this understanding of Calhoun, the statesman is a devotee of Enlightenment rationalism, serving as a prophet of a new age of political experimentation and analysis. A number of studies place Calhoun among the radical defenders of a "new science of politics," making him the precursor to modern positivism and "today's behavioral political science." Current suggests that Calhoun actually considered himself "the Newton, the Galileo" of politics.[45] The most influential of these assessments remain an essay and related works by Ralph Lerner, who recognizes the need for caution and exhibits an uneasiness in placing Calhoun among the more extreme American adherents to the Enlightenment: "Calhoun's science is not to be mistaken for an ethics or a particularistic empiricism or an arid 'scholastic refinement'; but it may be called metaphysics, if by that we mean as he did the mind's power of reducing a complexity to its elements and combining these into one harmonious system." The problem for Lerner lies more in the movement from the ascribed "metaphysical" abstractions and his general "scientific" theorems to the practical application of these ideas.[46] The critique he offers depends entirely upon the more theoretical presentation found in the *Disquisition*, and does not make any attempt to examine the *Discourse*, which provides insight into the

45. Ralph Lerner, "Calhoun's New Science of Politics," 931. While Lerner represents the most thoughtful and philosophically disciplined of this "school" of critics, others who should be included in overviewing this approach to Calhoun are James D. Clarke, Harry V. Jaffa, and Robert Jeffrey. In his more recent work, *The Thinking Revolutionary*, Lerner seriously misrepresents Calhoun's attitude toward Native Americans as being nearly synonymous with that of Andrew Jackson. For correctives from Calhoun's writings, see *Papers*, 13:436, 453; 14:279; 15:492. Current, *John C. Calhoun*, 110.

46. Lerner, "Calhoun's New Science," 918. Calhoun described his study as a "science of government" (*A Disquisition on Government*, in *Union and Liberty: The Political Philosophy of John C. Calhoun*, ed. Ross M. Lence, 5 [hereafter cited as *Disquisition*]), suggesting simply that he had undertaken a systematic mode of inquiry. Contrary to the implication that he had attempted an esoteric stratagem of some variety, Calhoun followed a pattern of description common among American political thinkers. Publius, for example, made use of science to connote the thorough study of a particular concern (see Alexander Hamilton, James Madison, and John Jay, *The Federalist*, ed. George W. Carey and James McClellan, Nos. 8, 9, 18, 25, 29, 37, 43, 47, 66 [hereafter cited as *The Federalist*]).

role of the practical in Calhoun's thought.[47] But to Lerner's credit, he poses an important question: if Calhoun was a political theorist, and his work was truly "philosophical," could it be assimilated with a tradition concentrating upon the practical? The Calhounian response to Lerner's dilemma suggests the importance of the connection between the philosophical and the pragmatic; for Calhoun these considerations could not be separated without political thought suffering an epistemological crisis. For Calhoun, an imaginative appreciation of American politics necessitated an assimilation of the two, guided by philosophical discrimination. In anticipation of such a response, Lerner and other critics of Calhoun note the natural gravitation of Calhoun to Edmund Burke's political theory as an inspiration; there is, nevertheless, a suggestion of overcompensation in Calhoun, an overly abrupt initial movement from the practical, human dimension to a denial of the "efficacy of human understanding" as it applies to politics.[48] The use of Burke as a political and philosophical mentor resounded throughout Calhoun's life and writings, doubtless encouraged by his association with John Randolph, but probably intact from a previous, formative period. As early as 1816, Calhoun referred to Burke as "a statesman of great sagacity" in supporting the means necessary to fortify the financial base of a country in time of crisis. For Calhoun, Burke's greatness was to be witnessed in his contribution as a statesman responding to the exigencies of everyday political situations, but also in Burke's status as the "greatest of political philosophers."[49] The political and philosophical acumen of Burke encouraged Calhoun to rearticulate the vision of the Founding during a period of increasing regional conflict and social upheaval.

On one hand, Calhoun's critics with great persistence hold his presumed penchant for abstraction in disdain, while on the other hand, more recent appraisals of Calhoun's political theory have critiqued his inadequate appreciation of the role human reason plays in

47. It is interesting to note that many critics who attempt to depict Calhoun's political theory as purely abstract completely neglect consideration of the *Discourse,* which Calhoun intended as an elaboration upon and supplement to the earlier *Disquisition.* The purpose of the *Disquisition* was to present the "elementary principles of Government" (Calhoun to Andrew Pickens Calhoun, July 24, 1849, in *Correspondence of John C. Calhoun,* ed. J. Franklin Jameson, 769–70 [hereafter cited as *Correspondence*]). For prominent examples of the failure to assess the *Discourse,* see Harry V. Jaffa, *Defenders of the Constitution; Original Intent,* 47; and *A New Birth of Freedom,* 462–71.

48. Lerner, "Calhoun's New Science," 921.

49. "Speech on the Revenue Bill," January 31, 1816, *Papers,* 1:319 (also see 1:386; 13:601; 14:71; 15:151, 482, 718); *Papers,* 11:254.

political life. We shall examine the criticism of Calhoun's presumed bent towards abstraction first, then proceed to offer an estimation of Calhoun's reliance upon human reason in defining the conceptual structure of his political theory. From Senators Henry Clay and John J. Crittenden during his lifetime to recent scholars, a chorus of complainers have found fault with the abstract quality of Calhoun's political theory. Usually in a summary manner, these critics imply that the obtuseness of Calhoun's philosophical orientation in his speeches and treatises prevented an adequate incorporation of the practical, the needs of everyday politics. There is among these critics nearly universal celebration of the practical as against the theoretical or philosophical, not unlike the subordination of the study of political theory in contemporary political science. Calhoun, in effect, reversed the proposition, urging the compatibility of the two aspects of his political thought; to separate the philosophical from the practical would destroy the necessarily dualistic character of a prudent political philosophy. Calhoun argued for a similarity of effect: the philosophical informs the practical, and conversely, the practical informs the philosophical.[50] To reflect upon the human condition, or the nature of politics, or the essence of a democratic regime, along with many other important concerns, was impossible for Calhoun without the coexistence of the philosophical search for truth, augmented by a conception of volition, which provided for moral action. So we can suggest that Calhoun served as an advocate of the duality of theory and praxis, and not as a philosopher of their opposition.

The emphasis upon the philosophical in Calhoun's political thought was motivated by a desire to discuss the great problems of politics in as comprehensive a manner as possible. The need for reflection on such an elevated level served as Calhoun's impetus for probing the depths of the American experience in a search for the ordering principles of the regime. Some concerns demanded the incorporation of a philosophical and historical dimension that was obviously neglected by many prominent statesmen of the day. Against claims of the uselessness of such a penetrating examination, Calhoun defended his path on the grounds that the search for truth necessitated more comprehensiveness:

> The fact is, that it is abstract truths only that deeply impress the understanding and the heart, and effect great and durable

50. See Benedetto Croce, *Philosophy of the Practical*, 293–305.

> revolutions; and the higher the intelligence of a people, the greater
> their influence. It is only the ignorant and the brute creation over
> whom they have no control.[51]

Most political discussions and activities were not based upon a dedication to principles of any sort, but were the result of a perceived need to advance the temporal, egoistic desires of particular politicians. For Calhoun the decomposition of political theory was the result of a flight from principles, and the decline was present among many of his critics. In fact, most of Calhoun's criticisms of Henry Clay, Andrew Jackson, and Martin Van Buren, among a host of individuals, were founded upon his concern that these prominent leaders had abdicated their devotion to disciplined reflection on the nature of the regime. By failing to develop and follow a principled approach to politics, these figures had fallen from the honor of their positions and had failed to meet the responsibility incumbent upon them.[52]

When united with a deeper appreciation of the regime, practical political reflection was to be understood as a sacred obligation. Unfortunately, to concentrate solely upon the practical without the inclusion of the philosophical led to the abrogation of a statesman's mission. When an effort was made in 1837 to amend a universally accepted tariff agreement, largely based upon the desires of President-elect Van Buren and his partisans, Senator William Rives of Virginia praised Van Buren as a practical politician. The appellation of "practical" implied for Calhoun a willingness to compromise principle for expediency, degrading the twofold basis of political reflection. Van Buren was certainly a politician, but for Calhoun genuine practicality must be inseparable from the philosophical: "[W]e are told he is a practical politician. Now, sir, what sort of an animal is a practical politician? I will endeavor to describe it. It is a man who considers the terms justice, right, patriotism, &c. [sic], as all being so many abstractions, mere vague phrases . . . [which are] shaped wholly by circumstances."[53] Calhoun had penetrated the dark veil of interest-driven politics. Instead of signifying a connection to the living dynamics of political life, *practicality* served as merely a euphemism for the movement towards opportunism and the refusal to return the regime to its original design.

51. "Remarks in Debate on His Fifth Resolution," *Papers*, 14:72.
52. *Papers*, 12:474.
53. "Speech During Final Consideration of the Bill to Reduce Certain Tariff Duties," February 25, 1837, *Papers*, 13:474–75.

To argue for a connection between the philosophical and the "real" was an effort to defend republican government as the best possible alternative to other types of political rule. Calhoun identified such a principled understanding of America with the "sacred regard for the letter and spirit of the Constitution, and a determination to protect the rights of the mass in opposition to the moneyed and manufacturing" elements of society.[54] Without an approach consisting of a composite duality of emphases, the "ultimate tendency" of politics could not be discerned in its totality, and the eventual degeneration of the regime could follow.

A guide to understanding Calhoun's use of reason, as well as his devotion to the theoretical, is found in the application of his inherited worldview to the political crises he faced. Obviously, Lerner believes reason is devalued in Calhoun's political theory. Instead of portraying humankind as the primary participant in politics, guided by some form of reason, Lerner argues that Calhoun valued "fortunate historical accidents" more than reason. For Lerner, Calhoun's reason encourages selfish motives within politics, while omitting a concept of virtue. To scrutinize Calhoun on such grounds presents a serious, if not overwhelming, flaw in approach. "Sound reason" for Calhoun was an integral part of political participation. The nurturing of human reasoning could be found in an individual's own community, among other locations, although not all members were willing to rely upon reason as a guide, preferring instead to succumb to "gross appeals to the appetites."[55] As one who shared the classical and Hebraic-Christian understanding of the role of reason in politics, Calhoun appreciated its capacity for defining both the concreteness and the universality of political life, as it illuminated the higher potentialities of humankind that balanced the needs of the individual with those of his community. In fact, Calhoun's understanding of reason was underpinned by a concept of justice and an insistence upon the rememorative role only experience could provide. From time to time Calhoun was most willing to defend human reason as a means of assessing the enduring and temporal problems facing the American republic. He often challenged those who would relegate the importance of reason to academic discussions, and always affirmed the centrality of a properly constituted conception of reason as a guide for political theory. In the

54. "Remarks on the Bill Relating to Duties and Drawbacks," August 27, 1841, *Papers*, 15:741–42.
55. Lerner, "Calhoun's New Science," 921; Calhoun, *Disquisition*, 33.

debate over the embargo with England during the War of 1812, at an early juncture in his public life, he provided an example of the vitality of reason when he pleaded against the propensity to "renounce our reason" when it was temporarily expedient to do so.[56] In failing to ascertain the precision and centrality of Calhoun's use of human reason and its role within his political thought, Lerner, along with other critics, has misunderstood a primary aspect of Calhoun's position. We will return to the proposition regarding the role of selfishness and the supposed lack of a concept of virtue in Calhoun's thinking in our discussion of the *Disquisition* in chapter 3, but as a preliminary note, we will again suggest that Calhoun was working within a South Atlantic republican understanding of the American regime that was influenced by a classical and Hebraic-Christian worldview.

Also attached to this major current of Calhoun criticism are efforts to deride Calhoun as an opportunist, as a man controlled by personal "insecurity," as well as criticism of his alleged "assault on majoritarianism."[57] In his description of Calhoun as an opportunist, among other failings, Gerald Capers offers the most vehement and unusual attack upon Calhoun's political theory. As a study, Capers's work provides an amalgamation of every negative, unreflective criticism of Calhoun ever written. Capers also underestimates the role Calhoun's inherited worldview assumed in his political thought. Prominent among these inherited sources were the Kentucky and Virginia Resolutions. According to Capers, the Resolutions, authored by James Madison and Thomas Jefferson, were merely a "political maneuver" to influence a temporal political objective. In fact, the Resolutions were a brilliant presentation of republican political theory designed to reduce the "appetite for tyranny" encouraged by the Alien and Sedition Acts.[58] For Calhoun, the Resolutions were also a primary source of the "old Republican States right doctrine of '98," the "daughter and mother" to a vibrant alternative understanding of American politics— especially in regard to the early political successes of the Federalists. And it was to this vision that Calhoun always turned, guided by a duty to preserve the republic. Calhoun's considerations about assuming

56. "Speech on the Albany Petition for Repeal of the Embargo," May 6, 1812, *Papers*, 1:107.

57. Gerald M. Capers, *John C. Calhoun, Opportunist*; John Niven, *John C. Calhoun and the Price of Union*; George Kateb, "The Majority Principle" (quotation from 600).

58. Capers, *Calhoun, Opportunist*, 97; Senator Henry Tazewell to James Madison, July 12, 1798, unpublished, Rives Papers, Library of Congress, Washington, D.C.

positions of responsibility were always guided by his principles, as compared to Capers's eccentric thesis.[59]

More recent interpretations by John Niven and George Kateb view Calhoun as a politician and theorist who self-destructed before a willing audience of his countrymen. Niven offers the novel approach of attributing Calhoun's failing to his insecurity as a political thinker, suggesting a gentler version of the personal denunciation initiated by Hofstadter and Hartz. By following such a course of insecurity, Calhoun "impaled" himself upon a cross of logical contradictions, according to Niven. While Niven's description underestimates the strength of Calhoun's personality, it more importantly distorts the centrality of the *Discourse* as part of Calhoun's contribution to political theory. Without any effort at refinement, Niven claims that the *Discourse* contains only one newfangled idea, the dual executive, indicating a reluctance on his part to undertake a systematic examination of the treatise and an eagerness to accept a certain normative, but superficial, interpretation of the text.[60]

Distinct from Capers and Niven, but nevertheless part of a current of criticism that portrays Calhoun as a theoretical anomaly, George Kateb describes Calhoun's political thought as the "theory of a permanent minority." To a degree Kateb's assessment accurately places Calhoun within a minority political framework, but he fails to distinguish Calhoun's original interpretation of popular rule from an attempt to destroy majoritarianism in any form. Calhoun's imaginative proposals regarding the use of extra-constitutional measures for ameliorating conflict are also not appealing to Kateb. He prefers instead to critique Calhoun from within a philosophical framework of pure majoritarianism. As does every critic who is part of this current, Kateb ultimately judges Calhoun as a force that "demoralizes" political theory.[61] Unfortunately, this current of criticism misunderstands and misrepresents Calhoun as a political theorist, especially neglecting the importance of the *Disquisition* and *Discourse* to his political thought. We will now turn to a second current of criticism that offers more assistance in our effort to understand Calhoun the political theorist.

59. *Papers*, 13:310; Calhoun to George Sanders, June 19, 1840, *Papers*, 15:282; *Papers*, 20:538.
60. Niven, *Calhoun and the Price of Union*, 329, 333. The suggestion of dual or multiple executives did not begin with Calhoun. It was introduced by Edmund Randolph and others at the Constitutional Convention (Max Farrand, ed., *The Records of the Federal Convention of 1787*, 1:66).
61. Kateb, "Majority Principle," 583, 605.

## Calhoun as Tragic Politician

Throughout the twentieth century a second current of criticism has emerged, one that stresses the importance of Calhoun as a wise statesman who supported lost causes. The works in this current praise Calhoun for a variety of reasons. However, the central problem undermining these criticisms is the unwillingness to appreciate Calhoun as a participant in the perpetuation of the inherited understanding of the republic, as well as a disregard for his approach to popular rule as contained in the *Disquisition* and *Discourse*. To the credit of those who contribute to this current of scholarship, they do make an effort to comprehend Calhoun as a political theorist and to place him within the American political tradition.

The principal figures who attempted to interpret Calhoun in this way were academic luminaries of a previous generation: Charles Merriam, Vernon Parrington, Ralph Gabriel, and Merle Curti. Calhoun's work assumed a special significance for Merriam, who most prominently attempted to "sketch the principles of his political philosophy."[62] Offering an adequate overview of Calhoun's political theory, Merriam correctly identified Calhoun as working within what this book describes as a South Atlantic republican cosmos, and suggested the connection between Calhoun's work and the writings of the legal philosopher St. George Tucker, the American editor of Blackstone. Merriam also presented, as the key to Calhoun's thought, his movement towards exposing and remedying the "despotism of the majority," and he "rank[ed] Calhoun as among the strongest of American political theorists in the first half of the nineteenth century."[63] Among the students of Calhoun associated with this current, only Merriam appreciated the connection between the *Disquisition* and the *Discourse*,

62. Charles Merriam, *A History of American Political Theories*, 252–88, and an earlier version of that essay, "The Political Philosophy of John C. Calhoun" (quotation from 319); Vernon Parrington, *Main Currents in American Thought*, 2:69–82; Ralph Gabriel, *The Course of American Democratic Thought*, 103–10; Merle Curti, *The Growth of American Thought*, 442–53.

63. Merriam mistakenly attributed the editorship of *Blackstone's Commentaries* (1803) to Henry St. George Tucker, who was the son of St. George Tucker. Calhoun sent his son, John C. Calhoun, Jr., to the University of Virginia to study under Henry St. George Tucker (see *Papers*, 17:117–18), but he was later dismissed from the university. St. George Tucker's youngest son, Nathaniel Beverley Tucker (half-brother of John Randolph), composed a novel entitled *The Partisan Leader* (1836), with Calhoun as its hero. See Beverley D. Tucker, *Nathaniel Beverley Tucker*; and Merriam, *American Political Theories*, 266–67, 271, and "Political Philosophy," 328.

and his exposition has invited further analysis of Calhoun as a political thinker.

If Merriam encouraged the study of Calhoun's two major works, Vernon Parrington also evinced a willingness to carefully study Calhoun's thought, but he concluded that Calhoun did not conform to the romantic, "middle-class" mode of Jeffersonian political thought at the core of the American political and literary experience. While praising Calhoun as the "outstanding political thinker" of his time, Parrington came to view his political theory as the "child of necessity," the result of Calhoun's personal and political predicament. In another vein, Ralph Gabriel argued for an idealist Calhoun, attached to the Union at all costs.[64]

Although Calhoun never was elected president or led a major political party, his role as statesman warrants celebration in these studies. This sentiment accords with the self-understanding of Calhoun, who recognized the statesman as representing the antithesis of the politician: "The distinction between the statesman and the politician is broad and well defined. The former is an ornament and blessing to his country, but the latter a pest." Merle Curti presents Calhoun's support of Stephen Long's explorations of the Rocky Mountains while secretary of war as an indication of his administration's prophetic nature. But Curti also underestimates the enduring quality of Calhoun's political theory by describing it as purely "realist" in contrast to the Jeffersonian philosophical tradition.[65] By making such a dichotomy, Curti performs a disservice to both Calhoun and Jefferson.

Others in this current of criticism have suggested paths by which a better understanding of Calhoun's political theory could be achieved, though they have never directly shown the way to such an appreciation. Alan Grimes's once-fashionable survey of American political theory summarized some aspects of Calhoun's insight, drawing the egregious conclusion that his political theory deserves a Hobbesian label. A greater comprehension of Calhoun's political world has been provided by William Freehling, although his argument for Calhoun as a "revolutionary" does not deserve serious consideration. It was Calhoun, after all, who helped contain the truly revolutionary Bluffton Movement in 1844, when many leading South Carolina politicians threatened drastic responses to a troublesome new tariff and the

64. Parrington, *Main Currents*, 2:69, 72; Gabriel, *American Democratic Thought*, 108.
65. Calhoun, *Papers*, 11:141; Merle Curti, *Growth of American Thought*, 223, 442.

questionable status of Texas.[66] Calhoun's success at moderating the conflict demonstrated both his restraint in a crisis situation and his lack of control over the politicians described by Freehling as "Calhounites" because of their intimate ties to the statesman. A recent assessment, written from a Marxist perspective, of Calhoun as a political actor and thinker acknowledges his propensity for statecraft, citing his celebrated union with Webster and Clay in the Senate.[67] Calhoun's location in the theoretical landscape of political thought has been widely debated, and a recurrent theme within this controversy has been the relationship of Calhoun's ideas to modern theories of pluralism; this book will put these studies under close scrutiny in due course.[68] In an effort to overcome the obstacles presented by previous scholarship and to understand Calhoun afresh, we now briefly survey a third current of studies that offers a greater appreciation of the Carolinian as a political thinker.

### Calhoun, Republican Philosopher

The last current of Calhoun criticism connects a small grouping of scholars who appreciate Calhoun's critique of popular rule as well as the *Disquisition* and *Discourse* as important contributions to political theory. Against the frequent practice of either denigrating or dismissing Calhoun as a political thinker, these scholars overcome the tremendous historical and philosophical prejudices created by the other currents of scholarship to view Calhoun as an original theorist whose work transcended his own time and place and continues to be of importance to American politics.

As with the more vehement denunciations of Calhoun as a theorist, the more favorable assessments of his ideas follow no discernible pattern in regards to place or time. During the nineteenth century, both John Stuart Mill and Lord Acton praised Calhoun for his appreciation of the diffusion of political authority and for his defense of liberty. In

66. Alan Grimes, *American Political Thought,* 246; William H. Freehling, *Prelude to Civil War,* 172. For an example of Calhoun's antirevolutionary notions of statesmanship, see *Papers,* 19:525.

67. Freehling, *Prelude to Civil War,* 134 (also see Freehling, "Spoilsmen and Interests in the Thought and Career of John C. Calhoun"); John Ashworth, *Slavery, Capitalism, and Politics in the Antebellum Republic,* 203.

68. See Peter F. Drucker, "A Key to American Politics: Calhoun's Pluralism"; Darryl Baskin, "The Pluralist Vision of John C. Calhoun"; and Peter J. Steinberger, "Calhoun's Concept of the Public Interest."

his *Representative Government*, Mill applauded Calhoun's understanding of "federal representative" government as a means of providing for the greatest participation from the populace while avoiding conflict, and offering a disincentive to the growth of a corruptive central governing authority. According to Mill's interpretation, Calhoun encouraged a return to the division of political power and "principles" designed by the Founding generation.[69] The moderating influence of the states within the union could be implanted by the "extension of the practice of co-operation through which the weak, by uniting, can meet on equal terms with the strong," suggested Mill. By protecting the role of minority elements in the regime, Mill argued, Calhoun was offering a means of reinvigorating the federal concept that had "broke[n] down in the first few years of its existence."[70] The English historian Lord Acton expanded upon Mill's exposition of Calhoun and described his work as "the very perfection of political truth" and as "profound and so extremely applicable to the politics of the present day." For Acton it was not Calhoun's theory of representation, but his presentation of an authentic constitutional tradition as distinct from "pure democratic views" fashionable in the nineteenth century that made Calhoun "the real defender of Union," and conversely of democratic theory.[71]

Calhoun's concept of popular rule has also been assessed by recent scholarship in America, including works by Charles Wiltse, Margaret Coit, August Spain, and Russell Kirk. The even more recent scholarship of Theodore Marmor, Irving Bartlett, Eugene Genovese, Clyde Wilson, David Ericson, Lacy Ford, Winston McCuen, and Guy Story Brown, among others, extends and revises the earlier, groundbreaking scholarship. Wiltse's massive biography set the standard for all

69. John Stuart Mill, *Considerations on Representative Government*, 237–49. Mill appeared to refer only to the *Disquisition* as a "work of great ability," but he may have intended for the *Disquisition* and *Discourse* to be viewed together as an extended meditation on the problem of representation (*Representative Government*, 244). Writing to his wife in 1854, Mill more clearly expressed his view of the works: "I am reading the American book, a Treatise on Government generally & on the institutions of the U. States in particular—it is considerably more philosophical than I expected, at least in the sense of being grounded on principles" (J. S. Mill to Harriet Mill, February 18, 1854, in *The Collected Works of J. S. Mill: The Later Letters, 1849–1873*, 14:163). Our theory receives additional confirmation from the publishing history of these works. The *Disquisition* and *Discourse* were posthumously published together in 1851 and republished in 1853 as the first volume of *The Works of John C. Calhoun* (1853–1855).

70. Mill, *Representative Government*, 246, 240.

71. Lord Acton, "Political Causes of the American Revolution," in J. Rufus Fears, ed., *Selected Writings of Lord Acton*, vol. 1, 240, 245.

subsequent studies of Calhoun by providing a trenchant commentary on Calhoun's own understanding of the American regime, as well as his principled political theory.[72] Coit's survey of Calhoun's life and political thought points out a consistency of moral and prudent statesmanship in Calhoun. Additionally, the redirection of scholarly attention to the central problem of popular rule and its importance to republican government in Calhoun's political thought is greatly aided by the works of Spain and Kirk. The more recent assessments improve our understanding of the historical situation, as well as the enduring significance, of Calhoun's political theory.[73]

The approach of this book, as indicated, is a departure from all earlier works by its focused and comprehensive study of Calhoun's theory of popular rule as presented in the *Disquisition* and *Discourse*. As we shall observe, Calhoun's search for a proper understanding of popular rule coincided with his increased appreciation for and elucidation of the limitations of the emerging plebiscitarian spirit within American democracy. We will now proceed with an examination of the republican antecedents of the *Disquisition* and *Discourse*.

72. Charles M. Wiltse, *Jeffersonian Tradition in American Democracy; John C. Calhoun: Nationalist, 1782–1828; John C. Calhoun: Nullifier, 1829–1839; John C. Calhoun: Sectionalist, 1840–1850;* and "Calhoun's Democracy."

73. Margaret L. Coit, *John C. Calhoun;* August O. Spain, *The Political Theory of John C. Calhoun;* Russell Kirk, *The Conservative Mind,* 7th rev. ed.; Theodore R. Marmor, *The Career of John C. Calhoun;* Eugene D. Genovese, *The Southern Tradition;* Clyde N. Wilson, ed., *Papers,* vols. 10–25; Clyde N. Wilson, introduction to *The Essential Calhoun;* David F. Ericson, *The Shaping of American Liberalism;* Lacy K. Ford, Jr., "Inventing the Concurrent Majority"; Winston Leigh McCuen, "The Constitution of Man"; Guy Story Brown, *Calhoun's Philosophy of Politics.*

2

# Calhoun's Early Republicanism

## A Prologue to the *Disquisition* and *Discourse*

To explicate Calhoun's understanding of popular rule embodied in the *Disquisition* and *Discourse*, we must first attempt to apprehend the tradition and mode of political reflection of which John C. Calhoun was part, namely, the South Atlantic republican experience. Calhoun served as a participant in the larger tradition by explaining and presenting an enduring appreciation of popular rule as well as the importance of statecraft and community to a country embroiled in a new "revolution" that was directed towards re-creating political experience.[1] To place Calhoun within the heritage of the Founding and the earliest manifestations of American political thought, one must attempt to appreciate the sources of political insight and philosophical sophistication that nourished his understanding, as well as his assimilation of and transferal of this wisdom to posterity. Moreover, as this chapter will demonstrate, Calhoun was an important and sometimes lonely defender of the older ethos of the American vision of diffused authority. Instead of serving as the "last of the classical republicans," Calhoun articulated not only an authentic recapitulation of the South Atlantic republican vision of politics, but also an application of these principles to his own and future generations.[2]

1. John C. Calhoun, *A Discourse on the Constitution and Government of the United States,* in *Union and Liberty: The Political Philosophy of John C. Calhoun,* ed. Ross M. Lence, 266 (hereafter cited as *Discourse*).
2. J. William Harris, "Last of the Classical Republicans."

35

The troubled legacy of republican thought in America remains a
fashionable and highly controversial scholarly concern among historians and political theorists, although recent debates over the origins
of American republicanism do not directly affect this book except that
we need to identify those works that affirm the value of the social
nature of political life and the related need for community as primary
republican virtues. Accordingly, the hotly contested approaches to
early American historiography and political thought commonplace
in contemporary academic discussions assist our study by identifying the resilient strains of republican thinking. To supplement our
presentation of the scholarly conundrum regarding republicanism
offered in chapter 1, we shall briefly survey the two leading schools of
research. Both schools are useful in understanding Calhoun's concept
of republicanism, although only in a partial manner, as they exhibit a
self-contradictory pattern of encouraging and restricting the cardinal
qualities of Calhoun's notion of republicanism as exemplified in the
political thought of the Founding. We shall use the competing theories
of republicanism as a tool for better appreciating Calhoun's own
understanding of it, as well as the importance of the concept for mid-
nineteenth-century American political thought.

Perhaps the most influential figure in the revival of interest in republicanism, J. G. A. Pocock, traces the spirit of republicanism from Aristotle and Machiavelli—who were united by concern for the social nature
of political life and the need for cultivating a concept of virtue among
the citizenry as an alternative to the patterns of decay so common
in antiquity—and from eighteenth-century British thinkers including
James Harrington and the Commonwealth Party of the early 1700s.
Pocock depicts the "Machiavellian Moment" as a persistent theme
in American politics from the Revolutionary period to Jefferson's
Revolution of 1800, as the regime experienced a renewal based upon
a recovery of the older principles of political order combined with a
synthesis of the newer elements of political power. This approach to
American political theory was originally promulgated by Bernard Bailyn and was expanded by Pocock, Gordon Wood, and others.[3] These
studies aid our understanding by placing republicanism within a tradition of ennobling the role of liberty, personal and societal restraint,
and the importance of community as the primary experiences and

---

3. J. G. A. Pocock, *The Machiavellian Moment*, and *Virtue, Commerce, and History;*
Bernard Bailyn, *The Ideological Origins of the American Revolution;* Gordon S. Wood, *The
Creation of the American Republic, 1776–1787.*

sources of a virtuous political life. Tracing the roots of republicanism in the ancient world as well as in modern England—and examining the transferal of these habits to America—allows for a quality of circumspection and depth of perception hitherto unavailable.

But the "republican synthesis" of earlier scholarship has come under intense scrutiny during the last thirty years, encouraging some academics to posit a presentation of the Founding as less narrow in focus and more fundamentally liberal in its view of social and political life.[4] Enlarging the nature of republicanism then becomes the basis for viewing the Founding and subsequent political movements as grounded more in a devotion to economic expansion and capital fluidity than in a desire for political and constitutional stability and the development of a virtuous community. The critics of the older thesis who propose a "liberal republicanism," premised upon the promotion of self-interest as the guiding force in political society, conclude that republicanism served as the precursor to the modern liberal state with its dedication to protecting individual interests.[5] The individualistic focus of liberal republicanism challenges the stress upon community within the civic version, and ultimately suggests a transformation from "the classical ideology of the new republic into its modern opposite" during the nineteenth century. While the advocates of various republican perspectives, including the persistent thread of scholars who continue to attribute the genesis of the Founding to a solitary Lockean influence, no longer form a consensus of any sort, the need for understanding republicanism as an important force in the minds and hearts of the Founding generation and its successors in the nineteenth century remains a vital enterprise.[6] As a statesman working within a republican worldview, Calhoun took an approach to popular rule that allows us to better distinguish republicanism as it was interpreted by his generation, while shedding new light

4. Robert E. Shalhope, "Toward a Republican Synthesis," and "Republicanism and Early American Historiography"; Michael Lienesch, *New Order of the Ages*, 3–37; Garrett Ward Sheldon, *The Political Philosophy of Thomas Jefferson*, especially 1–18, 53–82, and 148–70.

5. Joyce Appleby, *Capitalism and a New Social Order*, and "Social Origins of American Revolutionary Ideology," 954.

6. "[C]lassical ideology" quotation from Rowland Berthoff, "Peasants and Artisans, Puritans and Republicans: Personal Liberty and Communal Equality in American History," 585. On republicanism and Locke, see Thomas Pangle, *The Spirit of Modern Republicanism;* Steven Dwortz, *The Unvarnished Doctrine: Locke, Liberalism, and the American Revolution;* and Ronald Hamowy, "Cato's Letters, John Locke, and the Republican Paradigm."

on the meaning and importance of the concept for American political thought. To more fully appreciate Calhoun's republicanism, we
naturally turn to the wellsprings of the tradition that nourished his
worldview: namely, Thomas Jefferson's Kentucky Resolutions and
James Madison's Virginia Resolutions and Report of 1800; a formative
early life and career; and Calhoun's participation in an important
pseudonymous public debate during his tenure as vice president.
In these documents and in Calhoun's education the fertile seed of
republicanism that would come to its fullest expression in the *Disquisition* and *Discourse* is first visible; it matured over the course of four
decades of reflection and sustained Calhoun's political thought for
the remainder of his life.

Calhoun's republicanism was instinctive, what we might describe
as "bred in the bone" of his character. He inherited the social and
political tradition of his South Atlantic world, and this inheritance
was confirmed by his participation in a community and intermediary institutions that encouraged a republicanism with the moral and
philosophical overtones necessary to bring about a just polity and
the ethical life. Contrary to the fashionable and persistent maligning
of Calhoun's thought as a departure from the republican tradition—
especially the republicanism of a Jeffersonian cast—his lifelong dedication to restoring the regime to its "republican simplicity and virtue"
actually found much wise counsel in the political thought of Jefferson. The promise and perils of comparing Jefferson and Calhoun are
legion, although this discussion will concentrate on the Jeffersonian
documents most influential to Calhoun, the Kentucky Resolutions of
1798 and 1799.[7] As Jefferson and Madison had faced the crisis posed
by President John Adams and the Alien and Sedition Acts of 1798,
Calhoun's devotion to republican principles also forced his separation
from the extremes of the Jacksonian consolidation of all aspects of
the regime and the Whig accommodation of "interest group" politics regardless of the costs. Having resolved the nullification crisis
through maintaining a commitment to the republican idea of diver-
sified liberty, as well as a spirit of moderation amidst great turmoil,
Calhoun could toast the Jefferson of the Kentucky Resolutions as the
"true interpreter and faithful advocate" of a still-vibrant American
republicanism dedicated to

---

7. Calhoun, *Papers*, 14:302. See Priscilla Ann Atwell, "Freedom and Diversity: Continuity in the Political Tradition of Thomas Jefferson and John C. Calhoun," 1–143.

*States Rights and State Remedies,* as interpreted by Mr. Jefferson, and as contained in the Virginia and Kentucky Resolutions, the rock of our political salvation; he who admits the one and denies the other, exposes himself to the imputation of the want of intelligence or insincerity.[8]

For Calhoun, the "old Virginia school of politics" was the philosophical epicenter of South Atlantic republicanism. He wrote that Virginia was graced with "leaders of clearest discernment and purest patriotism," and he believed that these leaders' Founding principles were rightly resurrected and restored to prominence in the "Carolina Doctrine" of the 1820s and 1830s.[9] Virginia provided America with presidents for nearly a quarter century and dominated the political history of the nation during this period (1801–1825). The political and theoretical struggles of the next quarter century would mark a shifting of influence towards South Carolina, with Calhoun destined to represent the earlier generation's tradition of statecraft for a different age. Instead of a derailment of the tradition, the second quarter of the nineteenth century introduced new challenges, and Calhoun attempted to address these various crises as a political thinker who possessed a thoroughly republican understanding of politics. Furthermore, Calhoun's republicanism was neither anachronistic nor ill-suited for the conditions he faced or those confronted by republics in the twentieth century. In essence, Calhoun presented a compendium of republican alternatives to the Age of Jackson that was intent upon undermining the revolutions of 1776 and 1800. Thus, Calhoun must be appreciated as operating within and extending the older tradition, as well as suggesting the importance of republicanism for modern American politics. The originality of Calhoun's thought lies in his understanding of this republicanism and his presentation of it to his place and time. To more fully discern Calhoun's worldview, we must turn to the formative influences upon his political thought, with the Sage of Monticello as an important figure who directs us toward and helps define the larger tradition, followed by Madison's Virginia Resolutions and Report, and concluding with the initial manifestations of Calhoun's republicanism and the "Patrick Henry"–"Onslow" debate.

8. Calhoun to John Naglee and Others, April 12, 1834, *Papers,* 12:298–99 (italics in original).

9. "Speech in Reply to Daniel Webster's Rejoinder," March 22, 1838, *Papers,* 14:240.

JEFFERSON AND THE KENTUCKY RESOLUTIONS

According to Calhoun, Thomas Jefferson served as the "Republican Patriarch," the political thinker who had incorporated the South Atlantic republican understanding of liberty into a theory of federal relationships most conducive to the life of the community and political order. Interestingly, studying Jefferson the political philosopher also confirms and reinforces the idea that there were two evolving republican traditions in America, supplementing the more classical, republican stream of thought, while at other junctures abetting the advocates of a liberal, economically determinate America. Regardless of historians' desire to accentuate the uniformity of Jefferson's political thinking and to depict the antebellum periods of Southern political theory as "Jeffersonian" and "post-Jefferson," Calhoun's obvious utilization of Jefferson identifies the willingness of Americans to accept and complement the essential ambiguities of his thought.[10] Of course, Calhoun concentrated upon the Kentucky Resolutions as representing the core of Jefferson's conception of republican liberty, even though Democratic and Whig critics disputed Jefferson's authorship of the works until it was acknowledged publicly in 1821. Further supplementing this revelation, Jefferson's grandson produced two draft resolutions in Jefferson's handwriting in 1832.[11] Calhoun's use of the resolutions connected his concept of republicanism with Jefferson's. The political theory embodied in the Kentucky Resolutions was always present in Jefferson's thought, a concept that directly contradicts Calhoun's critics, who have sought to devalue his interpretation by relegating the resolutions to the status of a "political maneuver" of temporary importance.[12] More important, the Kentucky Resolutions remain a vivid witness to Jefferson's republican notions of liberty as including state responsibility; they also provide a useful introduction to this persistent theme in political thought. For example, in his first inaugural address Jefferson could again plead for "the support of the state governments in all their rights, as the most competent

10. Calhoun to Bolling Hall, April 3, 1832, *Papers*, 11:565; Robert E. Shalhope, "Thomas Jefferson's Republicanism and Antebellum Southern Thought."

11. For a partial rendering of the Resolutions' history, see Adrienne Koch and Harry Ammon, "The Virginia and Kentucky Resolutions"; the most insightful assessment can be found in K. R. Constantine Gutzman's "The Virginia and Kentucky Resolutions Reconsidered"; *Richmond (Va.) Enquirer*, March 13, 1832, 2–3 (as cited in Clyde N. Wilson, introduction to *Papers*, 10:xliv).

12. Gerald M. Capers, *John C. Calhoun, Opportunist*, 97.

administrations for our domestic concerns and the surest bulwarks against anti-republican tendencies." The states retained a mediatory role between the people of the states and the general government, according to Jefferson. Even in later life Jefferson reiterated the capacity of state responsibility as allowing for a state veto on a limited basis, as in the case of internal improvements. Calhoun argued consistently throughout his public career that an adequate understanding of Jefferson's political theory necessitated an appreciation of the Kentucky Resolutions as a primary text in the American republican canon. In these documents Jefferson provided a means for restoring the regime to its "simple" design of state authority, allowing for "mutual security, and more perfect protection of their liberty and tranquillity."[13] To appreciate Calhoun's inherited republicanism, as well as his own understanding of the concept, we turn to the Kentucky Resolutions.

The Kentucky Resolutions were penned during a period of great political turmoil resulting from the introduction of various Federalist Party initiatives, including the "XYZ affair" (1797) and, more important, the passage of the Alien and Sedition Acts (1798). These actions confirmed the Republican Party's worst fears regarding the centralization of political power in the country. The Alien and Sedition Acts were actually four pieces of legislation enacted in a time of nationalistic fervor related to the Quasi-War with France. In a general sense, the uproar over the acts centered upon the apparent Federalist abrogation of the fundamental concept of liberty as applied to political life: to restrict freedom of speech and the press and to repress aliens was to retreat from the Founders' design. The response of Jefferson and Madison to the crisis served as an important personal and philosophical example to Calhoun. Thus, the importance of the Kentucky Resolutions resided not only in the form of the protest, but also in the manner in which it was presented.

For Jefferson, the Kentucky Resolutions of 1798 and 1799 were a defense of the South Atlantic republican vision of American politics as incorporated in its most profound representation, the Constitution. The resolutions were composed to offset the Federalist effort at disparaging this South Atlantic understanding and experience, which Jefferson perceived as "palpably in the teeth of the Constitution." The first Resolution in the initial set framed republicanism as grounded

13. Thomas Jefferson, "First Inaugural Address," March 4, 1801, in Merrill D. Peterson, ed., *The Portable Thomas Jefferson*, 293; on state veto, *The Writings of Thomas Jefferson*, ed. Paul L. Ford, 10:348–52; Calhoun, *Papers*, 14:565.

in the division of authority for governing among the national government and the governments of the "several states."[14] The federated
nature of this primary republican arrangement was mirrored in a
slightly different form in Article VII of the Constitution, where ratification was defined as establishing a government "between the states."
As a formal aspect of authority between the elements, states were to
serve as copartners in the operation of the regime, as they shared a
common bond "not united on the principle of unlimited submission to
their general government."[15] The Constitution functioned as the sinew
of the compact, binding the regime together, which was the result of
establishing perimeters of authority for popular rule. The designation
of this governing authority, according to the first Kentucky Resolution,
was originally articulated in the Ninth and Tenth Amendments to the
Constitution, but the political crisis of 1798 required the reclamation of
responsibility as a means of protecting the autonomy and fundamental liberties of the states' "definite reserve powers" from usurpation by
the general government. In case the general government trespassed
the boundaries of the powers not delegated to it, a state could rightly
declare its actions as "unauthoritative, void, and of no force." As an
even more profound commentary on the Ninth and Tenth Amendments in light of the Resolution's steadfast aim of protecting reserved
powers, states assumed a parallel status with the general government
in terms of delineating delegated power, as "each party has an equal
right to judge for itself, as well of infractions, as of the mode and
measure of redress."[16]

The central section of the first set of Kentucky Resolutions responded more directly to the provisions of the four Alien and Sedition Acts, offering an explicit critique of the general government's
willingness to punish crimes beyond the purview of the Constitution
and to pursue punishment reserved to the states. As the primary
repositories of political liberty under the Constitution, individual
states were actually better able to judge the efficacy of the essential
freedoms enumerated in the First Amendment. The general government's propensity to assert authority in the area of protecting freedom

14. Thomas Jefferson to James Madison, June 7, 1798, *Writings*, 7:266–67; "Resolutions of Kentucky Legislature," in *The Virginia Report of 1799–1800 Touching the Alien
and Sedition Laws; Together With the Virginia Resolutions of December 21, 1798, The Debate
and Proceedings Thereon in the House of Delegates of Virginia, and Several Other Documents*,
162 (hereafter cited as *Report*).

15. *Report*, 162.

16. Ibid.

would be counterproductive, thus reaffirming the Founders' plan for
including the First Amendment in the Bill of Rights as protection for
long-established practices in the states. The understanding of diffused
authority embodied in the resolutions was identical to that in the
Constitution: states possessed the reserved power to form relationships with religious bodies, thereby prohibiting interference from the
general government. The connection between churches and various
states, particularly the Episcopalians throughout the country and the
Congregationalists in Massachusetts and Connecticut, remained one
of great intimacy after the ratification period. "Respecting" these associations and prohibiting the general government from subverting
them for the sake of a national church was a pressing concern among
the states. The necessity of state protection regarding these basic
liberties of religion, speech, and the press served to "throw down
the sanctuary which covers the others [freedoms]" and allowed states
to hold their ground against perceived attempts at appropriation.[17]
The protection of these rights and state authority rested more upon
moral than legal and procedural grounds. After all, states had formed
and ratified the compact and were closer to the essence of the country,
the citizenry.

The Kentucky Resolutions also incorporated the concept of subsidiarity as operating between states and the general government,
and among the states themselves. Commingling the needs of the
community and the individual allowed the states to ensure a system of popular rule that incorporated an appreciation of the collective will, as well as the dignity of the individual. As this study
argues, Calhoun's political thought continued to exhibit an attachment to the notion of subsidiarity, linking the wisdom of the ancients
with the republicanism of the Founding, and with his own political thought. A stable polity and social harmony could be secured
only when each part of the community was "just to each other,"
assuming a role in governing proportionate to its form.[18] Such an
appreciation of subsidiarity was supported by Jefferson's willingness
to argue that protecting aliens also came under the responsibility
of the states and was not delegated by the Constitution. With few

17. *Report*, 163.
18. Calhoun to Richard K. Crallé, April 15, 1832, *Papers*, 11:566–67. For a more
comprehensive presentation of subsidiarity, see Yves R. Simon, *Nature and Functions
of Authority*; and as a reassessment in response to recent developments, see Bruce
Frohnen, *The New Communitarians and the Crisis of Modern Liberalism*, 204–35.

restrictions having been placed upon states regarding the status of
"alien-friends," consisting mostly of Irish and French immigrants
sympathetic to republican principles, the Alien and Sedition Acts
were a blatant infringement upon the reserved powers of the states.
Any measures "not delegated are reserved" to the states, and any
abrogation of the compact could have resulted in the general government's offense being declared "void and of no force" as an infraction
against the Constitution within the confines of the respective state
or states.[19]

In defending state action as a partial remedy to the general government's propensity for overstepping the established boundaries
of responsibility, Jefferson noted that the Alien and Sedition Acts
encouraged the executive to abuse the balance of power regarding
the judiciary. To allow the president to become directly involved
in judicial decision making was to destroy the fragile equilibrium
provided by the separation of powers explicitly detailed in Article
III of the Constitution. Most efforts to transfer distinctive judicial
responsibility from the courts resulted in the consolidation of power
in the executive. Because of the connection between the judiciary
and the executive, Calhoun later argued that judges were tempted
to assist the executive, which had the effect of increasing executive
power and influence. The reserved powers served as a check against
the abuse of the separated powers because the limitations applied
to each branch, "as strongly against the judicial as against the other
departments, and of course, were left under the exclusive will of the
states."[20] Executive aggrandizement of judicial responsibilities could
become a recipe for disaster; the president already possessed the
power to appoint judges and the ability to veto initiatives from the
legislature, and the additional convergence contained in the Alien
and Sedition Acts and subsequent measures overturned the critical restraint in the Constitution's delineation of reserved powers.
Again, the abject subversion of constitutional limits upon political
authority, as well as a devotion to the perpetuation of the republic,
entitled states to declare such acts "utterly void and of no force" in
their locales.[21]

19. *Report*, 164.
20. "Speech on the Force Bill," February 15 and 16, 1833, *Papers*, 12:50.
21. *Report*, 164. The voiding of federal initiatives could also take place when several
states or a majority of states responded to an unconstitutional assumption of power
by the executive.

While executive and judicial aggrandizement of all governing authority under the Alien and Sedition Acts constituted a dire situation, the expansion and centralization of the political life increased exponentially when the "necessary and proper" clause (art. 1, sec. 8, clause 18) was interpreted as enabling greater involvement by the central government. Jefferson foresaw the problems associated with the imprudent expansion of implied powers, and in the *Discourse*, two generations after the first Kentucky Resolutions were introduced, Calhoun revised and extended the Jeffersonian critique of the "elastic clause." Sharing a philosophical habit of mind, Jefferson and Calhoun both believed that states should not remain passive in such a critical debate; instead, they argued, an attitude of persistent vigilance against and regular reexamination of intrusions by the general government into state authority would prove advantageous for the preservation of liberty. Looking far beyond the crisis of the Alien and Sedition Acts, Jefferson pleaded with his fellow Americans to follow a habit of "revisal and correction" when confronted with the abuse of federal power.[22] Calhoun would later concur with Jefferson's exhortation, counseling states to assume an attitude of jealousy in protecting their power and mediatory role within the government.[23] On a rudimentary level the survival of the regime and a properly constituted mode of popular rule demanded trust between the parts: a mutual attitude of balance and restraint on the part of the general government and the states. President Adams and the Federalists had temporarily destroyed this trust, Jefferson argued. Eventually Calhoun's disdain for the disembodiment of mutual trust—between the states and the general government—from a proper conceptualization of popular rule, subverted by increasing facile and abstract notions of power and liberty, would develop into the central concern of his political thought.

The first set of resolutions ended with a plea directed to the rest of the states on the behalf of a self-defining "union for specified national purposes" under the Constitution that safeguarded the citizen from the abuse of federal power through a hermeneutic of original protection. "In questions of power, then, let no more be heard of confidence in man, but bind him down from mischief, by the chains of the Consti-

22. *Report*, 165.
23. "Remarks on the Bill to Incorporate and Establish the Smithsonian Institution," February 25, 1839, *Papers*, 16:577. Near the end of the first Kentucky Resolution, Jefferson also implored states to assume an attitude of "jealousy and not confidence" in the use of federal power (*Report*, 166).

tution," Jefferson declared.[24] The original protection of freedom and liberty provided by the Constitution needed the continued support of the states and the citizenry. And the collective will of the citizenry, best exhibited through the medium of their respective states, was to be assimilated in a system of popular rule grounded in the protection provided by the original Constitution. Republican constitutionalism prescribed a return to foundational concerns, as well as adaptability when facing the exigencies of political life.[25]

The original set of resolutions was followed by the Kentucky Resolutions of 1799, authored by Jefferson and endorsed by the state's legislature and governor. Responding to the less-than-enthusiastic reception given by various state legislatures to the first set of resolutions, the second set clarified Jefferson's devotion to the cohesiveness of the republic, while critiquing the implacable Federalist disregard for concentration of power:

> To again enter the field of argument, and attempt more fully or forcibly to expose the unconstitutionality of those obnoxious laws, would, it is apprehended, be as unnecessary as unavailing. We cannot, however, but lament, that, in the discussion of those interesting subjects, by sundry of the legislatures of our sister states, unfounded suggestions, and uncandid insinuations, derogatory to the true character and principles of the commonwealth have been substituted in place of fair reasoning and sound argument.[26]

Instead of contemplating the inherited tradition and design for the protection of the states and their citizens contained in the Constitution, the Northern state legislatures succumbed to momentary political considerations, and drafted resolutions in support of President John Adams's endorsement of federal authority as presented in the Alien and Sedition Acts. The Northern legislatures' inability to heed Jefferson's argument from principle could lead to despotism, Jefferson

24. *Report,* 166.
25. While less an argument for original intent so often encountered in contemporary political theory and constitutional commentaries than a means of adjudicating disputes in accordance with the Constitution, the importance of original protection was as a theoretical aspect of republican political theory, Jefferson and Calhoun suggested. Of course, this concept is antithetical to strategies that insist upon a continued revision of the mode of constitutional interpretation as the basis for circumventing the need to place restraints upon the forms of popular rule (see John Hart Ely, *Democracy and Distrust*).
26. "The Kentucky Resolutions of 1799," February 22, 1799, in Henry Steele Commager, ed., *Documents of American History,* 4th ed., 183–84.

wrote, if the process were not arrested by the prudential judgment of these states. The Northern states, according to Jefferson, had confounded their primary role as members of the compact with the need to support the general government, which compromised the states' role as judges of federal expansionism in proportion to the amount of emoluments and patronage to be received for supporting "the discretion of those who administer the [general] government."[27]

Closely following the first Kentucky Resolutions, the second set reaffirmed the "sovereign and independent" quality of "the several states" that inaugurated the founding "instrument," the Constitution.[28] Jefferson continued to argue for the states as arbiters of disputes regarding the status of delegated power; in fact, it was the states that first allowed the general government to share in this aspect of popular rule. In assuming the role of protectors and delegators of power, the states ameliorated political and constitutional divisiveness. In other words, the states, individually and collectively, possessed responsibility for resolving conflict and preserving political order.

However, proper mediation required the states to establish clear lines of demarcation concerning the judgment of transgressions by the general government. Resolutions, public declarations, and related measures aided the overall purpose, but to adequately assume the states' constitutional duty regarding protection demanded a return to "the unquestionable right to judge . . . infractions." The states' ability to adjudicate conflicts was both limited and intensive. On one hand, the resolutions assumed strictures against state action, allowing protest only in those cases where "palpable violations" occurred, thereby confining state resistance to the most critical constitutional concerns facing the republic. On the other, the states, as the sovereign building blocks of the American nation, had to reject attempts to encroach upon their reserved powers. As noted, protection allowed the states to apply the "rightful remedy" when threatened. To describe this process of state action, Jefferson supplied a new term, *nullification*, to note the immediacy and severity of the "remedy" necessary to prohibit the general government from absorbing state authority.[29] The inextricable linking of state protest with nullification had begun, followed

---

27. *Documents,* 184.
28. Ibid.
29. Ibid. Efforts to portray Calhoun's political thought as overly "mechanistic" appear to ignore the strict constructionist foundation he inherited from Jefferson (see Lerner, "Calhoun's New Science of Politics").

by the Federalist effort to depict the term as a mantra for an overly protective, extreme state response against the general government. Eventually, the Federalist attempt to discredit Jefferson's thoughtful and prudential understanding of the appropriate role for states within the original design, especially that referred to by his term *nullification*, would prevail. Jefferson's second presentation merely fueled the Federalist ire against state authority, prompting denunciations from several state legislatures controlled by Federalist or related factions. Even though Jefferson mounted a consistent rebuttal to the more extreme attacks on nullification, the Federalist effort to devalue the concept prevailed. As a label to describe an authentic state response, *nullification* suggests an organic and protective role states can assume in relation to the general government. Jefferson's "Solemn Declaration and Protest," written several months before his death, evidenced a return to this defense of state authority, depicting the relationship between states as "free and independent" and as preserving state sovereignty within the federal arrangement.[30] As a recent study suggests, the "Declaration and Protest" formed a "second Declaration of Independence," as it defended an enduring theme of Jefferson's political thought: that the protection of states and the basic liberty of the citizenry required a vigilance against centralized government. It also supported the republican notion of popular rule that operated within a fundamental division of power.[31]

In the shadow of Jefferson, Calhoun rearticulated this understanding of popular rule and American republicanism for a new generation who found the term *nullification* distasteful but accepted the concept's fundamental assumptions. For Calhoun, *nullification* was a much-abused term in American politics, making the use of it problematic unless properly defined in light of Jefferson, the Kentucky Resolutions, the Virginia Resolutions, and the Report. Calhoun also knew that nullification was frequently misunderstood. He remarked to David Caldwell, Speaker of the North Carolina Senate: "If [supporting nullification] means [I am] a disunionist, a disorganizer or an anarchist, then so far from being in favour of nullification, I am utterly opposed to it."[32]

---

30. Thomas Jefferson, "The Solemn Declaration and Protest Of The Commonwealth Of Virginia, On The Principles Of the Constitution Of The United States, And On The Violations of Them" (December 1825), in *The Complete Jefferson*, ed. Saul K. Padover, 134.
31. Sheldon, *Political Philosophy of Thomas Jefferson*, 88–94.
32. *Papers*, 11:375.

Unfortunately, by the time Calhoun confronted the crises in American politics, a generation after Jefferson, nullification had lost most of its evocative power, thanks in part to the Jacksonian onslaught against state authority and the muddled legacy of Jefferson's original partner in the effort to battle the Alien and Sedition Acts, James Madison. We now move on to a consideration of Madison and his contribution to the South Atlantic republican understanding of popular rule.

## MADISON, THE VIRGINIA RESOLUTIONS, AND THE REPORT OF 1800

A month after the first Kentucky Resolutions were passed, the Virginia General Assembly adopted the Virginia Resolutions on December 21, 1798. As the author of the Virginia Resolutions, James Madison aided Jefferson's effort to elucidate a shared republican vision of American politics, although he presented his understanding in a more turgid and labyrinthine fashion. On one hand, Madison drafted and supported the "Virginia Plan"—with its national veto over state legislation—at the Constitutional Convention. And, along with John Jay and Alexander Hamilton, Madison was a coauthor of *The Federalist*, a series of essays supporting the proposed Constitution and the need for a stronger central government. At the end of his life, Madison also published a thorough denigration of state authority in his "Notes on Nullification." On the other hand, Madison was a thoughtful critic of concentrating too much power in the national government at the Virginia Ratification Convention. Madison also authored two classic defenses of state authority: the Virginia Resolutions and the Report of 1800. Madison's uneven affirmation of state authority suggests either a remarkable inconsistency of opinion or an inordinate faith in republican theory alone without the necessary counterbalance of republican institutions. A less charitable account recently portrayed Madison at the Constitutional Convention and perhaps at other junctures as "a classically comic figure," lacking the ability to discern and then insist upon the proper path for the republic. More problematic from our point of view are Madison's shifts from consolidation to states' rights and back again: the evasiveness of Madison's constitutional principles presents almost insurmountable obstacles, making it difficult to digest his work into a coherent whole.[33] We will now attempt to relate

33. For a defense of Madison as a "consistent" political thinker, see Lance Banning, *The Sacred Fire of Liberty*. On Madison as a "comic figure," see M. E. Bradford, *Original*

Madison's defense of state authority to Calhoun's larger and more consistent theory of popular rule.

The Kentucky and Virginia Resolutions served as the theoretical inspiration for Calhoun's attempt at replicating an older political order and preserving the republic. Calhoun understood the Resolutions to form a theoretical family of sorts, "daughter and mother," within the South Atlantic political tradition. The Report complemented the Resolutions and was "by far the ablest document that issued from the pen of Mr. Madison," containing in Calhoun's opinion more insight than any other work by Madison.[34] Obviously, Calhoun's high regard for the Virginia Resolutions and the Report was due in part to their locale of origin: the great Commonwealth served as the supplier of presidents and as the South Atlantic political tradition's living center. Such devotion to Virginia and the principles of the Resolutions and the Report came naturally to Calhoun: "Virginia has the honor of having taken the lead in the development of those principles, and making the first great successful effort in their favor." As noted, the "Virginia school" of Jefferson and Madison was for Calhoun the core of the American political tradition.[35] Jefferson's and Madison's multifaceted political thought was distilled into the "principles of '98," as embodied in the Kentucky and Virginia Resolutions and the Report, and these principles served as the animating force behind the political theory of the *Disquisition* and *Discourse.* Moreover, his thorough devotion to Jefferson and Madison prompted Calhoun to come to their respective defenses. In the case of Jefferson, American politics usually dissolved for Calhoun into a dispute between Hamiltonians and Jeffersonians, with the disciples of the Virginian more apt to choose the proper means of resolving a conflict or presenting the appropriate republican alternative. With Madison, the settling of issues concerning the diffusion of power was more complex. As pointed out above, Madison was quite inconsistent in his defense of state authority. When called upon to explain Madison's understanding of popular rule from within an apparent web of contradictions, especially his recanting of the Report, Calhoun attributed Madison's discrepancies not to a theoretical

---

*Intentions,* 6. On Madison's inconsistency, see Kevin R. Gutzman, "A Troublesome Legacy: James Madison and 'the Principles of '98.'"

34. Calhoun to George Sanders, June 19, 1840, *Papers,* 15:282; Calhoun, "Remarks on the Proposed Purchase of James Madison's Notes on the Philadelphia Convention," February 18, 1837, *Papers,* 13:444–45.

35. Calhoun to William P. Taylor, July 2, 1840, *Papers,* 15:292; Calhoun, *Papers,* 14:240–41.

"turn," but to advancing years. As an honorable statesman in the republican tradition, Calhoun could also admit that Madison committed a great injustice to the cause of state authority and the meaning of the Report by his actions.[36] To appreciate Calhoun's Madison is to understand the Sage of Montpelier's contributions of 1798 and 1800, and to recognize that the integrity of this "Madison" remained intact for Calhoun and could not be relegated to political accommodation or understood as an action limited to a particular period of his life.

While the Kentucky Resolutions began with an offensive measure, stating a condition of disunity in state–federal relations, the Virginia Resolutions' initial proposition assumed a defensive posture, declaring the state's willingness to support the Constitution.[37] The second and third Virginia Resolutions also supported the "union of states" and affirmed the compact theory of union. The defense of the compact connected the Virginia Resolutions to the Kentucky Resolutions on more solid philosophical ground than one might initially imagine. As parties to the original compact, states were limited by the uniting "instrument," the Constitution. Employing technical phraseology similar to that in the Kentucky Resolutions, Madison introduced the concept of interposition to protect the rights of states against the "deliberate, palpable, and dangerous exercise of other powers not granted by the said compact" to the general government.[38] Madison's presentation of interposition as a means of "arresting the progress of evil" lacked precision when examined in light of the second set of Kentucky Resolutions. Nullification required immediate and deliberate state action against interference from the general government, or potentially from other states, while interposition resulted from a call to duty on the state's behalf to protect its citizens. In terms of our thesis regarding protection, interposition as depicted by Madison initially appears to have a more tentative quality than nullification; however, the Virginia Resolutions admit that the only "basis of the union" results from properly opposing "every infraction of those [interpositioning] principles" contained in the Constitution.[39] As with the Kentucky Resolutions, the Virginia efforts primarily focused upon state action to protect the states, although Madison's later equivocal style of argument in the Report, attempting to reformulate and ex-

36. *Papers*, 15:415.
37. *Report*, 22.
38. Ibid.
39. Ibid.

tend the provisions of the Virginia Resolutions, may have obfuscated the enterprise.

According to the fourth Resolution, the general government sought to "enlarge its power by forced [constitutional] constructions," relying upon the "necessary and proper" clause, among others, to revise and extend its control beyond the limitations defined by the Ninth and Tenth Amendments. In making such an argument, Madison was in substantial agreement with Jefferson, although he added a distinctive element: he argued that the Articles of Confederation explicitly confined the power of the general government and served as the model for the Constitution. For Jefferson, the original insight regarding limitations on the general government became visible only in the Constitution, aided by the clearer presentation of state responsibility.

The interpretation of sovereignty within the Virginia Resolutions also suggested a significant departure from the Kentucky Resolutions. Contrary to the Kentucky Resolutions' theory of discernment as allowing each state independently to exert great autonomy in operation and judgment as a deterrent to unified control and administration, Madison's Virginia counterpart preferred instead to protest consolidation in a single sovereignty. In an effort to explicate the "republican system" existing in the United States, Madison deplored the tendency to "consolidate the States by degrees."[40] The Kentucky Resolutions more closely approximated Calhoun's own view of sovereignty as resting in the people, but being represented most profoundly in the states. A sovereignty of the people, constituted in the states, was the basis for judging infractions by the general government against the states. Only approximating unanimity with Jefferson and Calhoun, Madison's enigmatic fourth Resolution did not resolve the problem regarding the location of sovereignty, although his clarifying statements in the Report again connected his understanding with Jefferson's and Calhoun's.[41]

The second half of the Virginia Resolutions mirrored the Kentucky Resolutions, with an emphasis upon the specific foibles associated with the Alien and Sedition Acts. Madison, like Jefferson, lamented the uniting of the legislative and the judicial. Madison's Resolutions affirmed the separation of powers as an integral "positive provision"

---

40. Ibid.
41. Calhoun, *Papers*, 10:506. In his *Report*, Madison described the "sovereign capacity" of the states as the highest tribunal of judgment, further clarifying and refining his earlier position (192).

of the constitutional "organization." Madison continued to reiterate that Virginia's ratification of the Constitution depended upon the expressed freedom of conscience and the press. These "essential rights" were threatened by the Alien and Sedition Acts. More than an artifact, the Constitution served as a living "pledge of mutual friendship," the basis for appealing to other states for support and for asserting state authority. Madison concluded with a defense of state responsibility and an appeal to state legislatures to follow Kentucky's and Virginia's example:

> [T]he General Assembly doth solemnly appeal to the like dispositions of the other states, in confidence that they will concur with this commonwealth in declaring, as it does hereby declare, that the acts aforesaid are unconstitutional, and that the necessary and proper measure will be taken by each, for co-operating with this State in maintaining unimpaired the authorities, rights, and liberties reserved to the States respectively, or to the people.[42]

The Virginia Resolutions ended as they had begun, in fundamental agreement with the Kentucky Resolutions. Madison's treatise closed with a request for Virginia's governor to share the Resolutions with his fellow governors, with instructions for submitting the Resolutions to their respective state legislatures. While containing slight differences of emphasis, the Kentucky and Virginia Resolutions presented a unified front, a fact that contradicts contemporary scholarly opinion suggesting the need to compare one set of resolutions in light of the other, as if major discrepancies of either a theoretical or a practical nature exist between the two. The Kentucky and Virginia Resolutions present a lasting critique of diffused authority, celebrating the protective attributes of the American constitutional tradition and the fundamental liberties associated with the American regime. In the aftermath of the Resolutions' negative reception by the other states, the continuing political crisis, and Jefferson's own presidential campaign, Madison was prompted to expand upon his earlier theory of authority and constitutional interpretation in his Report of 1800.

As a commentary on the Kentucky and Virginia Resolutions, the Report shed light on some concerns, while it added complications to the understanding of others; it was a cloudy window for viewing the Resolutions in particular and Madison's political theory in general.

42. *Report*, 23.

It is impossible to study the *Disquisition* and *Discourse* without appreciating the political tradition that inspired these works—notably
the Kentucky and Virginia Resolutions and, to a substantial degree,
the Report of 1800. The extraordinary praise Calhoun reserved for the
Report suggests the importance of the treatise to his political theory.
For Calhoun, the Report validated and clarified Madison's true genius
as the person responsible "for the form of the government under
which we live." Calhoun also believed Madison had confronted the
excesses associated with popular rule, and the Carolinian confirmed
the gratitude due Madison for penetrating the depths of the problem:
"[But] [t]here was another great act, which would immortalize him in
the eye of posterity—the profound and glorious views which he took
of our Government in his celebrated Virginia report."[43]

Calhoun, however, viewed Madison with intellectual blinders that
limited his appreciation of Madison's political thought to the Virginia
Resolutions and the Report; nevertheless, the Report provided significant insight into the appropriate role for the states to assume in
the Union, as well as the dangers associated with the consolidation of
power. And these aspects of the Report encouraged Calhoun's own
philosophical mission amidst political circumstances not dissimilar
to the situations that Madison confronted. It was to these central
problems, among others, that Calhoun returned at the end of his life.
We now begin a look at some of the critical issues first introduced by
the Report and later elaborated upon in Calhoun's two major works.

The Report allowed Madison and the Virginia House of Delegates
another opportunity to expand upon the themes initially presented
in the Virginia Resolutions and to frame new responses to the "dis-
approbation" that Kentucky and Virginia had received from various
states following the Resolutions' introduction.[44] The Report began by
expressing allegiance to the Constitution, again showing a profound
attachment to the American constitutional order and a willingness to
work within its framework without seeking to circumvent or derail
it. Calhoun would follow Madison's example two generations later in
his attempt to recover what he understood to be the salient aspects of
the South Atlantic political vision.

Echoing the second Virginia Resolution, Madison returned to the
tradition's most vital elements—the means by which the regime might

---

43. "Remarks on the Proposed Purchase of James Madison's Notes on the Philadelphia Convention," February 18, 1837, *Papers*, 13:444.
    44. *Report*, 189.

enhance its chances for survival. The design of original protection for the country could "secure its existence," if faithfully discerned.[45] The political order took the form of a compact, secured through the Constitution and endowing America with a structure grounded in state authority. As the building blocks of the political system, the states could rebuild and reconfigure the arrangement. More important, the states served as buffers against consolidationist and irredentist forces. The states as parties to the compact confirmed the Constitution through the ratification process, while acknowledging a responsibility to serve as its protectors in perpetuity. It was precisely such an appreciation of state authority and responsibility that Calhoun would affirm and revisit in the *Discourse*. Naturally, "powers not given to the [general] government, were withheld from it," and this division of authority allowed for the necessary checks to exist and function within the political system.[46] As noted, the states, as the constituent elements in the compact, functioned as mediators between the general government and the citizenry regarding constitutional issues. In this capacity, states could "interpose" between the citizenry and the general government to protect basic liberties and the integrity of the original compact by refusing to enforce or comply with the general government's dictates. Due to the "intimate and constitutional" relationship between the states and the general government, interposition could be employed only when a truly "dangerous" abuse of power was witnessed.[47] As a valid response and potential remedy to a crisis, interposition was a strong action and not to be taken lightly. For interposition to be deemed a legitimate response, the situation would require a severe and final reaction on a state's behalf, Madison argued. In assuming an interposing posture, a state would be acting in a conclusive, ultimate manner.

In disputes over authority, interposition theory was a challenge to national judicial supremacy. The limitations under which the judiciary must function restricted the usefulness of the branch for ameliorating or precluding the usurpation of authority, according to Madison. The judiciary was also inhibited by an intrinsic deficiency regarding jurisdiction, which further limited oversight responsibility. More important, the judiciary was an inadequate arbiter for such disputes because the assumption of these duties would tend to elevate the

45. Ibid., 190.
46. Ibid., 191.
47. Ibid., 192.

courts above the position occupied by "the sovereign parties to the Constitution," the states.[48] Even those critics most unwilling to accept interposition as an appropriate response recognized that the usurpation of power by the general government was a tremendous problem for the polity. The Federalist legal philosopher and jurist Joseph Story, who sought to relegate interposition to the dustbin of history in his *Martin v. Hunter's Lessee* opinion, agreed with Calhoun in principle, but preferred collective rather than state action.[49] As the genius behind the Marshall and early Taney Courts, Story shared much common ground in his political theory with Jefferson and Madison in the Kentucky and Virginia Resolutions and the Report, and with Calhoun, while he maintained an extreme Federalist frame of reference. Historian Eugene Genovese has argued that a philosophical kinship existed between Story and Calhoun, suggesting that "[b]oth sought to control rather then arrest 'progress' in human affairs. Of the two, Calhoun was the more optimistic and hopeful."[50] While traveling in the same theoretical direction, but along different paths, Story and Calhoun were united in their labors to counter the intense attack on constitutional popular rule introduced by Andrew Jackson.

Both Story and the troika of Jefferson, Madison, and Calhoun affirmed the Report's argument that the mode of deliberation within the constitutional order rested upon "the authority of constitutions over governments, and of the sovereignty of the people over constitutions," but they differed on the formula of popular rule. This indicates the great and persistent divide in American political thought delineated throughout this book. For Jefferson, Madison, and Calhoun, only the states could adequately represent the people; no other assemblage, and certainly not the population en masse, could represent the needs and diversity of Americans. The return to state authority signaled a recovery of the connection between the protective qualities of the constitutional system and its most receptive organs, the states. The systematic enterprise devoted to enlarging the general government's power through the "necessary and proper" clause (art. 1, sec. 8) was initially condemned by Jefferson in the Kentucky Resolutions and Madison in the Report, but Madison also challenged, in the Virginia

48. Ibid., 196.
49. James McClellan, *Joseph Story and the American Constitution; Joseph Story, Commentaries on the Constitution of the United States*, vol. 1, ed. Thomas M. Cooley, 294–337, 346–75; *Martin v. Hunter's Lessee*, I Wheaton 304 (1816).
50. Eugene D. Genovese, *The Southern Tradition*, 42.

Resolutions and Report, the related expansion of the "general welfare" provision (art. 1, sec. 8). In the *Discourse* Calhoun thoroughly challenged the use and eventual abuse of the "general welfare" clause as an unjust and unconstitutional initiative pursued by the forces of centralization within American political life. The pursuit of an expanded "general welfare" provision negated the intended purpose of the clause, which was to promote the common good of the citizenry. Calhoun as well as Jefferson and Madison argued that the new "general welfare" was not synonymous with "individual and local welfare," and that the new version ultimately compromised the basic liberty and fundamental freedoms hitherto dependent upon a theory of protection perpetuated within South Atlantic political theory.[51]

According to Madison's Report, the tendency to abuse the clause's true intent was habitual: Alexander Hamilton's "neomercantilist" *Report on Manufactures* (1791) and a related congressional report encouraging a national agricultural plan (1797) provided examples of the tendency to violate the meaning of "general" welfare to such a degree as to make it almost meaningless. These measures, among many others, were promoted under the general welfare rubric. Both Madison and Calhoun, who envisioned general welfare as most prudently predicated upon promoting local well-being, with the local begetting the sectional and the section encouraging national social and political stability, clearly disputed the validity of Hamilton's interpretation. In defending such a hierarchy of needs and authority, Madison and Calhoun again asserted the central republican virtue of subsidiarity based upon an organic view of political existence. This notion of subsidiarity strongly reverberated within an American context, affirming the critical roles assumed by the family, the community, and the regime—with each unit possessing an autonomous or nearly autonomous status while providing the ordering principles a society required.[52] In relating the philosophy of subsidiarity to governing, the Report also offered a maxim for appropriations: "Money cannot

51. *Discourse*, 257.
52. An eloquent statement of subsidiarity can be found in Pope Leo XIII's *Rerum Novarum* (1891), the first modern encyclical: "Experience of his own weaknesses both impels and encourages a man to ally his forces with those of another. As the Bible puts it: 'Better two than one by himself, since thus their work is really profitable. If one should fall, the other helps him up; but woe to the man by himself with no one to help him when he falls down' (Eccles. 4:9–10); and in another place: 'Brother helped by brother is a fortress, friends are like the bars of a keep' (Proverbs 18:19). Just as a man is led by this natural propensity to associate with others in a political society, so also he finds it advantageous to join with his fellows in other kinds of

be applied to the general welfare otherwise than by an application
of it to some particular measures, conducive to the general welfare."
Through the power of the purse, government affirmed the localist
spirit and the natural division of authority by following constitutional
restrictions upon unenumerated appropriations, refraining from any
attempt to endow the "general welfare" with a truly national character,
and recognizing the importance of associations and governing bodies
nearest the situation under review. In effect, the Report and Calhoun's
arguments in the *Disquisition* and *Discourse* portrayed the exploitation
of the "general welfare" clause as a ruse intended to disestablish the
protective and subsidiary qualities of the Constitution, while coalescing government and other associations into a more centralized
configuration. Without safeguards, it became more likely that this
consolidation would occur and that the general government would
begin to dominate political life. To destroy these protective aspects of
the political heritage by the "appropriation of money to the general
welfare would be deemed rather a mockery than an observance of
this constitutional injunction" granted providentially to the American
republic. To interpret the "general welfare" clause as a provision for
national activity was to "supersede [the states'] respective sovereign-
ties" and disavow legitimate state action, argued Madison.[53]

Transitioning from a theoretical critique to a more descriptive assessment, the remainder of Madison's Report continued as a rejoinder
against central control and the unification of all aspects of popular
rule. While Jefferson's and Calhoun's explicit theory of state action
served to define a sphere of liberty, Madison's understanding assumed
a more ambiguous quality. Madison preferred to list the ramifications
of a republican system's retrogression into monarchy via uncontested
opposition to consolidationist measures. For Madison, the down-
ward spiral towards monarchy united executive power on two levels:
prerogative and patronage. Prerogative allowed greater control over
governmental mechanisms, while patronage confirmed the limits of
human nature. The judiciary, usually more insulated from everyday
politics than either the legislative or the executive, was corrupted

societies, which though small and not independent are nevertheless true societies"
("§49, *Rerum Novarum*," in Michael Walsh and Brian Davies, eds., *Proclaiming Justice
and Peace*, 35). For a contemporary rendering of *Rerum Novarum*'s themes after the
collapse of communism, see Pope John Paul II's *Centesimus Annus* (especially §29 and
chaps. 5 and 6 in *Proclaiming Justice*, 432–78).
  53. *Report*, 201.

by the executive's usurpation of legitimate authority. This led to an abrogation of basic freedoms, the suspension of habeas corpus, and drastic limitations upon the protection provided by states and the Constitution's Ninth and Tenth Amendments.[54] While the subversion of state authority was most disastrous, the "union of power" further disrupted original protection provisions by uniting all three branches into one; denigrating the "general principles" buttressing the American political order; and lastly, the "union of powers subverts the particular organization and positive provisions of the Federal Constitution."[55] Madison's mode of interpretation in the Report drew a straight theoretical line from the political theory of the Articles to the Constitution; two generations later, Calhoun retraced these steps in the *Disquisition* and *Discourse.*

Jefferson and Madison also brought the status of the common law under increased scrutiny. Jefferson affirmed a creed of natural rights. As chapter 4 will survey, Calhoun possessed reservations about the common law theories he encountered as a student and a statesman, while refusing to accept the natural rights philosophy of Jefferson and John Taylor of Caroline in its totality.[56] To Madison's credit, his republicanism appreciated the corrosive quality of centralized power, although Jefferson and Calhoun interpreted the struggle against federal hegemony more dramatically—as nearly identical to war. Even though much ambiguity existed within Madison's republicanism as witnessed in the Virginia Resolutions and the Report, these works contributed substantially to a defense of South Atlantic republicanism. Madison's republican theory included a doctrine of original protection, which attempted to define authentic political community and

54. Ibid., 203, 204, 208–9.
55. Ibid., 210.
56. Much confusion abounds regarding Calhoun's relationship to natural rights. A recent article on Calhoun argues that "[t]he South's defenders [Calhoun] thus gave first priority to the demolition of the theory of natural rights" (Robert A. Garson, "Proslavery as Political Theory: The Examples of John C. Calhoun and George Fitzhugh," 200). To discuss rights in contemporary society, one must acknowledge the tremendous influence of liberal notions of rights, as well as the increasing devaluation that modern liberalism is experiencing as a result of competing theories of rights, namely, the distance between established rights and the means necessary to preserve them in American society. This issue will receive treatment in chapters 3 and 4, where we will argue that Calhoun should be appreciated as a theorist who integrated rights and duties into a reciprocal relationship (*Papers,* 13:59) and who was closely connected to the "chartered rights" theorists within the English tradition. Calhoun's political thought was influenced in this regard by Edmund Burke. See David Walsh, *After Ideology: Recovering the Spiritual Foundations of Freedom,* 241–78.

to perpetuate an understanding of political existence so essential to Calhoun's thought. The influences upon Calhoun's work were many, and academic genealogists of one variety or another have attempted to uncover these "sources" from time to time. Unfortunately, these potentially insightful searches are usually inconclusive and sometimes misleading scholarly enterprises.[57] To truly appreciate the *Disquisition* and *Discourse* as a great achievement of American political thought, one must employ the Kentucky and Virginia Resolutions and the Report as interpretative lenses for viewing the soul of South Atlantic republicanism. As we have demonstrated, whenever Calhoun explored the formative intellectual forces upon his understanding of political life, he returned to the "principles of '98" found in these works.[58] Having accepted and applied the counsel of Jefferson and Madison, we now consider the first examples of Calhoun's applied republican concept of popular rule, his early career, and the "Patrick Henry"–"Onslow" debate.

### PREVENIENT REPUBLICANISM: THE EMERGENCE OF CALHOUN AS STATESMAN AND THE "PATRICK HENRY"–"ONSLOW" DEBATE

Calhoun's attachment to Jefferson's and Madison's "principles of '98" came naturally to a political thinker whose worldview was nursed from birth by the South Atlantic republican tradition. The great republican exemplar for Calhoun was his father, Patrick Calhoun, an Irish-born surveyor and judge who served as a member of the South Carolina legislature. Through Patrick Calhoun, John imbibed the heritage he was to represent and articulate during his lifetime: representation for political minorities, of which Patrick Calhoun and upcountry South Carolinians were part during the colonial era; the need for virtuous personal and communal life, predicated upon personal restraint and prudence; and an ultimate purpose—a republican vision for preserving constitutional democracy by reconciling popular rule with the ethical life—that would persist when determination and diligence failed.

57. For the most reliable attempt, see August O. Spain, *The Political Theory of John C. Calhoun*, 48–74.

58. The number of references to the Resolutions and the Report as framing the "principles of '98" in the works preceding the *Disquisition* and *Discourse* is amazing. For representative examples see *Papers*, 1:151; 10:428; 12:8, 74, 75, 140; 13:310; 14:16, 241; 21:52.

At every personal and political threshold John Calhoun crossed, the republican vision imparted by his father guided his path. Opposing the Constitutional Convention's perceived interference upon the liberties of states in terms of taxation and representation, the older Calhoun could not initially support ratification. If the republican political order was disrupted in some manner, Patrick Calhoun believed that restorative measures were to be employed, and John Calhoun's recapitulation of this vision as depicted in the partly autobiographical *Life of John C. Calhoun* (1843) provides greater elaboration:

> We have heard his son [John Calhoun] say that among his earliest recollections was one of a conversation when he was nine years of age, in which his father maintained that government to be best which allowed the largest amount of individual liberty compatible with social order and tranquillity, and insisted that the improvements in political science would be found to consist in throwing off many of the restraints then imposed by law, and deemed necessary to an organized society.[59]

Regarding liberty, both personal and societal, the most demanding challenge was not in securing it, but in preserving it. Patrick Calhoun had devoted his life to representing the long-neglected upcountry of South Carolina against the political hegemony of the east, namely, Charleston and the coastal region. The republican creed Patrick bequeathed to John was simple in form, although demanding in practice: he believed it was essential "to learn to control our dispositions; to restrain those that are too strong, and to strengthen those, that are too weak."[60]

John Calhoun was born in 1782, when upcountry South Carolina was still a frontier, so his educational opportunities were limited, albeit advanced by the occasional tutelage offered by his brother-in-law, the Reverend Moses Waddel, and ravenous study. Following the deaths of his father and sister, Calhoun, barely a teenager, began reading the tomes in Reverend Waddel's library, which included "Rollin's *Ancient History*, [William] Robertson's *Charles V*, his *South Carolina*,

59. *Life of John C. Calhoun, Presenting a Condensed History of Political Events from 1811 to 1843*, in *Papers*, 17:7 (hereafter cited as *Life*). For the best effort at resolving the authorship question, see James L. Anderson and W. Edwin Hemphill, "The 1843 Biography of John C. Calhoun: Was R. M. T. Hunter Its Author?"

60. John, in turn, shared these habits with his favorite child and soul mate, Maria (Calhoun to A[nna] M[aria] Calhoun, December 30, 1831, *Papers*, 11:531).

and Voltaire's *Charles XII*. After dispatching these, he turned with like eagerness to [Capt. James] Cook's *Voyages*, a small volume of *Essays* by [Sir Thomas] Browne, and [John] Locke on *Understanding* [*An Essay concerning Human Understanding*], which he read as far as the chapter on infinity."[61]

After a period of self-education, Calhoun entered Yale College, studying under the arch-Federalist Timothy Dwight, who could not dissuade the young man from his understanding of popular rule. On one occasion, against Dwight's objections, Calhoun defended sovereignty as residing in the people. Following the discussion, Dwight noted to a friend that Calhoun "had talent enough to be President of the United States," and he predicted Calhoun's eventual accession to the office. With his studies completed, Calhoun was selected to deliver a graduation thesis entitled "The Qualifications Necessary to Constitute a Perfect Statesman" at the Yale commencement in 1804.[62] He proceeded to study law for two years under Judge Tapping Reeve at the Litchfield Law School, the most prominent institution devoted to legal training during this period. Again, Calhoun withstood an extreme alternative republican critique of American political existence, this time offered by Reeve, a radical Federalist and member of the "Essex Junto." Reeve also advocated Northern secession and was indicted for libel against President Jefferson, a candidate he loathed, choosing to support his brother-in-law, Aaron Burr. Calhoun, the South Atlantic republican, accepted the comprehensive training Litchfield provided while retaining a view of politics at odds with the school's approach to social and political life. Returning to his native South Carolina to practice law, a pursuit he considered "both dry and laborious," Calhoun married and served two terms in the South Carolina legislature before being elected to the U.S. House of Representatives in 1811.[63] As a congressman, Calhoun continued to embody republican principles, regarding republicanism and patriotism as synonymous: he supported the War of 1812; he revised Madison's original national bank proposal and backed limited internal improvements; and he continued to praise a free economy and a regime founded upon "reason and equity" even when surrounded by a world of "fraud,

---

61. *Life*, 8. In other words, Calhoun read Book I and half of Book II, completing Locke's "history of ideas" sections.

62. *Life*, 9. Because of illness, Calhoun was unable to present his paper before his fellow graduates, and no copy exists among his papers.

63. Calhoun to Andrew Pickens, Jr., May 23, 1803, *Papers*, 1:9.

violence or accident." Defending a "purely republican" system of government against factionalism when "the attachment to a party becomes stronger than that to our country," Calhoun continued to articulate a theory of protection and strict constitutionalism, as evidenced by his first speech in Congress: "The senate was a diplomatic corps, who represented the states; who were sent here to protect the states' rights, and to preserve the federative principle. The members of the house were the guardians of the national principle incorporated, and wise incorporated . . . into this government."[64] In the years to come, Calhoun would champion the federative principle not simply as a doctrine of politics, but as a comprehensive incorporation and presentation of his understanding of popular rule.

As many historians and political theorists have noted, Calhoun supported "national" legislation during his early career; this fact has encouraged these scholars to inappropriately divide his life into stages based upon the perceived degree of his attachment to a centralized political order. The "young Hercules" who sustained the war effort looked to the future, disavowed temporal political gain or advantage, and envisioned that his role as a republican statesman was to encourage prosperity and the welfare of the republic. To secure the regime, a genuinely federal peacetime military establishment and some internal improvements were temporary and limited necessities. Possessing this prophetic quality, Calhoun sought to defend the country and to protect popular rule against the tide of more limited and destructive political arrangements presented by others, including his sometime mentor John Randolph, the leader of the Quid, or Old, Republicans. Calhoun even supported what he believed would be a temporary tariff in 1816 for the purposes of establishing a much-needed peacetime military organization and appeasing Northerners whose manufacturing industries were most displaced by the war. Along with sixteen other Southern congressmen, Calhoun voted for what he believed would be a revenue-raising measure sponsored by Northerners, asserting the need to recognize regional distinctiveness and cooperation: "Neither agriculture, manufactures or commerce, taken separately, is the cause of wealth; it flows from the three combined."[65] In the years to follow,

64. "[F]raud, violence" quotation from "Speech on the Commercial Treaty with Great Britain," *Papers*, 1:313; "attachment to a party" quotation from "Speech on the Dangers of 'Factious Opposition,' " January 15, 1814, *Papers*, 1:194–95; "[t]he senate" quotation from "Speech on the Apportionment Bill," *Baltimore American and Commercial Daily Advertiser*, December 6, 1811, in *Papers*, 1:75.
65. "Speech on the Tariff Bill," April 4, 1816, *Papers*, 1:349.

Calhoun would often explain his support of the tariff as based upon the need for revenue and not protection, although his critics and modern scholars have frequently presented unfair and inaccurate criticisms in this regard. For Calhoun's part, he saw, in hindsight, that the tariff actually "reduced the duties, and in truth exacted from the people no more than the constitutional wants of the Government then required." The rising protectionist spirit in America would also affirm Calhoun's wisdom in supporting the 1816 measure, even though he held subsequent tariffs in disdain:

> I then, and now believe, the policy was wise and just; nor do I believe there ever would have been a contrary opinion, had not the unconstitutional and unjust measures of protection, afterwards followed. I mean the Tariff[s] of 1820, 1824, and 1828, for which that of 1816, with a character and object entirely different, cannot be fairly considered responsible.[66]

Amidst the tariff frenzy after 1816, Calhoun continued to advocate free trade, maintaining his initial understanding.[67] The controversy regarding Calhoun's consistency of opinion has been debated at length and wisely summarized in a recent essay as evidencing short-term change, but lifelong congruity with the "goal always . . . to enhance the success of the American experiment in federal republicanism by harmonizing its potentially conflicting parts."[68] Calhoun maintained a consistent view and application of the South Atlantic republican vision throughout his life. This interpretation complies with Calhoun's own understanding, although he was also a statesman greatly attached to the philosophy and example of Edmund Burke, who recognized the need for confronting the challenges of time and place. If incorporated into a theory of politics as "uniform adherence to one policy" even amidst different circumstances, consistency was little more than "political quackery," denoting an inability to confront the more profound crises facing the regime.[69] Like Burke, Calhoun realized that change serves on some occasions as the basis for preservation, and the deeper social and political problems require more than

66. Both quotations from Calhoun to B[ernard] A. Reynolds, June 5, 1832, *Papers*, 11:592.
67. See *Papers*, 10:403; 11:267, 544, 656; 12:45, 50, 52, 62, 125; 13:272, 554; 14:193, 437, 571; 15:302, 633; and 16:72, 471.
68. Clyde N. Wilson, introduction to *The Essential Calhoun*, xx.
69. "Speech on the Abrogation of the Joint Occupancy of Oregon," March 16, 1846, *Papers*, 22:691–92.

an ideological framework for their resolution. As one who confronted ideological approaches to politics in America, Calhoun sought a reorientation that incorporated a refined republican worldview with the ever-changing political situation in which America found itself. In fact, to separate universal theory and practical particularity as opposing poles of ethical reflection within Calhoun's political thought divorces the Carolinian, who affirmed historical particularity as the proper amalgamation of these two experiential modes, from his essentially dualistic epistemology. Combining the universal and the practical proved to be an all-consuming task when President Monroe asked Calhoun to assume the helm at the War Department in 1817.

Calhoun was generally considered too philosophical for such a practical post, but he accepted the appointment out of a republican sense of duty. Upon hearing of Calhoun's cabinet nomination, Jefferson wrote commending his decision to assume the responsibilities and "confident that the abilities displayed in another branch [legislative] of it's government will be exercised to still greater advantage in this new scene of their employment."[70] In the course of two terms in office Calhoun completely reorganized and revitalized the War Department and its general staff, resolved its financial problems resulting from the war, and demonstrated a new, more compassionate approach to Native American affairs. Calhoun also began reforming West Point through a new spirit of openness in terms of admissions and administrative procedures. Brilliantly reconciling the republican worldview he had inherited with the practical and relentless decision making necessary to direct the government's largest and most demanding department, Calhoun has been described as "the ablest war secretary the Government ever had till Jefferson Davis." During Calhoun's tenure in office, President Monroe applauded his vision and considered him "remarkably well organized," causing a tremendous improvement in the department's operations and reputation.[71] The Constitution provided constraints upon the activity of executive officers, and Calhoun accepted the limitations even though such devotion compromised the temporary political advantages he could have reaped from refining his "public image" and using patronage opportunities for personal

70. Thomas Jefferson to Calhoun, December 31, 1817, *Papers,* 2:48.
71. "[A]blest war secretary" quotation from William E. Dodd, *Statesmen of the Old South,* 109. Monroe, quoted in Noble E. Cunningham, Jr., *The Presidency of James Monroe,* 128. Also see David Heidler and Jeanne Heidler, *Old Hickory's War: Andrew Jackson and the Quest for Empire,* 115.

gain.[72] After Monroe's eight years in office, the Virginia presidential "dynasty" ended, but not before a raucous political struggle took place to find a successor.

A broad spectrum of supporters encouraged Calhoun's candidacy for president in 1824 against his fellow cabinet members William H. Crawford and John Quincy Adams, Speaker of the House Henry Clay, and war hero and newly elected senator Andrew Jackson. Initially entering the presidential field, Calhoun realized he lacked adequate support and withdrew after Pennsylvania nominated Andrew Jackson. Accepting the vice presidential nomination, Calhoun was elected by a large majority. The results in the presidential contest between Jackson and Adams were inconclusive in terms of the electoral and the popular votes, and the election was thrown into the House of Representatives, where Jackson's nemesis, Clay, served as Speaker. In an unusual series of events, Clay came to Adams's aid, and the House vote secured the election for Adams. The president-elect proceeded to appoint Clay as secretary of state. Many Americans considered the supposed arrangement between Clay and Adams a "corrupt bargain," and Calhoun mirrored these sentiments a few months after the inauguration in a letter to former president Monroe's son-in-law Samuel Gouverneur: "Mr. Adams will find [in] the next election the people have too much sense to confirm the dangerous precedent, which he and Mr. Clay have created." Guided by a republicanism devoted to virtuous habits, Calhoun believed the unholy alliance was morally reprehensible and politically dangerous. The "corrupt bargain" had disrupted the balance between preserving liberty and assuming power explicitly reserved to the people; "improperly acquired" power would doubtless be "improperly used," Calhoun opined.[73]

Moreover, President John Quincy Adams's initial actions and pronouncements were discouraging to Calhoun, especially his inaugural address and first annual message to Congress. In a major effort to promote the administration's agenda, Adams proposed a dramatic expansion of the general government, including internal improvements and new regulations regarding industry, trade, and agriculture. For Calhoun, these innovations presented a departure from the worldview he cherished and sought to affirm. Adams was attempting a revolt from the South Atlantic republicanism of Jefferson, Madison, and

72. Theodore R. Marmor, *The Career of John C. Calhoun*, 53–69.
73. Calhoun to Samuel L. Gouverneur, June 10, 1825, *Papers*, 10:27; Calhoun to John McLean, September 3, 1827, *Papers*, 10:307.

Patrick Calhoun. Most historians appropriately notice the contending political forces at play within the emerging two-party political world, namely, the Old Republicans and the National Republicans, neglecting the deeper theoretical struggle between two implacable philosophical approaches to republican government. At the heart of the dispute was a conflict over popular rule. Celebrating the pursuit of happiness as resulting in democracy, Adams conflated his meager praise for popular rule and adoration of "pure democracy" into a democratic doctrine without the virtuosity and restraint that Calhoun envisioned as essential.[74] Adams can be seen as a "divided self," at one juncture praising abstract democracy, while at another criticizing the French Revolution as an obsessive and destructive model for democratic government. The confusion at the core of Adams's political thought concerning popular rule was his inability to recognize the need for a balance between personal and communal liberty and the integration of restraints against potential abuse. Adams's confusion led to the theoretical insecurity that prompted the "Patrick Henry"–"Onslow" debate and Adams's drift towards abolitionism. The rising consolidationist tide witnessed in the first sessions of the new Congress and in Adams's early initiatives alarmed Calhoun, who knew the "principles of '98" were threatened by this slow, steady increase of the general government's power and the erosion of constitutional integrity.

Assuming an office considered largely ceremonial, Calhoun took his vice presidential responsibilities seriously, bringing a new dedication to his position as Senate president. While elected a member of the executive branch, the vice president worked within the legislative branch. Calhoun began as a vice president elected in his own right, not as a disciple of John Quincy Adams. The office of vice president had previously proved to be a less-than-propitious springboard for political or personal advancement, with every vice president except John Adams and Thomas Jefferson either dying in office or becoming somewhat removed from their public responsibilities. From his first day as Senate president, Calhoun presided over the body's deliberations, breaking a long pattern of vice presidential inactivity regarding Senate proceedings.[75] Given the limited constitutional requirements

74. John Q. Adams, "Address to Constituents," September 17, 1842, in Josiah Quincy, *Memoir of the Life of John Quincy Adams* (1858), 382–83, as quoted in Russell Kirk, *The Conservative Mind*, 235.

75. The presiding power was usually yielded to the president pro tempore, a senator elected by his colleagues.

placed upon their office, vice presidents were not intimately connected
to the political struggles within their respective administrations, and
some rarely visited the Capitol. For example, Daniel D. Tompkins,
who preceded Calhoun as vice president, was conspicuously absent
from Washington during most of his five years in office. The previous Congress had given the vice president power to appoint Senate
committee chairmen, and Calhoun exercised this new responsibility
with great fairness, selecting friends of the Adams Administration
to chair eight major committees, with the remaining seven chairmanships given to senators not directly associated with the administration.
Calhoun's approach to making committee appointments and his increasingly critical posture towards executive control drove a wedge
between himself and President Adams regarding the use of power.
Calhoun consistently held that political power was a trust, given by
the people and moderated by the states primarily, but also in a more
limited degree by the general government; therefore, consolidating
power always led to political disorder, threatening the country's con-
stancy of mission and vision. In opposition to Calhoun's theory of
power restraint and diffusion, Adams believed in using power as
a tool for broadening one's sphere of influence, as the debate with
Calhoun would show.[76] Given such a divergence between Adams and
Calhoun on principle, the ensuing debate became a national event as
it brought their differences into the public arena, again dramatizing
the great philosophical divide in American politics.

The "Patrick Henry"–"Onslow" exchange should be understood as
a battle for the essence of American republicanism. While one can
argue that the debate traversed several levels, and indeed the exchanges themselves encourage such analysis, these reflections on the
nature of political authority actually took place on two interconnected
levels: the personal and the philosophical. In the course of eleven
turgid and often lengthy essays, the authors displayed a depth of
insight not encountered in contemporary politics, provided important
commentary on central concerns of political life, and offered remarkable insight on the tension between liberty and power. The debate
began on rather innocuous terms when Calhoun refused to preserve
order and interrupt Senator John Randolph's speech against President Adams and Secretary of State Clay, with whom Randolph had
recently dueled. Responding to Calhoun's failure to stifle Randolph,

76. *Papers*, 16:55.

an essay criticizing the vice president appeared in the "party press" paper, the *National Journal*, under the pseudonym "Patrick Henry." Some mystery persists over the identity of "Patrick Henry," although the attachment of the author to Adams's neo-Federalism cannot be questioned. For our purposes, we contend that the author was either Adams or a confidant acting under the president's direct tutelage.[77] It is unlikely that Calhoun would have participated in such a debate if he thought "Patrick Henry" was a surrogate for the president, and public attention to these issues and personages would also have been greatly diminished if some other individual besides President Adams was the acknowledged author of the "Patrick Henry" essays. Influenced by the reputation of Sir Arthur Onslow, a noted Speaker of the House of Commons whose expertise in parliamentary procedure influenced Jefferson's *Manual of Parliamentary Practice*, Calhoun took the nom de plume "Onslow" for his reply.

As we have noted, an incident occurred between Senator Randolph and Senator Mahlon Dickerson (New Jersey), and Calhoun refused to limit Randolph's speech, a prerogative supposedly provided by the presiding officer's "power of preservation." Furthermore, Randolph had introduced a motion to table and was probably entitled to speak on that legislative maneuver without reference to Dickerson's objections. Senator Dickerson later defended Calhoun's actions, noting that he did not lack "justice, decorum, or delicacy" during the course of the exchange, thus helping to deflate the claims of "Patrick Henry."[78]

During the period of the debate, the Senate rescinded some powers previously granted to the Senate president, provoking Calhoun to reaffirm the philosophical antecedents necessary for republican theorizing about power and the need for limitations upon political control first articulated in the Kentucky and Virginia Resolutions and the Report of 1800. With his endorsement of these new restrictions upon the Senate president, Calhoun reiterated the paramount republican virtues of diffused power and legislative dominance as elemental manifestations of his worldview. The republican heritage's evolving understanding again allowed for the orderly distribution of authority, with the citizenry connected to the parts, but concurrently supporting the whole. In the Senate's case, the whole was little more than an assemblage of parts, with each part maintaining the autonomy necessary

77. Charles Catlett, New York, to Philip B. Fendall, Washington, D.C., October 17, 1826, Special Collections, File 21-I, letter 24, Duke University, Durham, N.C.

78. *Washington, D.C., Daily National Intelligencer*, April 25, 1826, 3, in *Papers*, 10:91.

for authentic representation. Calhoun argued that the Senate president held "appellate power" as the beneficiary of the Senate's trust; such responsibility did not primarily dictate that the Senate president preside over legislative sessions. In fact, Calhoun cited Senate rules 6 and 7, which allowed the president to "call for the sense of Senate" when order was disputed, and for the recording of "exceptionable" speech before rendering a judgment about a member's comments. The approach that Calhoun defended as vice president was identical to the posture he encouraged the general government to take during all of his forty years in public office: "[A]ssume no power in the least degree doubtful."[79] Preserving liberty, he believed, required diligence in dividing authority and protecting the legitimate agencies of political power.

The first essay in the exchange found "Patrick Henry" inveighing against Calhoun personally, suggesting that the vice president promoted criticism of the Adams Administration and "sacrificed the proprieties of office to the sympathies of a desperate ambition."[80] "Patrick Henry" argued that the presiding officer must possess the power to preserve order, stressing the necessity of authority in relation to the Senate. In other words, the powers of the Senate president resided in the office, with the office also implying particular duties. Within the personal dimensions of the debate, "Patrick Henry" criticized Calhoun as a disciple of Jackson and one whose understanding of Senate procedure exceeded "scholastic absurdity" in its precision.[81] Defending his restrained demeanor in the Senate, Calhoun refused to "stand in the light of a usurper," exerting the power to preside when such a responsibility was "too high for the Chair [Senate president]."[82] Calhoun then offered his first response as "Onslow," addressing two questions—the necessity of calling Randolph to order and the more profound problem of using power when it is not explicitly needed or when it is reserved for other purposes. As Calhoun summarized this central philosophical thrust of "Onslow," he countered the emerging hegemonic theory of power in the essays of "Patrick Henry." The power to call to order was directly bestowed upon the Speaker of the House of Representatives, and the Speaker was selected from among

79. "Speech on the Rules of the Senate and the Powers of the Vice-President," April 15, 1826, *Papers*, 10:89; "assume no power" quotation in *Papers*, 10:90.
80. "Patrick Henry," May 1, 1826, *Papers*, 10:92–96.
81. *Papers*, 10:95.
82. "Remarks on the Power to Call to Order," May 18, 1826, *Papers*, 10:98.

the representatives. As an executive officer not elected by the Senate, the Senate president was not given the body's approval and consent for controlling its deliberations. In other words, the Senate president's role lacked legitimacy when compared to the Speaker of the House's obligation to preside. As rational agents on the behalf of the people and the states, the senators failed to entrust the Senate president with sufficient authority for calling members to order; although he had the power to determine and articulate the appropriate intervals for debate, he was not to interfere with the "freedom of debate."[83] Moreover, Calhoun argued, as a figure not elected from within the Senate, he could not appropriately referee issues concerning the "latitude" or limits of discussions; he cited the English House of Lords as precedent for such a posture. For Calhoun, defining and restricting vice presidential power tended, on the whole, to serve the republic by returning the power to the Senate at large, further republicanizing the regime.

By referring to constitutional provisos and the wisdom of the Founders, especially Jefferson, Calhoun offered a convincing and accurate appeal to the republican worldview. Of course, "Patrick Henry" also deferred to the Constitution and other sources in his opinions, but not with the intensity or determination found in the essays of "Onslow." Jefferson's *Manual of Parliamentary Practice*, the standard Senate procedure handbook, withstood selective exegesis from both "Patrick Henry" and "Onslow," with "Patrick Henry" attempting to expand the categories and commentary outlined by Jefferson. Conversely, the strict constructionist Calhoun accepted the severest limitations placed upon the Senate president. For Calhoun, rigid boundaries were the only prudent course, as he sought to serve "in the spirit that ought to actuate every virtuous public functionary: not to assume doubtful powers—a spirit, under our systems of delegated authority, essential to the preservation of liberty."[84] Operating within a republicanism dedicated to legislative supremacy, Calhoun was troubled by the "slide into monarchy" resulting from increased executive patronage and power, and he decried the growth of the general government's influence and power during his lifetime. As Calhoun explained to Andrew Jackson, the philosophical crux of the problem was whether power was to be exercised by the centralizing political forces, namely, an executive who assumed extra-constitutional powers and abused

83. "Onslow," May 20, 1826, *Papers*, 10:99–104, quotation from 102.
84. "Onslow," June 29, 1826, *Papers*, 10:153.

patronage, or by the forces of a more dispersed system that would provide for greater liberty and protection.[85]

"Patrick Henry" presented his arguments with copious quotations from Jefferson's *Manual* and arcane and tedious references to Hatsell's treatise on procedure in the English House of Commons.[86] While the struggle between "Patrick Henry" and Calhoun over the *Manual* and whose position most closely resembled its guidelines for organizing the Senate's work might appear to be of an inclusively procedural nature, the use by "Patrick Henry" of Jefferson and Senate history undermined his own theory of power.[87] Jefferson composed the *Manual* after studiously surveying various parliamentary works and serving a four-year stint as Senate president. Calhoun's "Onslow" recognized that primary responsibility for Senate deliberations as well as the work of American government depended on a more explicit and concise guide, the Constitution. According to the fundamental law, the Senate was to make its own rules regarding proceedings, and then obey these structures (art. 1, sec. 5, clause 2), in an effort to prevent disruption and stalemate. As a supplement to the Constitution, the *Manual* remains an important guide for American parliamentary procedure, although Jefferson relied more in practice upon his *Parliamentary Pocket-Book*.[88]

Despite numerous ambiguities, the *Manual* authenticated the claims of both "Patrick Henry" and Calhoun to a degree, although "Patrick Henry" frequently conflated House provisions with Senate rules. "Patrick Henry" also misrepresented the situations in which a senator could call a colleague to order as compared to when such a privilege required the Senate president's intercession.[89] More important, "Patrick Henry" failed to appreciate historical precedent within the Senate itself, which relied heavily upon the president pro tempore to preside during legislative sessions. This disregard for custom—a commentary of sorts by "Patrick Henry" on his view of the Constitution—and his

85. Calhoun to Micah Sterling, May 31, 1826, *Papers*, 10:108; Calhoun to Andrew Jackson, June 4, 1826, *Papers*, 10:110.

86. John Hatsell, *Precedents of Proceedings in the House of Commons*, vol. 2.

87. Both Calhoun and "Patrick Henry" could find support for their respective positions in the *Manual* (Thomas Jefferson, *A Manual of Parliamentary Practice for the Use of the Senate of the United States;* for the modern scholarly edition see *Jefferson's Parliamentary Writing*, ed. Wilbur Samuel Howell, 353–433). Of special importance to Calhoun's argument is Jefferson's commentary on the special provisions within Senate procedure found throughout the *Manual*, especially sections 15 (*Jefferson's Parliamentary Writing*, 373) and 17 (376).

88. *Jefferson's Parliamentary Writing*, 9–38.

89. "Patrick Henry," June 7, 1926, *Papers*, 10:113–27; text cited, 122.

persistent pleas for a greater concentration of power in the executive forced Calhoun to conclude that "Patrick Henry" sought to disrupt the natural balance and sharing of authority needed to preserve the constitutional order:

> [W]hatever right the Vice-President possesses over order, must be derived from the Senate; and, therefore, he can exercise no power in adopting rules or enforcing them, but what has been delegated to him by the Senate, and only to the extent, both in manner and matter, to which the power has been delegated.[90]

Power was diffused through delegation, which strengthened the parts and the whole, allowing the parts ample opportunity to mold popular rule within the whole. For Calhoun, the theory of power and ultimately of popular rule espoused by "Patrick Henry" tended to support the "uncontrolled and unlimited power" of the executive.[91] To articulate inherent power as intrinsic to a particular office neglected the sources and primary agency that genuine authority required. The people, acting through state legislatures, delegated a modicum of power to the Senate. A symbiotic relationship developed between the recipient of power and its original sources, encouraging deliberation and mutual respect. The Senate had evolved into an institution that was responsive to state preferences, but also sensitive to national needs. For the vice president, the Senate had crafted certain boundaries of authority through established legislative and procedural habits. In a fashion, the Senate entrusted the vice president as Senate president with certain delegated powers, while retaining most of its authority; this included keeping the power to maintain order "in the body, and not in the presiding officer."[92] Connecting the power to preserve order with enforcement duty, the Senate as a body reserved for itself the obligations placed upon the Speaker in the House of Representatives. To remove or obstruct the critical nexus between source and agency within a theory of power would threaten destabilization, Calhoun argued, endangering liberties and denigrating popular rule as an aspect of true constitutional democracy.[93]

When Calhoun presented a restrictive commentary on the Constitution, "Patrick Henry" countered with a more expansive critique. For

90. "Onslow," June 27, 1826, *Papers*, 10:135–46; quotation from 138–39.
91. *Papers*, 10:139.
92. *Papers*, 10:140.
93. "Onslow," June 29, 1826, *Papers*, 10:147–55.

"Patrick Henry" the creative power of the Senate president implied inherent power; once an office was created, the officer possessed the power of the position without compromise. The Senate, having vested the Senate president with the power to call members to order, "confer[red] on the office by the single fact of creating it, every power necessary for the performance of its duties." Once created, the Senate president's powers could not be taken away or modified, argued "Patrick Henry." The creation alone established the "Constitutional character of that officer." "Patrick Henry" concluded by accusing Calhoun of promoting anarchy, degrading the Senate, and compromising the Adams Administration with his appointment of opposition senators to committee chairmanships.[94] While the forceful essays by "Patrick Henry" provide a valuable assessment of Calhoun's South Atlantic republicanism and protection doctrine, connecting the worldview of John Quincy Adams with the earlier New England republicanism, Calhoun's "Onslow" remains the more perceptive and accurate translator of the Founders' vision. His profound reliance upon the Constitution and the freedom granted to the Senate and House for designing procedures fitting their respective bodies was a means of preserving dispersive power and constitutional restraints against governmental largesse.[95]

For Calhoun, Senate procedures served as a microcosm of the need for restraint within political life. The orderly diffusion of power and application of popular rule allowed for a political system that was more sustainable. Considering his opponent's willingness to abrogate Senate responsibility for a more general and consuming theory of control, Calhoun addressed the central issue, the failure to accept the exigencies of republican government:

> To avoid this [a true explication of Calhoun's ideas], you have plunged into distinctions that are absurd, dangerous, and unconstitutional. If you had not been thus diverted, by sinister motives, from following the plain application of your own principles, you

94. "[C]onfer[red] on the office" quotation from p. 169, "Patrick Henry," August 4, 1826, *Papers*, 10:165–75; "Constitutional character" quotation from p. 184, "Patrick Henry," August 5, 1826, *Papers*, 10:175–87; "Patrick Henry," August 8, 1826, *Papers*, 10:188–97.

95. "Onslow," October 7, 1826, *Papers*, 10:208–14, text cited, 210; "Onslow," October 10, 1826, *Papers*, 10:215–21; "Onslow," October 12, 1826, *Papers*, 10:223–32.

could not have failed to see that the Vice-President must preside wholly by the rules of the Senate.[96]

Eschewing the need to address the central problem, "Patrick Henry" also avoided reconciling his emerging understanding of popular rule with a republican framework. Failing to confront the need for self-imposed restraints upon the delegation and use of power, as well as upon the agency of control, "Patrick Henry" defended cronyism as an appropriate tool for extending and confirming political power. A vice president or legislative leader should install only committee chairs who are "friendly to the measures" of the president, encouraging a system for rewarding the concentration of power and limiting popular participation in governing.[97] Insofar as the version of popular rule that "Patrick Henry" endorsed explicitly precluded dividing power and appealing to the higher potentialities of the citizenry, Calhoun observed that such a theory of politics "must lead to a political state," suggesting an arbitrariness regarding constitutional "first principles." While recognizing the need to allow for self-interest as "Patrick Henry" had noted, Calhoun urged the inclusion of the moral dimension within a concept of popular rule. As a guide to these "first principles," Calhoun's "Onslow" again referred to the Constitution, Jefferson's "Republican struggle," and the need to persevere against efforts directed towards denigrating this republican worldview.[98] In a speech given at a dinner in his honor at Pendleton, South Carolina, near the end of the "Patrick Henry"–"Onslow" exchange, Calhoun provided a summation of the republicanism that guided his political thought and influenced his theory of popular rule as represented later in the *Disquisition* and *Discourse:*

> [T]o strengthen this control of the ruled over rulers, through the great instrumentality of election, and to prevent it from being weakened by accident or design, particularly in the highest instance of its exercise by the people of these States, has been my constant aim; and Gentlemen, I trust, that I will never shrink from this great object under any circumstance of difficulty or danger.[99]

96. "Onslow," October 10, 1826, *Papers,* 10:218.
97. "Patrick Henry," August 8, 1826, *Papers,* 10:191.
98. "Onslow," October 12, 1826, *Papers,* 10:232.
99. "Speech at Pendleton, S.C.," September 7, 1826, *Papers,* 10:202.

From these "first principles" of the Kentucky Resolutions, the Virginia Resolutions, and the Report of 1800, Calhoun translated the South Atlantic republican worldview to his own generation. We now turn to Calhoun's presentation and articulation of his theory of politics and an examination of his reconciliation of popular rule with the ethical life. The foundation of such a reconciliation, as chapter 3 will show, is to be found in the *Disquisition*.

$$\boxed{3}$$

# The Political Theory of the *Disquisition*

---

Working within an understanding of American politics influenced by the original diffusion of power and defense of liberty evidenced in Jefferson's and Madison's political thought, Calhoun confronted the crisis in which America found itself during the second quarter of the nineteenth century. Calhoun's many speeches, public reports, and personal letters articulated a remarkable philosophical and constitutional commentary on political events during the period, while also providing ruminations of a more enduring quality about human nature, the purpose of politics, and the American regime's chances of survival. Such reflections are important to this book's overall pursuit, but we must now direct our attention to the more philosophically significant materials available within the Calhounian literary corpus—his theoretical testaments, *A Disquisition on Government* and *A Discourse on the Constitution and Government of the United States.* As Calhoun confided to his daughter Anna Maria, the impetus for composing the *Disquisition,* and subsequently the *Discourse,* was to provide "a solid foundation for political science" to assist future generations of Americans:

> I finished yesterday, the preliminary work, which treats of the elementary principles of the Science of Government, except reading it over and making final corrections, previous to copying and publishing. It takes 125 pages of large foolscap closely written for me. I am pretty well satisfied with its execution. It will be nearly throughout new territory.[1]

1. Calhoun to Mrs. T. G. Clemson, June 15, 1848, *Correspondence,* 768.

In the *Disquisition* Calhoun presented a theory of politics that is both original and in accord with the mainstream of the American political tradition. More than any other thinker of his period, Calhoun sought to explain the enduring qualities of American political thought in light of the troubled world of the mid-nineteenth century. In characterizing his *Disquisition* as "new territory," Calhoun was merely attempting to describe his treatise on the foundations of politics as his first and only systematic examination of these primary concerns. Unlike other theorists who had preceded and would follow Calhoun, both American and European, he did not seek to invent a new mode of philosophical speculation or a "grand theory" for the human sciences. Instead, he attempted to offer a refinement of classical, medieval, and modern notions regarding the relationship between government and the social order. As an effort in philosophical retrenchment, the *Disquisition* strengthened many preexisting conceptions regarding political liberty and popular rule within the American regime, while offering such insight with a view towards the future that awaited America.

The roundabout and often unreflective manner of *Disquisition* criticism frequently portrays the work as a reactionary, liberal, or utopian framework for defending Southern institutions against the impending crisis in American society. In one sense the work is reactionary, as it sought a rememorative recovery of South Atlantic republican thought and institutions. The "reforms" associated with the Jackson presidency, abolitionism, and democratic theory were, for Calhoun, illusory, momentary, and counterproductive, and he identified the limitations connected with this metamorphosis of republican political thought into a democratic ideology throughout his life. The transition from a stable, disciplined mode of popular rule to an undisciplined "spoils" system convinced Calhoun that a recovery of the earlier ethos was necessary if the country were to survive. The "original" grounding of democratic ideas within a decentralized political order came under greater scrutiny during the 1830s and 1840s. With the election of Andrew Jackson to the presidency in 1828, the previously accepted understanding of the national government's "proper share" of authority as explained by the Constitution and political practice began to erode.[2] Long-standing provisions designed to promote aristocratic restraints upon uninformed or partisan opinion as a means of preserving the regime also came under attack. As early as 1826,

---

2. Calhoun to Samuel D. Ingham, July 31, 1831, *Papers*, 11:442.

Calhoun expressed his concerns to Jackson: "An issue has been fairly made, as it seems to me, between power and liberty; and it must be determined . . . whether the real governing principle in our political system be the power and patronage of the Executive, or the voice of the people." For Calhoun, the ensuing "Jacksonian Revolution" tended to denigrate these older principles within the polity, preferring instead to celebrate the assumption of powers and centralization of authority by the national government that was "neither conferred by the Constitution nor the laws, but in derogation of both."[3]

Calhoun's accomplishment was his diagnosis, although his death in 1850 prohibited a more integrated participation in the cure. Many who would attempt to assume Calhoun's philosophical and political mantle during the nineteenth and twentieth centuries actually committed a great injustice to his political theory by ignoring its more abiding qualities. In articulating the inherited understanding of properly constituted popular rule for his political situation, Calhoun may be called the last of the Founders. The worldview he imbibed from early life, his own republican understanding of popular rule, and his efforts directed towards preventing the dissolution of the regime are indicators of both an attachment to and a willingness to defend the American republic. While neither providing a programmatic transition to the future nor simply rearticulating an appreciation of constitutional restraint within popular rule, Calhoun presented an authentic and prescient American understanding of social and political life that could contribute even today to remedying problems associated with popular rule in America and elsewhere. Having alluded to several aspects of this potential contribution, we shall now proceed to examine the *Disquisition* as the primary theoretical guide for assimilating Calhoun's political thought into a philosophical whole.

To appreciate Calhoun, we must acknowledge that the *Disquisition* was a work of political theory, not a compendium of esoteric knowledge. While presenting the intrinsic limitations of the *Disquisition* here, we also recognize the treatise as part of a continuing conversation on America's political heritage. In this regard, Calhoun stood at the crossroads between the early republic and modern America. As this chapter discusses Calhoun's political theory in the *Disquisition*, modern Americans will find encouragement for confronting the persistent

3. Calhoun to Andrew Jackson, June 4, 1826, *Papers*, 10:110; "Speech on the President's Protest," May 6, 1834, *Papers*, 12:303.

and often bewildering problems associated with popular rule and perpetuating the Founders' design for dividing political authority.

Most theories of politics, including the *Disquisition*, attempt to provide an assessment of human nature. A prudent political philosophy must rest upon such a fundamental comprehension, reflecting the understanding of the author and his theoretical universe. According to the *Disquisition*, human nature is expressed in terms of the "constitution or law of our nature."[4] In describing the human predicament in this fashion, Calhoun affirmed the Hebraic-Christian conception of human nature, which views humanity as divided between the higher and lower ethical possibilities, and in need of personal and societal restraint as protection against the impulse of the moment. Calhoun's theory of human nature also rejected social-contractarian typologies devoted to promoting humankind's inert strength and virtue or ability to survive in isolation. As we shall see, Calhoun contended that humankind's primary obligation lies in community. Self-discipline and love of neighbor begin with the individual and spread to the community, and then to society as a whole. In other words, the "constitution or law of our nature" serves to define the limitations of society and politics for Calhoun, on one hand, while on the other it presupposes and defends the necessity of a properly constituted community for securing the moral and ethical results concomitant to society's perpetuation.

On an ontological level, Calhoun's "constitution or law of our nature" resembles the Declaration of Independence's "Laws of nature and of Nature's God," as both affirmed humanity's situation between the earthly and the transcendent. The implicit role of the transcendent at the beginning of the *Disquisition* becomes explicit as the work unfolds. However, the obvious tension between the concept of natural law and the explanation of a universal creative force is unresolved in Jefferson's draft of the Declaration.[5] As Jefferson would explain

4. John C. Calhoun, *A Disquisition on Government*, in *Union and Liberty: The Political Philosophy of John C. Calhoun*, ed. Ross M. Lence, 5 (hereafter cited as *Disquisition*). The Lence edition contains the most accurate versions of Calhoun's original *Disquisition* and *Discourse*. The more popular contemporary edition of the *Disquisition*, edited by C. Gordon Post, contains numerous typographical mistakes. Although no manuscript of the *Disquisition* exists, the work originally appeared in 1851 and was republished in 1853 in *The Works of John C. Calhoun*, edited by Richard K. Crallé, 1:1–107 (hereafter cited as *Works*).

5. The Continental Congress inserted the reference to the "Supreme Judge of the World" and an appeal to providence in the final version of the document (Carl L. Becker, *The Declaration of Independence*, 174–84).

near the end of his life, the "holy purpose" of the Declaration was to "burst the chains under which monkish ignorance and superstition" had previously hindered humankind's ability to understand the requirements of self-government. The incorporation of the role of the transcendent may not have been a primary consideration for Jefferson. While Jefferson used religious imagery in his draft of the Declaration, the text did not contain the invocation to the Divine that was commonplace in many state constitutions of the period.[6]

From an early point within the *Disquisition* Calhoun's concern for the transcendent is apparent, although it never became the predominant aspect of his political thought. The American republic possessed a providential quality, persevering against great obstacles, and warranting Calhoun's use of this tension for explaining the country's political endurance and prospects for its future. It is surprising that the theological doctrine of providence exhibited throughout Calhoun's writings has escaped the attention of nearly every student of his life and work, suggesting an inability within the scholarly community to acknowledge and appreciate Calhoun's philosophical and theological acumen, as well as the role these concerns assumed in his political thought.[7] To neglect Calhoun's relation with the spiritual, or to demean him as an antireligionist of some variety, implies a failure to adequately comprehend his self-understanding and his analysis of political crisis.[8]

Continuing to approach the fundamental questions of the human condition, Calhoun undertook a comprehensive and demanding process of examination. As it was for Aristotle, the practicality of everyday life for Calhoun often coincided with the need for contemplation and reflection.[9] Amidst a long and consuming public career filled

6. Thomas Jefferson, *The Writings of Thomas Jefferson*, ed. Andrew A. Lipscomb, 19:278; Jefferson to Roger C. Weightman, June 24, 1826, *Writings*, 7:450–51. See Pauline Maier, *American Scripture: Making the Declaration of Independence*, 186.

7. Both Clyde N. Wilson's introduction to *The Essential Calhoun* (xv–xxvii) and chapter 5 of James D. Clarke's "Calhoun and the Concept of the 'Reactionary Enlightenment'" (192–222) incorporate a more comprehensive elucidation of Calhoun's theological understanding and are exceptions to this rule. References to the importance of providence within Calhoun's writings are too numerous to cite, but for representative selections see his *Discourse on the Constitution and Government of the United States*, in *Union and Liberty: The Political Philosophy of John C. Calhoun*, ed. Ross M. Lence, 142, 198 (hereafter cited as *Discourse*); *Papers*, 10:239; 11:565; 12:80, 526; 15:163; 16:154.

8. See Robert Campbell Jeffrey, Jr., "The Thought of John C. Calhoun"; and R. J. Rushdoony, "The Disastrous War."

9. Aristotle, *Nicomachean Ethics*, trans. J. A. K. Thompson, 1106a20–1107a1.

with tremendous professional and familial obligations, Calhoun acknowledged the need for a serious study of the great principles of
politics and the moral life. Relying upon his lengthy involvement
in government and his capacity for contemplation, Calhoun began
his sustained meditations on the "elementary principles of political
science" in earnest nearly five years before his death, although his
initial foray into composing the work came much earlier. In 1841
Calhoun noted to Orestes Brownson that he had "commenced and
made some progress" towards developing his "views on Government." His lifelong study resulted in the *Disquisition*, a "science of
government" for apprehending the "nature and object" of politics for
the rising generation.[10]

### CALHOUN'S "SCIENCE OF GOVERNMENT"

As a work of political theory, the *Disquisition* incorporated a conception of science as denoting a systematic inquiry into the sources of political life, but Calhoun never envisioned the pursuit of science as the
solution to all human needs and concerns. Since the publication of the
*Disquisition*, it has become commonplace to infer that the methodology
supporting the treatise resembles the work of modern scientific exploration. For example, Ralph Lerner suggests that Calhoun's "models"
for the study were "Newton, Laplace, Galileo, and Bacon." In a similar
vein, other assessments contend that the *Disquisition* "represents the
claims of modern science" generally, and more specifically, "Darwin's
theory of natural selection."[11] These criticisms, among others, correctly
identify Calhoun's use of scientific language, but wrongly associate
Calhoun with the abuses of scientific study commonly described as
"scientism." As an intellectual movement, scientism was founded
upon reductionist premises and often promoted the dehumanizing
of the human subject once viewed as a unique or divine creation.[12]

10. Calhoun to John Alfred Calhoun, April 2, 1845, *Papers*, 21:465–66; Calhoun to
Orestes A. Brownson, October 31, 1841, *Papers*, 15:801; Calhoun, *Disquisition*, 5.
    11. Ralph Lerner, "Calhoun's New Science of Politics," 918; Harry V. Jaffa, *Defenders
of the Constitution*, 12; Theodore L. Putterman, "Calhoun's Realism?" 114.
    12. Calhoun clearly rejected any theory of politics that did not include an apprecia-
tion of the human condition. From another perspective, scientism is not a more rarefied
method of scientific study, but an attempt to control all discourse. As Father Stanley L.
Jaki has argued, "Scientism is never a genuine reverence for science but a harnessing
of science for a nonscientific purpose" (*The Road of Science and the Ways to God*, 218).

Unfortunately, Calhoun's direct correlation between the "science of government" and astronomy is also often misinterpreted as conflating these two systems of inquiry into a single pursuit. As with most theories of politics, Calhoun's attempts to prove the general applicability of his work lack the exactitude both assumed by and expected from modern proponents of the "scientific method."[13] Calhoun accepted a rudimentary association between cause and effect as witnessed in antiquity, while rejecting the determinism and argument from discovery essential to modern science. In fact, Calhoun's praise of human liberty, an "earthly blessing . . . in the first rank," further delineated his political theory from the extreme attempts to overcome the limitations of human nature found in modern science.[14] Calhoun also did not envision science as a tool for the manipulation and domination of humankind analogous to twentieth-century efforts, but as a means of providing for a greater intelligibility of human nature and the political world he had inherited. To associate the South Carolinian with the most pernicious aspects of modern scientific inquiry misrepresents his understanding and devotion to the systematic study of politics, and removes him from his historical context. If we are to comprehend the originality and importance of Calhoun's political theory, we must first apprehend his own understanding of science as a process of study and philosophical maturation, leading to the greater dispersion of knowledge and advancement of civilization. To approach such a level of comprehension, we shall first examine the statesman's dedication to improving agricultural practices as an example of the method he used throughout his life.

From an early age, Calhoun was attached to the agrarian life, and this prompted his intense devotion to all types of agricultural pursuits; he was continually improving and modifying his planting, harvesting, and farm-management practices. Agriculture served as the primary basis of support for his family, although Calhoun's devotion to farming cannot be explained merely in terms of pecuniary rewards or financial well-being. The same is true for his devotion to public service; Calhoun used his positions within government neither to advance his financial interests nor to amass great wealth. Responding to Duff Green, a political intimate and successful entrepreneur, Calhoun admitted, "Of all things in the world, I have the least taste for

13. *Disquisition*, 5–6.
14. *Papers*, 12:157. Also see C. S. Lewis, *The Abolition of Man*; Jaki, *The Road of Science*, 246–61; and David Walsh, *The Growth of the Liberal Soul*, 70–75.

money making." With the exception of a failed Georgia gold-mining venture during the 1830s and early 1840s, Calhoun demonstrated a spirit of timidity regarding investment opportunities, preferring to concentrate solely upon agriculture. "My highest ambition as to money is to be independent, in a moderate and plain mode of living," he professed to Green, as financial problems consistently plagued him.[15] A government salary and his Fort Hill plantation supplied the Calhoun family with a moderate income, but upon his death much indebtedness remained from loans and assistance given to others—especially his children—at least a decade earlier.

Calhoun's devotion to agriculture deserves more attention than it has received because the vocation represents his political theory in microcosm. Nourished by daily labors in the fields, the properly ordered plantation community produced a more stable and wholesome environment for families, workers, and slaves than Northern industrialism could offer, Calhoun argued. Even for an energetic and devoted planter like himself, agricultural pursuits also allowed greater opportunity for study, as he noted to his friend Senator Littleton Tazewell:

> You are not incorrect in supposing, that as much devoted, as I am to agriculture, which without affectation is my favorite pursuit, I am not so exclusively absorbed by it, as to have my attention wholly diverted from publick affairs. They are in fact too intimately blended to be wholly separated in the contemplation of any one, in the least disposed to trace the progress of events, and among the reasons of my attachments to agriculture is, that while it affords sufficient activity for health, it also gives leisure for reflection and improvement.[16]

According to Calhoun's worldview, an agrarian environment encouraged a mode of existence more conducive to the ethical life. In regard to farming, the living experience of tilling the soil and harvesting crops embodied a sense of self-sacrifice and an attachment to a shared community. Farming, according to Calhoun, was by its very nature a communal, rather than a solitary, act. The primary aesthetic and spiritual needs of humankind were best fulfilled by the structure and corporate nature of an agrarian society. A twentieth-century Calhoun

15. Calhoun to Duff Green, July 27, 1837, *Papers*, 13:526. For a summary account of the gold-mining venture, see Clyde N. Wilson, "Some Personal Matters," *Papers*, 12:xl–xliv.

16. Calhoun to Littleton Waller Tazewell, July 1, 1827, *Papers*, 10:292.

disciple, Andrew Lytle, convincingly reaffirmed Calhoun's original argument: "Agriculture is a limited term. A better one is farming. It is inclusive. Unlike any other occupation, farming is, or should be, a way of life."[17]

Calhoun's farming efforts, like his theoretical and practical labors, were dependent upon a process of reevaluation and emendation. Praising the propensity of his brother-in-law, James E. Colhoun, for applying innovations "desirous of improving our agriculture," Calhoun celebrated the accomplishment as appropriate and necessary: "I know nothing, by which our enlightened and wealthy citizens can more effectually place their country under obligation, than by contributing to its [agricultural] improvement."[18] The need to analyze and assimilate advances in farming practices was intimately related to his effort to appreciate and articulate the evolving political tradition, and Calhoun attempted to understand the significance of the unfolding crises within both American agriculture and politics from the perspective of a faithful steward.[19] For Calhoun, stewardship entailed reconciling the organic community with a universal moral order, and this unification was encouraged in an agrarian society that was dependent upon "the culture of the soil."[20] By accepting the challenge to study these movements, Calhoun provided ample evidence of his ability to examine the deeper inspirations behind social and political life. In developing a more thorough appreciation of these concerns, Calhoun followed a rigorous study regimen throughout his life. Furthermore, Calhoun's work in agriculture bore additional practical and intellectual fruit, and was frequently a more consuming interest than politics, forcing him to confess that he was sometimes "wholly absorbed in agriculture to the exclusion of politics."[21] Publishing an article on plough construction in the respected journal *American Farmer* in 1825 and receiving accolades from local farmers on his agricultural methods show Calhoun's devotion to improving rural life.[22] Farming, like politics, demanded systematic examination, circumspection, and patience. In relating this

17. Andrew Nelson Lytle, "The Small Farm Secures the State," in *From Eden to Babylon*, 34.

18. Calhoun to James E. Colhoun, April 28, 1832, *Papers*, 11:568.

19. For an exploration of the conjoining of ethics and the imagination in this manner, see Claes G. Ryn, *Will, Imagination, and Reason*, 65–77.

20. Twelve Southerners, "Introduction: A Statement of Principles," in *I'll Take My Stand*, xlvii.

21. Calhoun to Littleton Waller Tazewell, April 1, 1827, *Papers*, 10:283.

22. *The American Farmer* 6, no. 50 (March 4, 1825): 393–94; "Hon. John C. Calhoun's Farm," *Carolina Planter* 1 (April 1845): 219–21. In the course of an editorial, John

critical insight directly to politics, Calhoun recognized that penetrating the central problem associated with popular rule in America did not involve a new "metaphysics,"[23] but the recovery and articulation of a moral and intellectual foundation of politics. This pursuit would span Calhoun's public career and assume the status of a "science" or quest for a stable mode of popular rule. Consequently, one of the many contributions Calhoun imparted to modern political theory concerns the inefficacy of simply accepting existing formulations without acknowledging the need for engaging primary sources and confronting one's own world, as witnessed in the advice he gave regarding legal studies. The aspiring young lawyer should

> study attentively all the best elementary treatises; be assiduous in his attendance in court, and attentive to the routine of office. He will of course make himself master of the particular laws of the state where he intends to practice. But no previous preparation can supersede the necessity of the minutest & closest attention to the cases he may undertake after he is admitted to practice, both as to the facts and the law. On this point, the success of a lawyer mainly depends.[24]

One must study the past but also participate in the present to recover the necessary theoretical foundations. For Calhoun, the search assumed the form of a systematic inquiry, a "science"—ultimately, a quest for the truth; he was dedicated to sharing these developing political and philosophical meditations with his generation.

Science, as an early metaphor within the *Disquisition*, was encouraged and supported by Calhoun's tutelage at Yale College under Benjamin Silliman, a newly hired professor of chemistry and natural history, who would become an eminent teacher and mentor to a generation of geologists.[25] As a renowned scientist and a person of great religious faith, Silliman served as an important model for the young Calhoun. The professor's work suggested that the most probing questions regarding human existence could be encountered while maintaining a belief in the eternal. In Silliman, Calhoun found

---

S. Skinner, editor of *The American Farmer*, described Calhoun as "amongst the most accomplished practical planters, and enlightened promoters of the interests of Agriculture in our country" (*The American Farmer* 6 [February 4, 1825]: 362).

23. Lerner, "Calhoun's New Science," 918.
24. Calhoun to Thomas J. Johnson, March 20, 1836, *Papers*, 13:116–17.
25. See Chandos M. Brown's *Benjamin Silliman: A Life in the Young Republic*.

an able exemplar and inspiration for his own study of popular rule. As a model of how scientific study, human experience, and one's faith could be reconciled, Silliman was as much a moral philosopher as a natural scientist.

Calhoun and Silliman continued a friendship and exchange of ideas over the years. During his tenure as secretary of war, Calhoun received a prospectus from Silliman announcing a new scholarly publication, the *Journal of Science*. Calhoun expressed his support for the venture as he surveyed the nation's situation: "The utility of such a work, particularly in this country, must be apparent, and our number, wealth, and intellectual improvement have now attained that point at which there ought to be sufficient patronage." Acting upon Silliman's counsel three years later, Calhoun republished a paper that originally had appeared in the *Journal*, and he confided to his teacher a desire to secure a permanent chemistry professorship at West Point. Eventually, Secretary Calhoun invited Silliman to inspect West Point's academic and physical facilities. The professor obliged his former student, conducted an official visit, and filed a report with the secretary suggesting ways "for improving the condition of certain branches of the sciences" taught at the Academy.[26] Calhoun discovered in Silliman a continued witness to the need for the kind of systematic inquiry that he would employ in his political theory labors at the end of his life. Silliman's willingness to advance the critical processes while embodying an eagerness to work within a living tradition encouraged Calhoun's own efforts in this regard. For most modern thinkers such a predicament cannot be resolved without fear and trepidation, and Calhoun and Silliman were not exceptions to the rule; yet, they persevered.[27]

The combination of Benjamin Silliman's early influence and Calhoun's dedication to an unfolding understanding of social and political life as it related to popular rule encouraged Calhoun's lifelong devotion to advances in learning. Through the study of recurrent knowledge—his inherited republican worldview—and a process of

26. Calhoun to Benjamin Silliman, March 26, 1818, *Papers,* 2:211; Calhoun to Benjamin Silliman, January 13, 1821, *Papers,* 5:556–57; Calhoun to Benjamin Silliman, July 19, 1822, *Papers,* 7:216 (for the report of his visit, see 7:201).

27. Calhoun to Benjamin Silliman, January 13, 1821, *Papers,* 5:557. Silliman's response to the rise of critical biblical exegesis during the early nineteenth century provides some illumination in this regard. Instead of accepting or rejecting the view of the Genesis creation narrative as essentially a literary device, Silliman assumed a compromise position, arguing that the six days of creation were symbolic—denoting a great, infinite expanse of time (E. Brooks Holifield, *The Gentlemen Theologians,* 99).

scholarly refinement, the "science of government" and astronomy could be associated, albeit in a rather unorthodox manner: to apprehend the dynamics of politics or astronomy, one must study foundational concerns, experience the more enduring aspects of one's field of study, and finally develop an appreciation for those primary characteristics of our lives and work as we participate in a "chain of being" transcending our own limited ventures. For Calhoun, these concerns included a horizon beyond farming and politics, encompassing geology, linguistics, history, and other disciplines of humane learning. Calhoun also believed that a gradual advancement towards appreciating the full range of human experiences and accomplishments merited his steadfast attention, and he devoted much of his time to studying and recording these improvements in many fields of endeavor, as a few representative examples will demonstrate. On one occasion, Albert Gallatin, statesman, diplomat, and secretary of the treasury under Presidents Jefferson and Madison, sought Calhoun's counsel regarding his proposed study of Native Americans. Supplying corrections to Gallatin's draft overview of the study, Calhoun encouraged the enterprise and even offered his theory surrounding an "analogy of languages" among Native Americans. A year later, Gregory Perdicaris, a Greek acquaintance of Calhoun's, notified the senator of his election to the Archaeological Society of Athens, based upon his association with Calhoun and Calhoun's reputation for encouraging humane learning and as "one of the friends of Greece."[28] As a result of Calhoun's diverse interests, he either joined or was awarded honorary memberships in many major academic societies. By participating in the advancement of scholarly labors, Calhoun also remained faithful to the constitutional admonition furthering the "Progress of Science and the useful Arts" (art. 1, sec. 8), but more important, he developed a more "solid foundation" for the political theory of the *Disquisition* than he could have otherwise.[29]

The conception of science Calhoun incorporated into the *Disquisition* most closely resembles earlier work by Montesquieu, Pufendorf, and Burlamaqui, among others, as these thinkers sought to articulate habitual human experiences and responses into a "science of politics." While doubtless influenced by these political philosophers and their empirical approaches to the study of politics, the *Disquisition*, in Cal-

28. Calhoun to Albert Gallatin, May 25, 1837, *Papers*, 13:506; Gregory A. Perdicaris to Calhoun, September 12, 1838, *Papers*, 14:423.
  29. *Disquisition*, 5.

houn's own view, was a systematic inquiry into the deeper interplay between liberty and the diffusion of political authority throughout American political life. To accomplish this study, Calhoun was forced to penetrate the sometimes vulgar and often turgid political veneer of public discourse and the heavily partisan press he faced as a cabinet officer and senator. Within the previous generation of American thinkers, "Publius" too had attempted such an intricate analysis, suggesting the importance of "the science of politics" throughout *The Federalist*. For example, in *The Federalist*, No. 9, Publius explained that the "science of politics" was not to be thought of as a quantum leap towards a new empiricism; rather, this "science" would serve as an imaginative and systematic approach to the "distribution of power":

> The science of politics, however, like most other sciences has received great improvement. The efficacy of various principles is now well understood, which were either not known at all, or imperfectly known to the ancients. The regular distribution of power into distinct departments—the introduction of legislative balances and checks—the institution of courts composed of judges, holding their offices during good behavior—the representation of the people in the legislature by deputies of their own election—these are wholly new discoveries, or have made their principal progress towards perfection in modern times. They are means, and powerful means, by which the excellences of republican government may be retained and its imperfections lessened or avoided. To this catalogue of circumstances, that tend to the amelioration of popular systems of civil government, I shall venture, however novel it may appear to some, to add one more on a principle, which has been made the foundation of an objection to the New Constitution, I mean the ENLARGEMENT of the ORBIT within which systems are to revolve.[30]

Neither Publius nor Calhoun could have imagined the brave new theoretical world later critics would ascribe to their labors. This quotation from *The Federalist* demonstrates an explicit reappraisal and defense of republican principles, repackaged to fit the political situation. Significantly, *The Federalist* and the *Disquisition* share a common

---

30. Alexander Hamilton, James Madison, and John Jay, *The Federalist*, ed. George W. Carey and James McClellan, No. 9 (Hamilton), 38–39 (hereafter cited as *The Federalist*). *The Federalist*, Nos. 9, 18, 31, 37, 47, and 66 are important examples of Publius's "science of politics."

and interwoven thread in this aspect: both argue that popular rule, regardless of the particular form one inherits or envisions, must incorporate a notion of restraint to guard against potential excesses. It is to this end that both works are dedicated. But unlike *The Federalist*, Calhoun's *Disquisition* supplies a more comprehensive and uniform political theory for confronting the complexities of modern popular rule. Against a backdrop of great sectional and ideological animosities, the *Disquisition* attempts a reconsideration of the primary concerns that contribute to a more thorough depiction of human nature.

In considering the fundamental "law of our nature," Calhoun envisioned humankind "so constituted as to be a social being." He believed that the natural human condition is defined by its gregariousness, grounded in community, and devoted to encouraging the unfolding of "moral and intellectual faculties" so as to enlighten and develop civilization. In accord with Aristotle and the Hebraic-Christian tradition of political theory, Calhoun understood human existence as essentially social. Moral and spiritual development necessitate interaction, restraint, and reinforcement, and these elements are most acutely experienced in a society constituted to embody them. In other words, the ethical life cannot be sustained outside of a social framework. While not rejecting a role for self-interest within the community, Calhoun recognized the constant tension between the need for some degree of societal unity and the needs of the individual. He suggested that the properly constituted society could assist in ameliorating the selfishness associated with our "brute creation," and encouraged attachment to the common good as an alternative. Conversely, the statesman's concern within the *Disquisition* regarding the frailties of social and political existence demonstrates the true importance of community. For Calhoun, authentic community or the associating of communities into a larger society was neither humankind writ large without an appreciation for the philosophical and practical ordering of political life, nor an atomistic association devoted to the narcissistic advancement of the self above all other requirements. Authentic social life requires self-denial in some form, he contended, regardless of the level of enmity between the individual and the group, as humans are "irresistibly" drawn to each other.[31]

While Calhoun accepted and incorporated a Burkean notion of humankind's "ancient imperfections" to suggest that an element of

31. *Disquisition*, 5.

restraint is necessary within society, he rejected the radical individualism often associated with social contract theorists.[32] The primal
life of the savage, envisioned by some social contract theorists as the
precursor to society and politics, was for Calhoun the most unnatural
of states. Calhoun's defense of an authentic, moral community was
based upon acknowledging that the only natural state is the political
and social one to which a person is born. Instead of being born
free, humans are "born subject" to parental authority and the laws
of the country of their birth.[33] In presenting this theory of politics,
Calhoun extended his original proposition regarding humankind as
essentially social and political, adding the institution of the family
as the bonding element for this association. His argument in the
*Disquisition* remains implicit and must be read in light of his earlier
defense of community as a natural order where the parts remain
"just to each other."[34] When Calhoun surveyed his world, the most
conspicuous example of a living community was the plantation.[35]
Like the Aristotelian household, the plantation possessed a certain
hierarchy of status and responsibility, although Calhoun's lines of
demarcation are less distinct than previous studies have suggested.
Even though Calhoun was a slaveholder who defended the institution
as necessary for both the slave and the plantation owner, at least
temporarily, he incorporated slaves into his community as much as
possible and described slaves and their relations as "family."[36] The
plantation settlement certainly possessed tremendous shortcomings,
especially for its captives; however, Calhoun's use of the plantation
narrative to describe his conception of a true community further
distinguishes the roles of diversity and liberty within his political
theory. The older notions of autonomy and mutual accommodation
among communities—diversity and liberty in action—were already
weakened as the result of an expanding administrative regime. If a
stable mode of popular rule was to be recovered, the community
would have to be protected against efforts to incorporate its stake in
society and politics into a political structure that would diminish the

32. The most convincing, albeit flawed, argument for reading Calhoun as a disciple of Hobbes remains Frank M. Coleman's "American Constitutional Philosophy:
Madison, Thoreau, Calhoun, and Sumner," in his *Hobbes and America*, 121–47.
33. *Disquisition*, 52, 45.
34. Calhoun to Richard K. Crallé, April 15, 1832, *Papers*, 11:566.
35. *Papers*, 14:84.
36. Calhoun to Abbot Lawrence, April 9, 1845, *Papers*, 21:482–83. For examples of
Calhoun's concern for slaves, see *Papers*, 15:367, 510, 685; 16:9; and *Works*, 4:505.

community's most salient qualities. The preservation and protection of an organic, republican system of popular rule required accepting the natural diversity of the communities that formed the larger society, while enjoying the increased liberties that resulted from this diffusion of authority.[37]

Proceeding from the smaller to the larger aspects of Calhoun's reconstructed *koinonia*, we should note that Calhoun specifically avoided a gender-based theory of association, while reaffirming the importance of society. As we have argued, the *Disquisition* should be studied primarily as a work of political theory that concentrates upon the role and relation of the government to the social order. The work's dramatic transition from describing a rather nebulous social state to the political should be interpreted as the extension of Calhoun's plantation narrative to the larger society, while providing for a system of governance that would insure the larger society's survival.

In shifting from the social to the political, Calhoun omitted an adequate explanation of the intricacies of society; however, for Calhoun, the assemblage of smaller groupings of the citizenry, in communities, within the larger society was of greatest importance. He held that these communities served as the primary mode of association and were essential to the regime's survival. After all, a rightly ordered community consists of highly autonomous parts or divisions cooperating together for the welfare of the whole. The societal realm described in the *Disquisition* should be understood as the extension of the smaller community units, represented by the states, which serve as examples of how the larger society could be organized and political authority diffused throughout an extensive regime. For Calhoun, the United States of America did not exist as an aggregate, only as a confederacy of communities, ultimately forming states and eventually contributing to a union.[38]

---

37. The Aristotelian notion of superior and subordinate social functions greatly influenced Calhoun's understanding of slavery as a political condition. Given the slave's situation, Calhoun argued that protection was a goal superior to personal liberty. Although Calhoun's interpretation of slavery is beyond the scope of this book, any study of his views on the subject should include a comprehensive assessment of his various critiques. See *Papers*, 1:312, 371; 10:253, 254; 11:250, 464; 12:136, 197, 371, 531, 548; 13:62–67, 108, 262, 371, 389–90, 395, 504; 14:34, 65–66, 84, 123, 207, 549; 15:99, 139, 315, 366, 367, 510, 685, 830; 16:9, 17, 32, 105, 111, 112, 301, 341, 342, 349, 403; 17:136, 355, 425; 18:220, 276, 278; 19:534, 575, 613; 20:181, 290–91; 21:272–73, 482; 22:31, 172, 177; and *Works*, 4:346, 482, 505.

38. *Papers*, 11:494.

Society, as the natural assemblage of settlements or communities, is reinforced by the political order, Calhoun asserted: "[W]hile man is so constituted as to make the social . . . necessary to his existence and the full development of his faculties, this . . . cannot exist without government." To further the durability of society, government emerged in the evolution of human structures, usually linking existing sources of social and political organization into a more coherent totality. The perpetual human and community need for a governing authority of some kind is presented in the *Disquisition* as exemplifying "phenomena" for understanding the insight involved in evaluating the human "constitution" or "law." In presenting social and political development in this manner, Calhoun offered a coherent and connective description of the transition from the familial to the societal, and concluded with the governmental. As indicated earlier, Calhoun's formulation is more compact than Aristotle's four-tiered family–household–village–government movement in the *Politics*, although the *Disquisition* recognizes the role of the family by portraying the connection between a mother and an infant as "peculiar relations."[39] The attachment between mother and child demonstrates the vital interconnectivity fundamental to human relationships. In presenting the higher potentialities of social and political life, Calhoun laid the groundwork for a political theory dedicated to cultivating community within an environment where the potential disruptions to this order could be corrected from within. Government provides the necessary means for preserving family, community, and the larger umbrella of social webs that connect communities to each other; and while government is a necessity, it remains subordinate to the society. Calhoun's conclusion came as the result of much reflection and a comprehensive, "scientific" study of historical sources over the course of his life.

In addition to this historical and philosophical analysis, the *Disquisition* offered the idea that "universal experience" was to be appreciated as the accumulated insight of many generations imparted to the current generation.[40] This historical continuity confirmed and extended Calhoun's perception of providence at work in the world. "Universal experience" also formed the building blocks of Calhoun's conception of prescriptive knowledge and reason. The statesman's

39. *Disquisition*, 6.
40. Ibid., 6–8.

understanding of the unity of experience and reason provides additional evidence that he eschewed mechanistic and idealist theories of politics. In fact, Calhoun's use of reason was underpinned by a concept of justice and an insistence upon the reflective role experience could assume within the process of political decision making. Throughout his life, Calhoun defended human reason acting within a historical and communal framework as a means of addressing the country's ills. Frequently opposing the denigration of reason generally, and defending the centrality of a properly constituted conception of "sound reason," specifically as a guide for political theory, Calhoun warned his colleagues against the propensity to "renounce our reason" during times of upheaval.[41]

The compatibility between reason and "universal experience" also assumes great importance in the *Discourse*, in which Calhoun provides a multiplicity of histories to augment his presentation, including accounts of political parties, regime dissolution, and the Founding. In blending the *Disquisition*'s theoretical formulations and the *Discourse*'s refinement of American political experience, Calhoun affirmed the insuperable role played by the historical in understanding political order: the "past is the parent of the present."[42] More than a trite affirmation of the use of history as a guide to present troubles, Calhoun's integration of reason and the role of experience into a theory of politics resembled the earlier contribution made by Edmund Burke in this regard.[43] Through his assimilation of the Burkean notion of inherited wisdom, and his insight into the nature and practice of politics, Calhoun was able to articulate a profound understanding of the bonding of experience and reason.

Calhoun believed that reason must be guided by the full range of historical experience and must be available to successive generations as a guide for securing and maintaining a just regime. Calhoun's rather compact language of "universal experience" possessed two components: reason *(Vernunft)* and understanding *(Verstand)*.[44] Reason as the immediate, logical thought process of an individual was important, albeit potentially counterproductive. Apportioning human freedom

41. Ibid., 33; "Speech on the Albany Petition for Repeal of the Embargo," May 6, 1812, *Papers*, 1:107.

42. *Correspondence*, 753.

43. Calhoun's intellectual debt to Burke was tremendous, as suggested by the political theory of the *Disquisition* (for representative examples see *Papers*, 1:319, 386; 11:254; 13:601; 14:71; 15:151, 482, 718).

44. Ryn, *Will, Imagination, and Reason*, 91.

based upon an individual's ability to reason removed from any ethical considerations would introduce the possibility of arbitrariness and all too often would provide the opportunity for aborting the transmitted legacy of liberty and restraint in governing, especially as it concerned popular rule. The personal faculty of reason alone could not sustain societal liberty, or ultimately individual liberty. Against Locke's unencumbered man with the "power to think or not to think, to move or not to move, according to the preference or direction of his own mind," Calhoun presented a more intricate defense of reason as the culmination of individual reflection and corporate refinement and understanding. As the Carolinian argued, the notion of reason articulated by Locke was a denial of man's social nature. Accordingly, the Lockean state of nature was "a truism resting on a mere supposed state that cannot exist, and of course one of little or no practical value."[45] And while it must be admitted that a tension between the individual and the community is inevitable within Calhoun's concept of reason, this tension can be alleviated when the insight of reason is complemented by experience. The only appropriate means to counter or amend abuses within the body politic resulting from "irresponsible power" such as tyranny, illegitimate authority, or unrestrained popular rule was a theory of liberty ripened by reason and experience.[46] Among the various contributing factors initiating and inflaming these abuses in the society, no source was more destructive than an imprudent extension of individual liberty at the expense of the community and the moral order. Therefore, Calhoun argued that reason provided a balance between societal and individual pursuits and needs, and connected these concerns within a larger framework of liberty. Reason guided by experience promoted a mode of popular rule under self-imposed limitations and the growth of decentralized institutions of government. Calhoun's emerging theory of liberty, based upon the assimilation of reason and the insight of human experience, affirmed the social nature of politics and the necessary dispersion of authority.[47]

The interchange between reason (combining individual and communal insight) and experience manifests itself as the "earthly blessing" or the "essence" embodied in human liberty, namely, that "those, who make and execute the laws, should be controlled by those on

45. John Locke, *An Essay Concerning Human Understanding*, vol. 1, ed. Alexander C. Fraser, 315; "Speech on the Oregon Bill," June 27, 1848, in *Works*, 4:509.
46. *Papers*, 10:486.
47. *Disquisition*, 5.

whom they operate; that the governed should govern." The view of human nature and the ethical life that nourishes a diffused society is closely related to the type of leadership necessary for popular rule.[48] By again combining the notions of reason and experience into a theory of liberty, Calhoun urged moderation as the guide between the excesses of both intemperate communal and potentially oligarchic approaches to popular rule:

> I hold it to be a fundamental principle of our political system, that the people have a right to establish what government they think proper for themselves; that every state about to become a member of this Union has a right to form its government as it pleases; and that, in order to be admitted there is but one qualification, and that is, that the Government shall be republican. There is no express provision to that effect, but it results from that important section [art. 4, sec. 4], which guarantees to every State in this Union a republican form of government. Now, Sir, what is proposed? It is proposed, from a vague, indefinite, erroneous, and most dangerous conception of private individual liberty, to overrule this great common liberty which a people have of framing their own constitution![49]

The greatest danger before the young American republic resulted more from an expansion of individual liberty than from an imprudent structuring of community. For Calhoun, modern social contract theory as articulated by Hobbes, Locke, and Rousseau depicted humanity in the abstract, removed from the necessary restraints and ordering principles required for a truly "social" existence. As Calhoun subsequently argued in the *Discourse*, the social contract was a contradiction in terms, as it was neither social nor based upon a proper assessment of human nature and interaction or decision making.[50]

According to this interpretation, the social contract relied upon reason separated from its most sustaining source: the community. As the antithesis of Calhoun's concept of reason that combined both personal and communal insight, this individualistic reason might contribute to social and political fragmentation. Instead of searching for the nobler, enduring characteristics of popular rule, individualistic

---

48. *Papers*, 12:157; 10:490, 491.
49. *Works*, 4:345.
50. Calhoun did not believe Greece and Rome exhibited elements of a social contract. See *Discourse*, 116.

reason served only the isolated human being. Venerating the instant, deductive labors of individuals over corporate and prescriptive reason aided by experience paved the way for a truly mechanistic and overly procedural political theory, according to Calhoun. In a sense, modern social contract theory was more a justification for regimes of one variety or another than an explanation of human nature. Interestingly, Calhoun has often been criticized for proposing an "alternative" contract theory, reminiscent of these modern social contract theories. In depicting Calhoun as a disciple of Hobbes, Locke, or Rousseau, these critiques indicate both the inadequacies of previous assessments and an unwillingness to penetrate Calhoun's complex theory of social and political life. On the surface, Calhoun appeared to endorse certain aspects of modern social contract theory, especially Locke's right of revolution.[51] And at some junctures, Calhoun recommended Locke and Sidney as distinctive sources of political wisdom with whom "all the prominent actors in our revolution were familiar."[52] These references are of interest mainly to intellectual genealogists; they are rather cursory and of limited importance for appreciating Calhoun's political theory. As we have demonstrated, Calhoun should more appropriately be viewed as part of an older tradition that celebrated humanity as a divine creation.

The manner in which Calhoun addressed human nature may have more in common with the work of Sir Robert Filmer, the English royalist and contemporary of Locke, than anyone else. Although he rejected Filmer's "divine right to govern," preferring more participatory forms, Calhoun in his political thought nevertheless resembles Filmer in many ways. As with Calhoun, the works of "Aristotle, the grand master of politiques," were the most important influence upon Filmer's appreciation of the problems of political rule. Filmer proceeded to argue that the great lessons of humankind not found in scriptures are "in Aristotle."[53] For Filmer and for Calhoun, Aristotle's *Politics* presented a remarkable understanding of the inadequacies of the democratic state. Aristotle defended the life of moderation, based on the control of our natural appetites (of which the desire for unlimited personal freedom is our greatest weakness), to protect individuals from the extremes that could be produced in both social

51. "Remarks in Debate with James Buchanan on the Bill for the Admission of Michigan," *Papers*, 13:353.
52. *Works*, 4:509.
53. See *Papers*, 13:391, 17:285; and Filmer, *Patriarcha*, ed. Peter Laslett, 186, 193.

and political systems. While Aristotle was a proponent of diversity, albeit with some controls, he maintained that the importance of virtue in the good state predominated over simple adjustments in everyday life. In this sense, Filmer's search for political order brings us closer to an understanding of the contemporary dilemmas of representative government—and to an understanding of Calhoun's defense of authentic popular rule.

By rejecting the social atomism that results from separating human beings from their communities, Calhoun again affirmed reason as the product of a social nature. But a properly constituted notion of reason guided by experience alone—Calhoun's "universal experience"—was difficult to develop and preserve. The root problem lay within humanity itself.

As a proponent of organic, hierarchical community as the best earthly womb for nurturing social and political life, Calhoun also appreciated the role that individual action and will assume within the community and in politics. Understanding the political theory of the *Disquisition* requires a willingness to assimilate the statesman's praise for community with the community's need for individual responses to problems affecting the political order. Calhoun saw community as the most natural and enduring aspect of one's existence, but as "universal experience" had demonstrated, individualist forces could prove destructive without an element of restraint. The symbiotic relationship between the community and the individual proves that a dualistic vision sustains the *Disquisition*. This dualism cherished community as a concrete, autonomous, intermediary structure, while also praising the merits of individual responses. This vital merger challenges both the community and those persons within these autonomous groups to seek the higher potentialities of political life. But as we found Calhoun's concept of community to resemble more closely the ancient and medieval idea of subsidiarity than the modern notion of community as undifferentiated groups of persons, so does his concept of individualism differ from the social-contractarian and other varieties of individualism that depict humankind as independent, self-governing, and bound by little or no limitations. Calhoun's individualism connects the person with his community. Personal initiative becomes an asset when connected with the community's propensity to offer restraint and nurture. The individual and communal can be said to merge into an integrated whole, each promoting and encouraging the other. The combining of these human responses provides the basis for reaching a level of ethical insight hitherto prohibited by humankind's inability to adequately connect the community's love of neighbor with the particularistic claims of individuals. We can now appreciate the value of community according to Calhoun: it affirms the critical interactivity between group and personal identities, supporting humankind's social nature while blurring the lines of demarcation between our longings and the longings of those associations of which we are part. However, this personal and communal engagement is limited by humankind's original flaw, requiring the imposition of government:

> The answer [to the question why is "it impossible for society to exist with government"] will be found in the fact (not less contestable than either of the others) that, while man is created for the social state, and is accordingly so formed as to feel what affects others, as well as what affects himself, he is, at the same time, so constituted as to feel more intensely what affects him directly, than what affects him more indirectly through others; or, to express it differently, he is so constituted, that his direct or individual affections are stronger than his sympathetic or social feeling.[54]

While attempting to circumvent describing such an aspect of human nature as selfishness because the term "as commonly used . . . implies an unusual excess of the individual over the social feelings in the person to whom it is applied," Calhoun nevertheless recognized the critical human weakness. The delicate balance between the community and individual responsibilities and freedom could be disrupted by the egotistical or sinful impulse.[55] The persistent need to address this aspect of human nature forced Calhoun to contemplate the lower potentialities of politics. Calhoun affirmed the limitations associated with our "constitution," but he did not believe mere selfishness adequately explained the problem. Utilizing the language of politics, Calhoun had previously depicted the individual's operating

54. *Disquisition*, 6. For references within the larger Hebraic-Christian tradition, see Genesis 3, Psalm 51:5, and Romans 5:12–21. This critique of humanity's tainted nature influences all aspects of Calhoun's political theory.

55. *Disquisition*, 6. Calhoun defined this human weakness most concretely in the *Disquisition* as "the law of animated existence" (7), but the frailty closely resembled the understanding of original sin according to the older, inherited tradition. "Sinful impulse" and "animated existence" are used throughout this chapter to denote the same state of human decrepitude.

within the confines of the sinful impulse as resembling the situation that would develop if the general government were allowed to determine its own power: "[F]rom the known principles of human nature, encroachments would never cease, while any power worth absorbing, as the means of ambition or avarice, remained."[56] Calhoun held that by whatever name this weakness of human nature was identified—as an acquisitive desire, selfishness, sinfulness, or moral turpitude—it was a persistent flaw or defect in our constitution or nature. Describing these intrinsic imperfections of humanity in such a manner, Calhoun reaffirmed his devotion to the classical and Hebraic-Christian worldview. In this way, the Carolinian's theory of human culpability resembles St. Augustine's "earthly city" dominated by a "love of self" against the love of community and God.[57] St. Augustine's idea of sin and Calhoun's original flaw both resulted from misguided wills instead of an inability to follow a particular moral code. In another sense, readers are also presented with a study of misplaced loves, or "affections," according to Calhoun. The dilemma of an innate human weakness rests not in the created world, but in man's inability to seek the good at all possible levels. Asserting one's own desires in place of the community's welfare was, for St. Augustine, a sign of a deformed human will. Calhoun described the "phenomenon" of an original weakness as the "law of animated existence," affirming human nature's central flaw as he attempted a more comprehensive explanation of the role this failing assumes in politics.

In Calhoun's theory of human behavior, the law or nature of our constitution suffers from "animated existence," and mirrors the frailties associated with original sin. Both original sin and "animated existence" possess a tenacity to exert influence "throughout [the] entire range [of human experience], so far as our knowledge extends," declared Calhoun.[58] But he argued that political and social order can persevere amidst this devastating obstacle by guarding against momentary selfish, shortsighted, and tyrannical impulses. Again, what emerged is Calhoun's reaffirmation of the individual guided by a notion of restraint, separating his political theory from the extremes of atomism and abstract communitarianism, and en-

---

56. "Rough Draft of An Address to the People of South Carolina," December 1, 1830, *Papers*, 11:277.
57. St. Augustine, *The Political Writings of St. Augustine*, ed. Henry Paolucci, 8.
58. *Disquisition*, 7.

couraging a more intermingled view. Operating within a worldview distinct from those provided by social contract theorists, Calhoun offered an individualism that is particularly American, but inadequately explained by philosophical and political movements operating within the dichotomy of thought already mentioned. In fact, personal assertiveness possesses some merit when carried out within the appropriate context. "Animated beings" are "endowed each with feelings, instincts, capacities, and faculties best adapted to their allotted condition." From the "Creator of all," humans are given certain gifts and graces that allow for and abet enlightened self-interest.[59] This self-interest assumes its most concrete form in the desire for self-preservation. Reminiscent of St. Thomas's idea regarding every substance's penchant for seeking its own perdurability in the *Summa Theologiae*, Calhoun's argument affirmed that self-preservation must not be conflated to denote mere survival.[60] Moreover, self-preservation demands a level of ethical reflection usually excluded from these considerations. Contrary to the ahistorical and philosophically untenable claim regarding Calhoun's "anticipation" of Darwin and his disciples in America, especially Herbert Spencer and William Graham Sumner, the political theory of the *Disquisition* clearly rejects evolutionary naturalism and the Darwinist preference for "workable hypotheses," preferring again to examine politics as a search for truth.[61] Self-preservation actually served to counterbalance and augment the requirement to perpetuate a society composed of diverse and highly dependent communities:

> If reversed—if their feelings and affections were stronger for others than for themselves, or even as strong, the necessary result would seem to be, that all individuality would be lost; and boundless and remediless disorder and confusion would ensue. For each, at the same moment, intensely participating in all the conflicting emotions of those around him, would, of course, forget himself and all that concerned him immediately, in his officious intermeddling with the affairs of all others; which, from his limited reason and faculties, he could neither properly understand

59. Ibid., 9.

60. St. Thomas Aquinas, *Saint Thomas Aquinas: On Law, Morality, and Politics*, ed. William P. Baumgarth and Richard J. Regan, 48.

61. Putterman, "Calhoun's Realism?" 115; Edward A. Purcell, Jr.'s *Crisis of Democratic Theory: Scientific Naturalism and the Problem of Value* provides a useful survey and interpretation of the influence of the American Darwinists on politics.

> nor manage. Such a state of things would, as far as we can see,
> lead to endless disorder and confusion, not less destructive to our
> [human] race than a state of anarchy.[62]

Authentic community and individuality are dependent upon each other. The community needs the energy, imagination, and private action of the person, and the person benefits from living and working in the community. The individual becomes aware of the social character of politics through group involvement. Calhoun held that this communal and personal meshing takes place in smaller, more intimate associations than in a society at large. In these independent and local groups, individuals acquire the restraint necessary to function within the larger society and accumulate the moral and intellectual qualities that a person employs throughout his life. In other words, aided by the indispensable autonomous group/personal nexus, the community and the individual can prosper in a manner "necessary to the existence and well-being of our race, and equally of Divine ordination."[63]

Rather than framing self-preservation in the language of natural right or rights—for example, a right to life—Calhoun defined this innate human proclivity as a duty because it is the "supreme law as well with communities as with individuals."[64] In opposition to other theories of human nature that place all natural rights (and natural right) at least rhetorically under nature's canopy, accessible to everyone, Calhoun implied that rights are actually human responses to the divine imperative to live and work within the social dimension.[65] Therefore, legitimate natural rights can be recovered only as the more prudent and practical denouement of this relationship. Connecting natural rights with a prescriptive understanding of politics, the *Disquisition* sets the theoretical stage for understanding the limitations upon natural rights by concentrating upon the role of human and divine charters.[66] As compendiums of the filtered political heritage of humanity, charters served as an important source of prescriptive wisdom. In

62. *Disquisition*, 8.
63. Ibid. The use of the term *race* is intended to suggest the entirety of humanity or society, as opposed to a racial theory of politics (Clarke, "Calhoun and the Concept of the 'Reactionary Enlightenment,'" 274; Spain, *Political Theory of John C. Calhoun*, 92). Calhoun's ambiguous use of language in regards to race tends to complicate his discussion of these matters (*Papers*, 14:207).
64. *Disquisition*, 11.
65. Donald S. Lutz, *A Preface to American Political Theory*, 49–88.
66. *Disquisition*, 7.

other words, a charter was an acknowledgment and rearticulation of the best insight within one's social and political tradition. By applying this inherited understanding to new circumstances, as in the *Discourse*, the problem of "animated existence" could be examined with greater precision, and self-preservation could be appreciated in a new light as a duty.

Self-preservation is not, however, without limitations. The balance between society and the individual suffers a disruption when the pursuit of self-preservation becomes overly aggressive. Unfortunately, increasing regard for the self and neglect of society deteriorates the bonds that tie society (assembled in autonomous communities) together.

Obviously, Calhoun appreciated the most destructive dimensions of social and political life resulting from the sinful impulse, while presenting an alternative to the chaos that could prevail. In this regard Calhoun's view of human nature resembles St. Augustine's "earthly city" more than Hobbes's "war of every man against every man." As Michael Oakeshott observed, the Hobbesian conflictual scheme rests upon little more than the "proximity" of individuals under the social contract to one another.[67] Denying Hobbes's solipsistic view of human nature, Calhoun, like St. Augustine, contended that humankind retains a social quality resulting from the "peculiar relations" within the family. By integrating the community and the individual, guided by reason, Calhoun challenged the nonrational aspects of the Hobbesian state of nature. Calhoun's "universal state of conflict" also differs significantly from Hobbes's total war in several regards. Humanity enjoys a "twofold constitution"—social and individual, according to Calhoun, whereas Hobbes believed that human existence, as well as the state of nature, is defined by its solitude.[68] Even though the twofold constitution appears threatened as the result of the sinful impulse, or "law of animated existence," and conditions appear "destructive of the social state and the ends for which it is ordained," it remains operative. Political and social life can be maintained for a period through the social quality resulting from familial "peculiar relations"; or, they can be recovered via another level of restraint, namely, government. The possibility of moral, spiritual, and political advancement remained intact for Calhoun, but Hobbes's system presented an unacceptable

67. St. Augustine, *Political Writings*, 16; Thomas Hobbes, *Leviathan*, ed. Michael Oakeshott, 83; Oakeshott, ed., *Leviathan*, li.
68. *Leviathan* (chap. 13), 83.

dichotomy when examined in light of the inherited tradition: either go to war and suffer eventual death, or pay obeisance to an absolute sovereign. Amidst the crises induced by the sinful impulse, the social character of humanity persists, and the three varieties of "peculiar relations," or tendencies, represent the most important manifestation of the impediment to the impulse, according to Calhoun's perspective.

Calhoun posited that three basic human responses allow for some restraint, albeit inadequate, against the expansion of self-assertiveness to a point beyond self-preservation and towards a "universal state of conflict between individual and individual": the "peculiar relations" within the family, especially between a mother and child; "the force of education"; and the development of habits.[69] The first mode of restraint against overly aggressive self-preservation is that caused by the "peculiar relations" of the family and possibly other natural, intimate relationships. The family serves as the normative and primary group mode of association, providing a foundation for "social feeling" and responsibility, while introducing the individual to the nobler tendencies in the range of human experience, including interpersonal fellowship and politics.

Second, Calhoun appreciated education as helping order the soul and providing a moral framework for one's life. In describing the best form of education, Calhoun was neither an academic curmudgeon nor an abstract metaphysician removed from the rigors of everyday life. He believed education must be comprehensive, including the mind and the body; he described the problem of confining it to the mind to his friend Micah Sterling: "Our young men often study too much and take too little exercise. There is a radical defect in our system of education, which in time must tell in its bad effects on the constitution of our people. We want more attention to health & vigour of body."[70] Along with this integrated regimen, historical studies formed an essential footing for all schooling. In advising a young correspondent regarding such study, Calhoun shared a comprehensive and "lifelong" study plan, suggesting his great devotion to humane learning and education as a persistent enterprise:

> [S]tudy all the ancient classicks [sic]; to be followed by Gibbon's decline & fall of the Roman Empire. To which the history of England & that ["of" interlined] our own country ought to succeed.

69. *Disquisition*, 6, 34.
70. Calhoun to Micah Sterling, February 18, 1841, *Papers*, 15:506.

> Both ought, not only to be read, but studied. Add to these some
> good general History, and a foundation will be laid, which may
> be built on, from time to time, by reading at leisure, the histories
> of the more celebrated States of modern times.[71]

Calhoun held that the great object of education is to help individuals gain control over their tainted and defective nature, or "dispositions."[72] Education further illuminates the insight contained in "universal experience" by extending the conversation among generations to include "universal principles." The "universal principles" encouraged by education cultivate the higher potentialities of humanity by exposing individuals to concrete examples of virtue and moral restraint.[73]

Last, self-preservation gone awry is countered through the development of habits against our destructive "peculiar constitutions," resulting from the "animated existence" or sinful impulse found in all persons. The sinful impulse is impeded through habituated practices grounded in restraint. As the result of a proper conception of reason and the "twofold constitution" of humanity, participation in social and political life becomes habit, assisted and nurtured by these considerations. Aristotle and St. Thomas had earlier described moral development as synonymous with habit, and Calhoun accepted and extended this understanding, albeit with less precision and explanation than previously supplied.[74] The vitality or usefulness of habit can be witnessed in individual action (or, in Thomistic terms, "operation"). Although the functioning of habit alone cannot insure that a person might grasp the higher potentialities available to him, habits nevertheless serve as a moral guide or compass. For example, Calhoun recognized that participation in politics frequently produced exigencies hitherto uncontemplated, and some adjustment or modification was then necessary. "Life is a journey," Calhoun remarked to his daughter, suggesting the importance of the struggle directed

71. Calhoun to Thomas J. Johnson, March 29, 1836, *Papers*, 13:117.
72. *Papers*, 11:531.
73. "Speech in Reply to Criticisms of the Bill to Prohibit the Circulation of Incendiary Publications Through the Mail," April 12, 1836, *Papers*, 13:161. In Calhoun's idiom, education allowed the lower inclinations of humanity to "yield" to the higher, "the convenient to the necessary; mere accommodation to safety and security. This is the universal principle which governs in all analogous cases, both in our social and political relations" (*Papers*, 13:161). See Claes G. Ryn, "Universality and History."
74. Aristotle, *Nicomachean Ethics*, trans. J. A. K. Thompson, 1103a; St. Thomas Aquinas, *Treatise on the Virtues*, trans. John A. Oesterle, 50–66.

towards sustaining moral habits amidst a world fraught with change. Even during turbulent periods the sinful impulse is deterred by virtue concretized in habits. Drawing on the older tradition, Calhoun prominently reaffirmed virtue's critical role in the *Disquisition*.[75] On some occasions virtue manifested in the form of habits "overpower[s]" the sinful impulse, and "animated existence" is stymied, albeit only for limited periods.[76] In essence, habits allow the individual and society to assemble the pieces of a moral worldview into a practical, useful guide for living: "[The ethical life] is, with good moral & virtuous habits, the only perennial source of health, happiness & enjoyment. Without it any other advantage will fail to bestow their [*sic*] blessing."[77]

While the "peculiar relations" among family members, education, and moral habits can hinder and sometimes abrogate the sinful impulse's control upon individuals and communities, ultimately these restraints are insufficient to counter "the all-pervading and essential law of animated existence."[78] The individual is entrusted with moral tools, although the limited usefulness of these gifts becomes clear when the individual is confronted with the human condition's weaknesses. But the individual's imperfections are also society's frailties, and society as well as the individual needs a restraint upon the passions. In other words, the sinful impulse or the influence of "animated existence" stretches from the individual to community and society, across all human boundaries, resembling the inherited tradition's interpretation of humankind's original state. Human beings, of course, remain captive to their own depravation. For our purposes, Calhoun located the problem of human corruptibility within human nature. In defending the universality of this predicament, Calhoun also stressed the particularity of human imperfection: it is present within each individual who composes the community and society.[79] Because the sinful impulse can overwhelm the individual's capacity for restraint and leave him with "a greater regard for his own safety or happiness than for the safety or happiness of others," the assemblage of individuals in communities, and society as a unit, are also vulnerable to this human

75. Failing to appreciate this dimension of the *Disquisition*, some theorists have thoroughly misinterpreted Calhoun (see Jaffa, *Defenders*, 19; and Jeffrey, "Thought of John C. Calhoun," passim).

76. Calhoun to Anna Maria Calhoun, March 10, 1832, *Papers*, 11:561; *Disquisition*, 6.

77. Calhoun to Lieutenant Patrick Calhoun, January 6, 1842, *Papers*, 16:38.

78. *Disquisition*, 7.

79. Calhoun shared such an insight with St. Thomas concerning the location of the weakness (*Summa Theologiae*, IaIIae.94.6.answer 2).

flaw.[80] Whereas the individual can, over time, exhaust his personal restraints against the passions, communities and society possess a more
dominating force against the weakness: government. The presence of
"animated existence" within the individual, community, and society is
offset by the evolution of restraint at each of these levels—beginning
with the personal capacities of restraint we have already discussed
at length, progressing to the community, and eventually leading to
society's imposition of government. As the concluding association,
government provides the needed resistance against the sinful impulse.
In this pursuit, the government and society are interjoined:

> But, although society and government are thus intimately con-
> nected with and dependent on each other—of the two society is
> the greater. It is the first in the order of things, and in the dignity of
> its object; that of society being primary—to preserve and perfect
> our race; and that of government secondary and subordinate,
> to preserve and perfect society. Both are, however, necessary to
> the existence and well-being of our race, and equally of Divine
> ordination.[81]

Benefiting from the codependency of government and society, the
individual can then advance unhindered by the disorder that had previously resulted from the absence of government. Some critics suggest
that government's role within the *Disquisition* is depicted as merely
the extension of society without definite purpose and no devotion to
the "higher purposes" of politics.[82] These accounts usually dismiss
the critical social dimensions of government. As Aristotle suggested,
government is "an association intended to enable its members, in their
households and the kinships, to live well; its purpose is a perfect
and self-sufficient life."[83] Government's substantive social mission
encompasses the nurturing of communities and society; it can achieve
this goal by fostering virtue and self-restraint among the citizenry.

As an outgrowth of and a component of communities and society,
government stands between anarchy at one extreme and total control at the other. In other words, government encourages moral and
political maturation by providing a stable polity. Calhoun envisioned

80. *Disquisition*, 7.
81. Ibid., 8.
82. Jaffa, *Defenders*, 16.
83. Aristotle, *The Politics*, 1280b29.

government as fulfilling an important although limited function: providing society with the "higher and holier purposes—liberty, security,
and perfecting the high moral and intellectual qualities with which our
Maker has thought proper to endow us."[84] Commingling society and
government into a coherent whole by relying upon the human bonds
that unite the individual to the community and society, government is
a natural development in accordance with humankind's fundamental
social nature. In addition, a social nature predicated upon self-restraint
and mutual respect encourages a system of government based upon
these principles.

Although government serves a virtuous purpose, the sinful impulse
also circumscribes its role in society. In particular, government faces
the same limitations as the individual, the community, and society.
"Intended to protect and preserve society," government has "a strong
tendency to disorder and abuse of its power, as all experiences and
almost every page of history testify," argued Calhoun.[85] The influence
of "animated existence" also penetrates government as part of the
social and political structure of human life. As with other human
arrangements, government requires some mode of restraint; after
all, each societal element already contains a check or an obstacle
prohibiting the sinful impulse from assuming complete control. In
due course, government, too, possesses an element of restraint, a
constitution, which completes Calhoun's theoretical circle:

> Having its origin in the same principle of our nature, *constitution*
> stands to *government*, as *government* stands to *society*; and, as the
> end for which society is ordained, would be defeated without
> government, so that for which government is ordained would, in
> a great measure, be defeated without constitution.[86]

In fact, linking society, government, and constitutionalism comple-
ments and reinforces each constituent part. Presenting an organic
understanding of politics and society, Calhoun further elaborated
a theory of popular rule and representative government. Disputing
those who propose necessity as the *Disquisition*'s cornerstone, the
work actually provides a coherent and refined framework for ap-
proaching and comprehending an inherited tradition of popular rule

84. "Further Remarks on the Loan Bill," July 16, 1841, *Papers*, 15:621.
85. *Disquisition*, 9.
86. Ibid. (italics in original).

that was at odds with the desultory theories that abounded in America during Calhoun's lifetime and that continue to influence American politics today. But the *Disquisition* provides more than a reaffirmation of accepted theories. The treatise attempts to confront the profound crisis of popular rule in the mid-nineteenth century: the erosion of a representative, decentralized mode of government. The dilemma Calhoun addressed in the nineteenth century remains a vital concern for the contemporary world. For Calhoun, a properly constituted mode of popular rule should allow for the fullest expression of the deliberate sense of people guided by self-restraint. Calhoun's original insight regarding the need for understanding the very nature of humanity receives further clarification in his desire to articulate a sense of political order that incorporates popular rule with the need to preserve the regime. To suggest incorrectly that Calhoun argued purely from necessity omits the most salient aspects of his critique of popular rule. Necessity cannot be disregarded completely, although one should not depict this obligatory characteristic of any theory of human nature as the fountainhead of the *Disquisition*'s political theory.[87] In a world dominated by "animated existence," Calhoun may be understood as pleading for an accurate assessment of human nature and suggesting that politics must remain an imperfect pursuit. Accordingly, government possesses a pivotal role but one that can reach its full potential only when accompanied by a spirit of moderation in all efforts. Avoiding the pitfalls of a regime without any ordering principles at one juncture, while distancing oneself from the multifaceted hazards of unitary control at another, again encourages personal and societal restraint in various forms. As a bulwark against these antinomies, a constitution is a human "contrivance," in contradistinction to government's "divine ordination."[88] Having supplied numerous precautions, Calhoun specifically decried the inefficacy of concentrating government in the hands of the few, regardless of form:

> It cannot be done by instituting a higher power to control the government, and those who administer it. This would be but to change the seat of authority, and to make this bigger power, in reality, the government; with the same tendency, on the part

87. As a concept, necessity can encourage the compromise and resolution of difficult issues, especially during periods of crisis (*Disquisition*, 48–50). Calhoun presented necessity as a prudent antecedent to statesmanship in some situations, which is a notably different interpretation from what either his critics or his contemporaries provide.
88. *Disquisition*, 10.

of those who might control its powers, to pervert them into
instruments of aggrandizement.[89]

Calhoun had maintained such a view throughout his life, suggesting that "all governments are actuated by a spirit of Ambition and
avarice . . . be the form of government what it may, monarchical, Aris-
tocratical or Republican."[90] Government needs some form of restraint,
although the imposition of a sovereign or ruling council cannot sustain
the political system and serves only to shuffle the authority from one
location to another. Alternatively, government warrants a modicum
of authority to adequately fulfill its proper role within the larger social
framework. To entrust the government with little or no dominion over
the affairs of state is to insure its impotence, making the institution "too
feeble to protect and preserve society."[91] In determining the powers
rightfully given to government, two considerations are always necessary: protecting the community from external and internal threats.
With the diversity of communities and the sinful impulse's intransi-
gence in human nature, conflict among various communities remains
a possibility. The search for a golden mean between an overzeal-
ous, domineering state and a weak, ineffectual regime led Calhoun
towards a constitutionalism that evolved out of the need to advance
moral concerns on a communal level, while offering a notion of restraint against self-indulgent behavior. "For, without a constitution—
something to counteract the strong tendency of government to disorder and abuse, and to give stability to political institutions—there
can be little progress or permanent improvement."[92] Calhoun should
be appreciated as a theorist of limited government who defended
the centrality of restraint as represented in a constitution for hin-
dering the coercive power that can accompany popular rule. Such
an insight again aids our apprehension of Calhoun's political theory
and certainly places his thought within the larger American tradition
that renounced political libertinism in all forms, while also holding
government's centralizing, aggrandizing tendencies in great disdain.
We shall now explore how Calhoun's constitutionalism contributed
to his theory of popular rule.

89. Ibid.
90. "Rough Draft of An Address to the People of South Carolina," December 1,
1830, *Papers*, 11:272 (capitalization in original).
91. *Disquisition*, 10.
92. Ibid., 12.

## CONSTITUTIONALISM AND POPULAR RULE

Providing a constitution as the appropriate and most useful means of limiting government's propensity for "disorder and abuse," Calhoun described the social and political evolution that prefigured the imposition of such restraint, including the transition of various constitutional "materials" from antiquity to the modern period. A constitution serves as an "interior structure" within society, "formed in order to resist" the usurpation of power.[93] As a guide for society and government, a constitution is most thoroughly identified with the restraint it contains and the proximity of the restraint to everyday life and the practice of politics. Calhoun described the restraining structure as an "organism," suggesting the vital and permanent characteristics associated with constitutionalism in a stable polity. As an organism, constitutionalism cannot be separated from the actual process of governing, in whatever form it might assume. Individuals and communities possess modes of restraint expressed through various practices, although most profoundly exhibited in day-to-day living.

The primary examples of these interrelationships between the moral demands of a properly constituted concept of popular rule and the need for practical ordering principles can be found in Calhoun's recommendations regarding individual habits and moral development, as noted above. The personal begets the communal and societal, and the communal and societal beget the governmental. Constitutionalism also forms an "interior structure" to resist "the tendency to abuse . . . power" within the government.[94] In this sense, it mirrors the imposition of personal and communal/societal limitations upon the sinful impulse's influence. When allowed to prosper, such a constitution provides explicit constraints upon the centralization and the related aggrandizement of political authority. Returning to the core tenet of American politics as articulated by the Founders, Calhoun suggested three ways in which the "organism" affirms the love of liberty and diffusion of authority, according to the original design. First of all, constitutional governments encourage liberty through genuine popular rule defined as active participation by the citizenry under self-imposed limitations—or allowing the governed to govern, as Calhoun so often described this essence of liberty.[95] Second, the diffusion of au-

93. Ibid.
94. Ibid.
95. *Papers*, 10:490.

thority again mitigates the sinful impulse's swaying of the individual from the critical matters associated with the community, society, and government. Finally, dispersing the sources of power, and ultimately the representation of sovereignty, ensures a stable system of popular rule and encourages the survival of the regime.

On a more practical level, Calhoun rejected the doctrine of the general will and related theories of extirpation dedicated to removing personal attachments to the most compelling social and political associations, including one's own community and government. Either to accept the inherent process of consolidation within these unitary approaches or to fail to incorporate restraint at each level of the political system denies the necessary qualities popular rule requires at all points. The perpetuation of liberty throughout human history has resulted from these checks operating at each division or level of society and government.[96] As a prize to be won through deliberate labors directed towards ameliorating the consolidation of political authority, liberty receives a grounding in community that it cannot extract from the society at large.[97] Of course, the constitution as "organism" supplies the foundational materials for any government dedicated to promoting liberty; and it serves as a theoretical and pragmatic beacon assisting government's effort to thwart the pervasive influence of the "constitution of our nature," and this impulse's related desire "which leads rulers to oppress the ruled."[98]

As intimated in earlier chapters, the Carolinian saw "constitutional" government as both nurturing popular rule and encouraging the moral life. To achieve these essential tasks, "constitutional" government (as an "organism") supplements the social, moral, and political development already active in families, communities, and society. A government possessing the ordering guide of a constitution also embodies the qualities needed to restrain the sinful impulse's movement towards tyranny. This potential abuse of power commonplace in the lower potentialities of politics is best countered through the ethical and political authority of a constitution. "Power can only be resisted by power—and tendency by tendency," Calhoun urged.[99] It would be incorrect, however, to suggest that Calhoun attached utopian qualities to a constitution. On the contrary, as the next chapter will show, he

---

96. Ibid., 12:361.
97. *Works*, 4:509–12.
98. *Disquisition*, 13.
99. Ibid.

was all too familiar with the limitations of the American Constitution, which he believed was the "genuine voice of the people" and vastly superior to any other guide.[100]

A constitution also equips society with a framework for hearing this "voice," thereby providing the protection and dispersal of political authority requisite to establishing popular rule and resisting consolidation in all forms. As a matter of even greater importance, the participation of the citizenry is essential to the survival of the "organism" and the regime. This unwavering interconnection between constitutionalism and popular rule is intimate and pervasive, and is the primary fixture of the republicanism Calhoun inherited from many sources and subsequently revised amidst the struggles he faced. The normative world of politics is envisioned as dependent upon deliberation, and capable of restraining momentary electoral majorities, which unites constitutionalism and popular rule in such a distinctively Calhounian fashion. By appreciating the "organism" as most intensely offering evidence of this mixing of participation and structure, one is able to comprehend more fully Calhoun's constitutionalism and, ultimately, his political theory.

Guiding and reaffirming the infrastructure of the "organism" comes most naturally through popular rule, imperfectly manifested in participation:[101]

> Such an organism, then, as will furnish the means by which resistance may be systematically and peaceably made on the part of the ruled, to oppression and abuse of power on the part of the rulers, is the first and indispensable step towards forming a constitutional government. And as this can only be effected by or through the right of suffrage—(the right on the part of the ruled to choose their rulers at proper intervals, and to hold them thereby responsible for their conduct)—the responsibility of the rulers to the ruled, through the right of suffrage, is the indispensable and primary principle in the *foundation* of a constitutional government.[102]

100. *Works*, 1:393.
101. As the ensuing quotation proves, Calhoun viewed participation through voting as a right and a duty, not to be dictated by the general government. The assessing of the importance of participation in voting continues to suggest the intrinsic limitations associated with relying completely on the "mechanism" to provide for a stable polity (Arend Lijphart, "Unequal Participation: Democracy's Unresolved Dilemma").
102. *Disquisition*, 13 (italics in original).

Although voting is "the indispensable and primary principle," it alone is not "sufficient to form constitutional governments." Moreover, voting as a participatory response contributes to Calhoun's theory of popular rule, but involvement in voting by itself cannot fully affirm constitutional government, and occasionally this "right of suffrage" entrusts "irresponsible rulers" with complete control of the regime.[103] The resulting "absolute" forms of political rule, in which authority is centralized and the citizenry denied their rightful role in governing, are actually the antithesis of genuine "constitutional" governments. As another important aspect of popular rule, voting contributes by identifying the rulers, those elected to office in a particular election, as agents on behalf of the supreme and sovereign source of government: the people. Serving as the central political authority, the people cannot be appropriately represented as an undifferentiated mass; lacking an element of discrimination eventually denies full participation, denigrating popular rule in practice. Voting entrusts the rulers with responsibility for representing the true or sovereign agency, the people, and not conflating the agency of the people into the government regardless of the regime's form. Even though its sovereignty resides in the people, America was not formed in the aggregate, as we have noted. Produced by the most accessible and only competent authorities within the original design, the states, the Constitution provides this diffused mode of authenticating popular rule in theory. As Calhoun reminded his Senate colleagues, "We must not forget that states and the people of the states are our constituents and superiors, and we but their agents; and that if the right in question be abused, or the freedom of election impaired, it is they, and not we, who must mainly suffer, and who of course are the best judges of the evil and the remedy."[104] In assessing the deeper problem, Calhoun recognized that the ethical claims of the people were mediated through the states. But a more demanding moral question remained before the regime: what were the limits of simple majoritarianism as an ideal form of popular rule?

The impracticability of ideal forms of participation and decision making tends to marginalize the importance of voting (and all other aspects of popular rule). Voting alone serves the purposes neither of diversifying the interests and depth of participation nor of resolving

103. Ibid.
104. "Speech on the Bill to Prevent the Interference of Certain Federal Officers in Elections," February 22, 1839, *Papers*, 14:562.

conflicts regarding the most critical issues before the land. To present voting as an ideal form of popular rule, possessing the capability to ameliorate long-standing and intense conflict, is questionable at best and improbable at worst. To depend too heavily on voting alone can prove counterproductive, and can potentially undermine the individual citizen's role within the political system by concentrating attention solely upon electoral success and supremacy. Calhoun argued that the sinful impulse encourages an aggrandizing spirit in all human endeavors, culminating in the quest to control government at any cost. The ideal form of voting and elections supports a view predicated upon equal, deliberate participation with predictable outcomes. Calhoun rightly dismissed such an approach, suggesting that the desire to control government, influenced by the sinful impulse, would always result in unequal participation, devaluing the people as the sovereign voice and turning elections into maneuvers directed towards assuming hegemony and commanding the "emoluments" of office. In confronting this inevitable problem, Calhoun revised Madison's extended republic theory in light of the usurpation of power he had witnessed in his lifetime, and proposed an alternative approach. Madison had opined, "Extend the sphere, and you take in a greater variety of parties and interests; you make it less probable that a majority of the whole will have a common motive to invade the rights of other citizens."[105] Agreeing with Madison's assertions regarding this "multiplicity of interests" thriving in America, Calhoun nevertheless rejected the possibility that a large republic through its vastness could lessen the intensity of conflict.[106] The desire to consolidate political power would result in unforeseen political unions dedicated to controlling the government for the purposes of compounding power and patronage. Against Madison's related portrayal of an independent political force that would function as a "judge" that opposed the merging of power, Calhoun confronted a political situation in which the twin attributes of expansion and independence from group interests had failed in practice. If extending the regime had proved fruitless at reducing conflict and preventing the coalescing of forces, Calhoun envisioned the solution for America (and other regimes) as a return to the original instrumentation of diffused authority:

105. *The Federalist*, No. 10.
106. *The Federalist*, No. 51; *Disquisition*, 33–34.

Without it, free states in the present condition of the world could
not exist, or must have existed without safety or responsibility. If limited to a small territory, they must be crushed by the
great monarchical powers or exist only at their discretion; but
if extended over a great surface, the concentration of power and
patronage necessary for government would speedily end in terror.
It is only by this admirable distribution that a great extent of territory, with a proportional population and power, can be reconciled
with freedom, and consequently that safety and respectability be
given to free states.[107]

Unencumbered by some limitation upon the concentration of power,
the desire for power would also result in the rise of a majority and
a minority party, with "incessant struggles on the one side to retain,
and on the other to obtain the majority and, thereby, the control of
the government and the advantages it confers."[108] Because of the
sinful nature of humanity and the increasingly lucrative benefits of
controlling the government, the majority would be tempted to usurp
power from the minority through all available means, resulting in the
"tyranny of the majority" decried throughout human history.

While both Madison and Calhoun sought to prevent the "tyranny of
the majority" within an American context, Calhoun proposed a more
tenable solution when faced with intractable divisions resulting from
the rise of an expansive government. The subsequent movement to
control government and the perquisites therein would increase the
intensity of the conflict, further dividing the two parties. The normative pattern regarding taxation and revenue allocation would slowly
adjust to this movement, reducing the tax indebtedness of the majority
party, while increasing the disbursement it received, with the minority
party suffering the antithesis—higher taxes, diminished returns, and
a depreciated political status. Throughout his public career, Calhoun
critiqued various tariff increases and abuses, correctly viewing tariffs
as the building blocks of an increasingly intrusive and domineering
general government. Interpreting this expansion spurred by tariffs as
a disease, the statesman surmised that "government, like a family,
spoiled by an extravagant income, can only be reformed by stinted
means."[109] The ensuing struggle, he argued, would divide the regime
into taxpayers and tax-revenue recipients, leading to violent conflict.

107. Calhoun to Robert Garnett, July 3, 1824, *Correspondence*, 219.
108. *Disquisition*, 16.
109. "Speech on the Loan Bill," July 19, 1841, *Papers*, 15:633.

Again echoing ancient, medieval, and modern reservations against the centralization and abuse of power, Calhoun explained how the persistence of the sinful impulse influenced this consuming spirit among the majority (as well as the minority once it became a majority). This endemic human weakness would lead to "oppression and abuse of power," finally subverting the political order.[110] Over time, the uncertainty of majority tenure within such a system would also contribute to this instability by increasing instead of relieving the amount of volatility. Accordingly, the intrinsic weaknesses of human nature provide the need for reconsidering the role of voting. The substantive importance of voting to popular rule cannot be diminished, although this mode and concept of participation must be examined anew, given Calhoun's tremendous discernment as it unfolds in the *Disquisition*. Calhoun's approach to voting specifically, and to constitutionalism and popular rule generally, reflected a breakthrough made possible by his wisdom concerning the fundamental human dilemma. Framing his insight in a distinctly American manner, Calhoun combined the most salient aspects of American political thought into a theory of politics that is both an endorsement and a critique, affirming popular rule and constitutionalism. In the process, Calhoun helped sharpen our understanding of republican government and, more important, the limits of spontaneous, plebiscitarian notions of popular rule.

## CONCURRENT POPULAR RULE EXEMPLIFIED

As this chapter has suggested, the *Disquisition* was an enterprise dedicated to reclaiming the Founders' vision for the American republic—primarily through an explication of the interrelationship between the two most vital characteristics of the original design: authority and liberty. Authority requires offering the resistance necessary to "guard the community against injustice, violence, and anarchy within, and against attacks from without." Numerous foreign and domestic threats merited the attention and action of the republic, united in what Publius described as "the preservation of the public peace."[111] When confronted with forces bent upon the destruction of the regime, the states constituting the republic depended upon each other's mutual collaboration to resist these antagonists. The pursuit of national

110. *Disquisition*, 20.
111. Ibid., 40; *The Federalist*, No. 23 (Hamilton), 119.

defense and domestic tranquility reached its highest potential for Calhoun when the states were united by concurrent elements. From Calhoun's perspective, the advantages of a concurrent response were obvious, but the harmony of spirit that accompanied the revival of concurrent measures was of paramount importance to a defense of the idea in action. Calhoun prudently feared the unchecked concentration of power in the general government. At the same time, the statesman argued that a republic free from domestic uprisings and the threat of invasion provided the greatest measure of liberty for its citizenry. But establishing a modicum of governmental authority so that a republic may protect itself, especially within a system predicated upon dispersed authority, is not easily accomplished. Calhoun located his solution to this conundrum in the obligatory interconnection between authority and liberty under the concurrent majority.

If the elements or states within a republic depend upon each other to safeguard the country from external and internal disruptions, it is the federative character of the regime that serves as a prescription and model for the sharing of these essential duties. Instead of presuming that the centralization of authority always promotes efficiency and a coupling of mission with regard to protection, the concurrent majority provides for mutual cooperation between authority and liberty by giving each "its appropriate sphere" of leverage and responsibility with a diffused framework.[112] The critical precondition for this sharing of authority and liberty requires viewing the republic's obligation towards authority in light of the need for personal and communal liberty. It is liberty that leavens the republic's authoritative (or protective) quality, enlarging personal and communal freedom while affirming the concurrent majority as its guide. To accommodate the greatest amount of liberty, individuals and states must be allowed to pursue those avenues they "may deem best to promote . . . interest and happiness." For Calhoun, interest and happiness were closely akin, as these pursuits linked humanity to a diversity of community and the advancement of "faculties, intellectual and moral," endowed by the Creator.[113] The union of interest and happiness can take place because the concurrent majority encourages a mode of social and political

112. *Disquisition*, 41. Calhoun extended his explanation to suggest that when authority and liberty occupy their appropriate spheres, guided by the self-restraint intrinsic to the concurrent majority, the forces of partisanship and control associated with numerical majoritarianism are also reduced.

113. *Disquisition*, 40.

life that has a common moral symmetry. The extremes of "pseudo-liberation" and social fragmentation are limited by a disciplined, albeit refined, obligation to a moral order grounded in community.[114] In regard to liberty, the concurrent majority also allows for an expansion of the concept in its particularity (individual) and its universality (community and society), as observed earlier in this chapter.

The crux of the problem, however, concerns those situations in which the desire for liberty must also be regulated by the need for order. In his return to the original recipe for acknowledging and assimilating the confluence of authority and liberty, Calhoun argued that some communities and states will need more authority, while others more liberty, depending upon their respective situations:

> But the principle, applied to different communities, will assign to them different limits. It will assign a larger sphere to power and a more contracted one to liberty, or the reverse, according to circumstances. To the former, there must ever be allotted, under all circumstances, a sphere sufficiently large to protect the community against danger from without and violence and anarchy within. The residuum belongs to liberty. More cannot be safely or rightly allotted to it.[115]

Although Calhoun remained devoted to this interconnection, he nevertheless submitted "that it is a great and dangerous error to suppose that all people are equally entitled to liberty."[116] In a decentralized republic, states become the primary arbiters of the relationship between authority and liberty. In turn, communities and individuals assume responsibility for moral and intellectual development. The survival of concurrent constitutionalism depends upon having a well-informed citizenry possessing personality traits in accord with the republic's ethos of self-restraint—traits that are inculcated throughout one's life. Even those who lack the necessary gifts to benefit initially may eventually demonstrate an appreciation for liberty, although "rising from a lower to a higher point in the scale of liberty is necessarily slow," resembling Plato's "myth of the metals" without the deceptiveness.[117]

Still, some states within a republic may need to prohibit certain practices or activities if the state's or republic's security is threatened,

114. Wilfred M. McClay, *The Masterless: Self and Society in Modern America*, 270–75.
115. *Disquisition*, 41.
116. Ibid., 42.
117. Ibid., 43; *The Republic*, Book III:414d–415c.

as long as these prohibitions are in harmony with the moral ethos and the constitution. As a useful example of this conjunction of authority and liberty, popular rule itself represents the value of Calhoun's insight. Popular rule is often defined simply as the acts of voting, campaigning, or running for elective office. From the perspective of numerical majoritarianism, this definition of popular rule is sufficient when augmented by the citizenry's participation in decision making as a homogenous mass, according to a "one man, one vote" formula. Calhoun asserted that the numerical majoritarian or simple democratic understanding of popular rule distorted the salient political and moral realities of republican government; and in the case of a republic consisting of many states and diverse communities, this understanding of the concept might prove unsatisfactory and potentially destructive. He also denied that popular rule can be interpreted as a collection of rules or devices. Instead, a properly constituted standard of popular rule (as well as a constitution or government) "must emanate from the hearts of the people, and be supported by their devotion to it, without support from abroad," and must "be adapted to the intelligence and character of the people."[118] In other words, popular government and popular rule express the ethos that has shaped them over time. As a moral and intellectual tradition, this ethos originates in the family, community, and state. The critical intersection between liberty and authority is best resolved at the level closest to the activity. For popular rule generally and elections specifically, state governments are better suited to protect and embody the needs and interests of their citizens than the general government:

> [I]n considering this general question, I shall assume, in the first
> place, what none will deny, that it belongs to the States separately
> to determine who shall, and who shall not, exercise the right of
> suffrage; and, in the second, that it belongs to them, in like manner,
> to regulate the right; that is, to pass all laws that may be necessary
> to secure its free exercise on one hand, and to prevent its abuse
> on the other.[119]

The states within the republic allow liberty and authority to be reconciled in a way that promotes substantive popular rule. Through

118. "On His Resolutions in Reference to the War With Mexico," January 4, 1848, *Works*, 4:405; *Disquisition*, 58.
119. "Speech on the Bill to Prevent the Interference of Certain Federal Officers in Elections," *Papers*, 14:560–61.

advancing the involvement of communities and individuals, states (guided by the constitution) serve as the most able facilitators of the concurrent majority in practice. In America, the states represent the premier exemplar of the concurrent "organism," although Calhoun offered four "comparative" examples of it to demonstrate the usefulness and profusion of the concept: the Polish Constitution, the Iroquois Confederacy, the Roman Constitution, and the British Constitution. Poland served as the most radical application of the "organism," or concurrent majority. During the seventeenth and early eighteenth centuries, the Polish gentry could exercise a personal concurrent check upon royal succession, described as a *liberum veto*. According to the historical account we are given in the *Disquisition*, if one citizen voted against the succession, the heir apparent was denied the throne.[120] An individual had the ability to check the decisions of a whole regime. Calhoun presented Poland, of course, as an extreme example of the protection of minority interests. Even though the Polish government was based on what appeared to be an overextension of the concurrent majority, it survived for nearly two centuries.[121] For Calhoun, this ability to endure proved that even the most extreme case of the concurrent majority possessed "power and permanency," albeit an overextended "organism":

> I will venture an assertion, which may be considered extravagant, but in which history will fully bear me out, that we have no knowledge of any people in which a power of arresting the improper acts of government, or what may be called the negative power of government, was too strong, except Poland, where every freeman possessed a veto.[122]

Calhoun offered the Iroquois Confederacy as his second example of the concurrent "organism." The Confederacy was composed of six nations, or tribes, including the Onondaga, Mohawk, Oneida, Cayuga, Seneca, and Tuscarora. The decision making body consisted of a chief delegate from each of the six tribes, with six additional voting members per tribe, for a total of forty-two members. As in the case of the Polish assembly, an individual vote could block a decision.

120. *Disquisition*, 53–54.
121. J. M. Roberts, *The Pelican History of the World*, 571–72.
122. "Speech in Reply to Daniel Webster on the Force Bill," February 26, 1833, *Papers*, 12:134; *Disquisition*, 54.

While the decisions of the league chiefs required unanimity, the Confederacy followed a system that nurtured compromise. In the course of debate, the younger chiefs expressed their views first, followed by the more senior chiefs. This protocol served as a means of restraint, as it allowed the more experienced leaders to veto potentially rash or ruinous proposals by the less experienced leaders. The Iroquois Confederacy also selected a chief who presided over these gatherings and most certainly possessed more authority than any single tribal representative. Presumably charged with conducting the sessions of the body, such an official could easily influence the direction and other aspects of the proceedings. In Calhoun's use of the Iroquois Confederacy, we witness another example of his remarkable historical and philosophical erudition. The effort to disparage the Carolinian's sources with the intention to devalue his political thought, led by the grouping of critics described in chapter 1 under the subheading "Calhoun the Aberration," including Hofstadter, Hartz, and Current, clearly underestimates the statesman's historical perceptiveness. His survey of the Iroquois also exhibits a willingness to examine all available materials, and demonstrates a profound understanding of Native American life.[123] The presentations of the Polish Constitution and the Iroquois Confederacy are certainly illuminating, but it is Calhoun's critiques of the Roman and English Constitutions that more clearly portray the qualities of the concurrent majority or "organism" in practice.

Calhoun opened his discussion of the Roman Constitution by describing the early bifurcation of the patricians and the plebeians. Slowly, over a period of centuries, the plebeians were integrated into the government. According to Calhoun, the balance that developed allowed the plebeians to gain control of the tribunate, but provided for the patricians to maintain their dominant position in the Roman Senate. The patricians and the plebeians were essentially given a negative check on each other's actions. Rome represented for Calhoun "an iron government" that could stand the test of time.[124] When the influence of these concurrent measures was diminished, the check on power dissolved, and Rome began to decline as a republic. Calhoun

123. For contemporary affirmations of Calhoun's survey, see E. Tooker, "The League of the Iroquois"; and Dean R. Snow, "Hiawatha: Constitution-Maker." Calhoun may be considered an "enlightened" advocate of Native Americans for his time and context. For illustrative examples of his interaction with Native American populations, see *Papers,* 13:436, 453; 14:279; 15:492.
124. *Disquisition,* 72.

considered Rome, with the balanced tribunate and Senate, to be one of the "best and strongest" governments ever to have existed, but the absence of these measures produced the most "oppressive and cruel" one in the course of history.[125]

The final example Calhoun offered in his comparative and historical defense of the concurrent majority was the British Constitution. The British system of government, with its checks upon authority, was the archetypal concurrent republic and had greatly influenced the American political experience. "I hold in high estimation the institutions of our English ancestors. They grew up gradually through many generations, by the incessant and untiring efforts of an intelligent and brave people struggling for centuries against the power of the Crown. To them we are indebted for nearly all that has been gained for liberty in modern times, excepting what we have added."[126] The British system balanced the monarchy, the predominant form of government during Calhoun's lifetime (and one he held in some disdain), with the needs of the aristocracy and the remainder of society. Calhoun observed that the activities of the three major institutions—the monarchy, the House of Lords, and the House of Commons—were balanced by the performance of each institution acting concurrently. The House of Lords served as the most "conservative" estate because it was "interposed" between the two reactionary bodies.[127] Each element was able to take action against the other, making England the penultimate example of the concurrent majority: "But the British government is far superior to that of Rome, in its adaptation and capacity to embrace under its control extensive dominions, without subverting its constitution."[128] And more important, the British system accomplished such a feat without succumbing to the desires of simple majoritarianism.

125. *Disquisition,* 72, 191; *Papers,* 10:494. For surveys that affirm Calhoun's basic insight, see Numa Denis Fustel de Coulanges, *The Ancient City,* 234–39; and Russell Kirk, *The Roots of American Order,* 97–136. As Eugene Genovese has pointed out, Calhoun relied upon Barthold Niebuhr's *History of Rome* as his guide for understanding the tribunate (*The Southern Tradition,* 59–60).

126. "Speech on Abolition Petitions," March 9, 1836, *Papers,* 13:98. The intimate connection between American and British political theory and constitutionalism provided another important theoretical thread that linked the Founding generation to Calhoun, Story, and other thinkers in the mid-nineteenth century (M. E. Bradford, "The Best Constitution in Existence: The Influence of the British Example on the Framers of Our Fundamental Law," in *Original Intentions,* 17–33; Russell Kirk, *America's British Culture*).

127. *Disquisition,* 75.

128. Ibid., 77.

In presenting these concurrent precursors to the American political tradition, Calhoun augmented the critical insight provided by the *Disquisition*, as he indeed laid a "solid foundation for political science" through revitalizing popular rule.[129] To complete his theoretical and practical mission, Calhoun proceeded to explicate the premier example of the diffusion of authority and cultivation of liberty: the American Constitution. The fundamental law of the American republic provided, after all, the "interior structure" for regulating the shape and scope of government.[130] As a guide for the states and the general government, the Constitution was also part of the "organism" that limited the centralization of authority and allowed for genuine popular rule; it is Calhoun's exposition of the connection between the moral demands of a properly constituted concept of popular rule and the need for practical ordering principles that we shall find in the *Discourse*.

129. *Correspondence*, 768.
130. *Disquisition*, 12.

# 4

## The Political Theory of the *Discourse*

*The stronger the pressure of the steam, if the boiler*
*be proportionally strong, the more securely the bark*
*buffets the wave, and defies the tempest.*[1]

The philosophical and practical mission Calhoun embarked upon in the "Patrick Henry"–"Onslow" debate, and continued in the *Disquisition*, came to fruition in the *Discourse*. Examined in tandem, the *Disquisition* and *Discourse* articulate Calhoun's understanding of the importance of popular rule and its obligatory relationship to republican government. Calhoun's *Discourse* also serves as an interpretation of the American political experience, with an emphasis upon the original dispersion of authority, sovereignty, and restraint, and the ways these vital qualities might be recovered amidst the impending crisis in nineteenth-century America. As a study of the "character and structure" of the republic, the *Discourse* attempts to nourish the political tradition in such a way as to facilitate a recuperation of the body politic.[2] As will become apparent, the *Discourse* differs from the *Disquisition* in terms of focus rather than substance. In many regards, the *Discourse* amplifies aspects of Calhoun's thought prevalent decades earlier. His remarkable speech in support of a presidential veto in 1842 provides a loose framework thematically anticipating the

---

1. John C. Calhoun, *A Discourse on the Constitution and Government of the United States*, in *Union and Liberty: The Political Philosophy of John C. Calhoun*, ed. Ross M. Lence (hereafter cited as *Discourse*), 219.
2. Ibid., 222.

*Discourse* and reaffirms his South Atlantic republican interpretation of American politics:[3]

> All this must appear anomalous, strange and unaccountable, on the theory of the Senator [Clay], but harmonious and easily explained on the opposite; that ours [republic] is a union, not of individuals, united by what is called a social compact, for that would make it a nation; nor of Governments, for that would have formed a mere confederacy, like the one superseded by the present Constitution; but an union of States . . . forming a Federal Republic, with the same equality of rights among the States composing the Union, as among the citizens composing the States themselves. Instead of a nation, we are in reality an assemblage of nations, or peoples . . . united in their sovereign character immediately and directly by their own act, but without losing their separate and independent existence.[3]

By returning to the fundamental law in the *Discourse*, Calhoun attempted to sustain the philosophical and constitutional bedrock of American politics. The absence of an adequate elucidation of these core elements distressed the Carolinian. In response to a query from a "young man," Calhoun addressed the predicament: "You ask me a question not easy to answer. There is no satisfactory work extant on our system of government. The Federalists [*sic*] is the fullest and, in many respects, the best, but it takes many false views and by no means goes to the bottom of the system. The Virginia and Kentucky resolutions & the report to the Virginia Legislature by Mr. Madison on the Alien and Sedition acts take far deeper & correct views, but are less full."[4] The *Discourse* was Calhoun's final effort to fill this perceived void.

Calhoun contemplated writing the *Discourse* for many years, informing his nephew that if he were to undertake any literary project it would "be on the elementary principles of political science, preliminary to a discourse on the Constitution of the U. States."[5] Against the scholarly and political currents of his time, Calhoun refused to present his critique of the American political tradition in "the shape of [constitutional] commentaries"; instead, he sought to recover these foundational elements through "a philosophical discussion on its

---

3. "Speech in Support of the Veto Power," February 28, 1842, *Papers*, 16:140.
4. Calhoun to A. D. Wallace, December 17, 1840, *Papers*, 15:389.
5. Calhoun to John A. Calhoun, April 2, 1845, *Papers*, 21:465–66; *Discourse*, 154.

character and constitution in illustration of the elementary treatise."
In June 1849 he finished the *Disquisition*, the "elementary treatise," and
was preparing to begin work on its sister volume, the *Discourse*. At
year's end his progress on the *Discourse* was the subject of much celebration: "The rough draft is finished," he proclaimed to his daughter.[6]
Calhoun continued to revise the work during the early months of 1850,
until his death on March 31. Just hours before his passing, Calhoun
asked his son John to read portions of the manuscript to him with
the intent to make further revisions.[7] Unfortunately, Calhoun died
before he could complete his final revision of the *Discourse*. The final
preparations for publication were completed after Calhoun's death by
Richard Kenner Crallé, his former chief clerk at the State Department
and longtime associate. Through the efforts of Crallé, the *Discourse*
was posthumously published (as was the *Disquisition*) in a limited
edition in 1851 and in a more widely circulated version two years
later. Although a journalist and man of letters himself, Crallé made
no substantive emendations to his mentor's work, choosing only to
add a few explanatory footnotes in reference to citations within the
text, along with noting an omission of "illegible" marginalia from the
published edition.[8] Critics have subsequently devalued the *Discourse*
in light of its purported textual, historical, or philosophical shortcomings. Even though these assessments offer considerable insight
into the work, critics have thoroughly neglected the deeper, more
profound interpretation of the American political tradition contained
in the *Discourse*.

As we have noted, the text of the *Discourse* did not benefit from
Calhoun's refining touch, prompting Crallé to remark that the draft
exhibited "marks of interrupted and hurried composition."[9] Margaret
Coit, one of Calhoun's finest biographers and a reliable student of his
political thought, argues for the stylistic superiority of the *Disquisition*
based upon the "diffuse, repetitive" qualities of the *Discourse*.[10] Other
useful accounts of the work have lamented the absence of the "logical

---

6. John C. Calhoun, *Correspondence of John C. Calhoun* (hereafter cited as *Correspondence*), 750, 768, 777. Earlier in his letter to his daughter Calhoun noted that the
manuscript totaled between 400 and 500 pages. In February he revised the number of
draft pages from the earlier estimate to between 350 and 400 pages (*Correspondence*,
782).

7. *Correspondence*, 782; William M. Meigs, *The Life of John Caldwell Calhoun*, 2:455, 461
n. 46 (for a somewhat less dramatic account, see Irving H. Bartlett, *John C. Calhoun*, 374).

8. *Discourse*, 227–28 n. 10.

9. *Works*, 6:vii.

10. Margaret L. Coit, *John C. Calhoun*, 519.

vigor and relative intellectual detachment" previously evidenced in the *Disquisition*, while depicting the *Discourse* as little more than "an appeal for the rules of the [political] game to be changed."[11] To a degree, these critics raise valid concerns about the *Discourse* as a text; however, the enduring importance of the treatise necessitates looking past Calhoun's often turgid stylistic veneer and confronting the intricate philosophical and historical idiom of the work. Embarking upon this task requires participation in two complementary pursuits: acknowledging that the American political tradition serves as the inspiration for Calhoun's insight; and employing the *Disquisition* as a lens for appreciating the philosophical worldview that nourishes the *Discourse*. Without the assistance of these "guides," the *Discourse* remains an elusive and perplexing treatise.

According to Calhoun, the foremost theoretical and practical distillation of authority and liberty was found within the American political tradition. The original system was predicated upon reserving the states' sphere of authority, while delegating sufficient authority for particular and limited responsibility to the general government. For Calhoun, this original diffusion, buttressed by a prudent mode of popular rule, was the primary achievement of American politics. A necessary corollary to his understanding of the regime's historical evolution was the need to perpetuate the original vision of the Union for posterity's sake: "The Union: Next to our liberty, the most dear; may we all remember that it can only be preserved by respecting the rights of the states and distributing equally, the benefit and the burden of Union."[12] If, as Calhoun argued, America had "departed" from its "original character and structure," this design or vision could also be restored, and the *Discourse* is dedicated to this purpose.[13]

In the *Discourse*, Calhoun convincingly traced the development of popular rule from the Declaration of Independence through the Articles of Confederation to the ratification of the Constitution. Calhoun's analysis enhanced earlier definitions of constitutional republicanism, emphasizing the American example as a "system of governments"

11. Bartlett, *Calhoun*, 356; James D. Clarke, "Calhoun and the Concept of the 'Reactionary Enlightenment,'" 103.

12. *Papers*, 11:148.

13. *Discourse*, 222. This study attempts to interpret those sections of the *Discourse* that illuminate Calhoun's theory of popular rule. Other aspects of the work, including its potential contribution to American legal history, the theory of law, and many related concerns, are deserving of scholarly examination, but not under the purview of this enterprise.

with the general government serving as the "representative and organ of the states."[14] To further his delineation of the American political tradition, Calhoun offered a critique of reserved and delegated powers evolving from the crucial political compact that formed the regime. Finally, the statesman suggested a return to the original design as a key to unraveling the growing confusion that abounded in America over popular rule and republican government, while providing his own elaboration of the tradition occasioned by the social and political predicament in which America found itself. By casting the "lamp of experience" over the exigencies of a troubled republic, Calhoun furnished both a sagacious theoretical defense of properly constituted popular rule and a remarkably cogent affirmation of American politics as laid out by the Framers. The *Discourse* could provide this insight because the *Disquisition* had established the philosophical groundwork for its assimilation of the American experience into a coherent whole.

Unfortunately, most appraisals of Calhoun's political theory concentrate solely upon the *Disquisition* rather than the *Discourse*. As a more succinct and accessible work, the *Disquisition* is usually considered a principal text in American political theory, and has continued to attract a steady stream of critiques since its initial publication. The *Discourse*, on the other hand, has not benefited from a corresponding measure of systematic examination. Nearly every study of Calhoun's political theory attempts to distinguish the *Disquisition* from the *Discourse*, defending the former as an authentic contribution to political theory and relegating the latter to a status of lesser importance. This prevailing, although flawed, approach to interpreting the *Discourse* deserves our scrutiny because it represents a significant departure from the author's own understanding. At several junctures, we have suggested that Calhoun's political theory deserves careful study due to its coherence and philosophical integrity. This proposition is especially important in terms of the *Discourse*. Calhoun sought, after all, to compose a sustained treatment of the American political tradition in "two parts."[15] The mutual compatibility of the *Disquisition* and *Discourse* in all critical respects was integral to Calhoun's project. In this light, studying either work without the assistance of the other presents significant, if not overwhelming, interpretive difficulties.

This study argues that the cooperative arrangement of the *Disquisition* and *Discourse* remains indispensable for comprehending the

14. *Discourse*, 133.
15. *Correspondence*, 770.

scope and the depth of perception involved in Calhoun's effort to recover popular rule, and Calhoun's own synergistic composition of these texts serves as the hermeneutical guide for our study. The attachment to Calhoun's method is not assumed out of deference to the author or a nostalgic devotion to the past. On the contrary, Calhoun's approach offers the most appropriate and rewarding mode of textual investigation, and assuming such a critical posture neither prohibits nor limits the exploration of potential divergences of the *Disquisition* and *Discourse*. Provocative challenges to this approach have been presented by James Clarke, among others, who has argued that the *"Discourse* is clearly not theoretical in the same sense that the *Disquisition* is."[16] Superficially, this distinction may seem to possess some merit, but again Calhoun's understanding and the text prove otherwise. The unique combination of the historical and theoretical within the *Discourse* should be appreciated as representing a quality of instrumentation endemic to texts in American political thought. As a guide to this genre of theoretical works, Donald Lutz has suggested that the student of American political thought must "move beyond the written word alone and supply the common understandings that any active citizen should possess."[17] When Lutz's discernment is appropriated for our purposes, we are presented with at least two key insights. The first concerns the distinctiveness of the *Discourse* as a work of American political thought. The manner of theorizing found in the *Discourse* emerges from an understanding of politics that is premised upon constitutionalism. The second key insight is that one must confront the possibility that many Americans during the mid-nineteenth century possessed an appreciation for the original design and political history of the republic that is either not comprehensible or not appealing to their late-twentieth-century counterparts.[18] In misconstruing the salient aspects of the *Discourse,* some critics depreciate the treatise as an "obsolete" work "outmoded by the passage of historical events" and unable to influence a presumably antagonistic Northern audience.[19] The case for the obsolescence of the *Discourse* is predicated upon the faulty notion that the crisis over divided authority in American politics was resolved by the Civil War. In actuality, the

16. Clarke, "Calhoun and the Concept of the 'Reactionary Enlightenment,' " 104.
17. Donald S. Lutz, *A Preface to American Political Theory*, 38.
18. See Jerry Combee, *Democracy at Risk;* and Diana Ravitch and Chester E. Finn, *What Do Our 17-Year-Olds Know?*
19. Clarke, "Calhoun and the Concept of the 'Reactionary Enlightenment,' " 35–61, 102–5 (quotation from 105); Gerald M. Capers, *John C. Calhoun, Opportunist*, 245.

postbellum history and political theory of the republic contradict any claim of obsolescence. The method and purpose of the *Discourse* regarding the need for a "restoration" of the regime and the continuing struggle for "reciprocal action and reaction" between the states and the federal government is called federalism today.[20] As a work in political theory, the *Discourse* also provides a valuable presentation of the South Atlantic republican vision that dominated Calhoun's thought, cultivating the discernment of the *Disquisition* for a distinctively American context. This chapter will pursue these matters while attempting to clarify the appropriate role for popular rule within American politics according to the *Discourse*.

## THE *DISCOURSE* AND REPUBLICAN DESIGN

For Calhoun the American political tradition was exemplified by a consistency of understanding and purpose. A direct path could be traced from the association of colonies under the Declaration, to a confederacy of states under the Articles, to the Constitutional Convention, and to the ratification process that established a constitution for the independent and sovereign states composing the United States. As a literary text, the *Discourse* commences and ends with abstracts of this interpretation of American politics; the introduction supplies a philosophical digest of Calhoun's project, while the conclusion presents a narrative account, centered upon South Carolina, of his theory in practice. The initial encapsulation summarizes the *Discourse*'s weighty purpose:

> Ours is a system of governments, compounded of the separate governments of the several states composing the Union, and of one common government of all its members, called the Government of the United States. The former preceded the latter, which was created by their agency. Each was framed by written constitutions; those of the several states by the people of each, acting separately, and in their sovereign character; and that of the United States, by the same, acting in the same character— but jointly instead of separately. All were formed on the same model. They all divide the powers of government into legislative, executive, and judicial; and are founded on the great principle of

20. *Discourse*, 222–23, 168.

the responsibility of the rulers to the ruled. The entire powers of
government are divided between the two; those of a more general
character being specifically delegated to the United States; and all
others not delegated, being reserved to the several States in their
separate character. Each, with its appropriate sphere, possesses
all the attributes, and performs all the functions of government.
Neither is perfect without the other. The two combined, form one
entire and perfect government.[21]

Within the "system of governments," authority was delegated from
the states to the general government, creating a "perfect," or diffused,
political system. The pursuit of perfection, according to the *Disquisition* and *Discourse*, denotes the need to provide for the greatest amount
of liberty possible under law. Two generations earlier Publius had
defended the departmental theory of government and its ability to
distribute power as an advancement "towards perfection."[22] Against
contemporary claims of perfectionism in the rhetorical and messianic
pronouncements of numerous ideological movements, Calhoun and
Publius incorporated the concept to suggest the cultivation of the best
possible political system for the republic. This contradicts the idea of
perfection as an instantaneous, idiosyncratic form of social and political gratification that disregards any fundamental suspicions concerning human nature. Moreover, as the *Disquisition* has already proved,
the limits upon politics imparted by the sinful impulse preclude the
possibility of perfectionism as a liberating device. Instead, popular
rule is defined by the imposition of self-restraints, advancing perfection as a model or reifying image of ethical discrimination instead of
a mandate for limiting constitutional and legal restrictions upon the
citizenry.[23] According to Calhoun, perfection encouraged self-control
as a guide to preventing the impulsive, potentially anarchic, attempt
to define republican government as the pursuit of unlimited liberty.
As an effort to nourish restraint among the citizenry and in the government, perfection was clearly identified with theological and political

21. Ibid., 81.
22. Alexander Hamilton, James Madison, and John Jay, *The Federalist,* ed. George
W. Carey and James McClellan, No. 9 (Hamilton), 39 (hereafter cited as *The Federalist*).
See Nos. 5, 6, 10, 15, 29, 33, 38, 41, 47, 64, 65, 68, 69, 72, 80, 82, and 85 for additional
examples of the use of *perfect* or *perfection* in the work.
23. A related approach to perfection from a theological perspective, and one that
is frequently misunderstood in the same fashion, can be found in the works of John
Wesley (see Wesley's *Standard Sermons* [any edition] and W. E. Sangster, *The Path to
Perfection*).

efforts to restore a troubled republic.[24] Genuine popular rule and political stability were predicated upon such a recovery of restraint or "perfection" among the citizenry. Calhoun translated the notion of the best possible or "perfect" government, "formed by the Constitution," into a more deliberate formulation: a "democratic, federal republic."[25]

Calhoun argued that America, as both a democratic and a federal republic, was devoted to "the great cardinal maxim, that the people are the source of all power," and was devoid of the "artificial distinctions" found within other typologies of political rule.[26] By *federal*, Calhoun suggested that America represented the middle ground between the potentially hegemonic consolidation of authority in a centralized government and the dissipation of a coherent political order manifested in a purely confederal arrangement. The American polity embodied the best possible situation for the preservation of popular rule because it avoided the extremes of consolidation on one hand and disunion on the other. America was allowed to overcome the foibles so often associated with popular rule throughout political history by maintaining a truly federal system of government. In presenting the case for an authentic federal configuration, Calhoun referred to George Washington's "Letter to Congress," which summarized and accompanied the original Constitution when it was distributed to the states for ratification.[27] The "Letter" evidenced the influence of a High Federalist worldview, even though the work can also be appreciated as anticipating Calhoun's notion of diffused authority.[28] It translated the Constitution's rather complex mission as

24. Richard J. Carwardine, *Evangelicals and Politics in Antebellum America*, 130.
25. *Discourse*, 81.
26. Ibid., 81, 82. Calhoun also subsequently defined a "democratic, federal republic" more thoroughly as "democratic in contradistinction to aristocratic, and monarchical—federal, in contradistinction to national, on the one hand—and to a confederacy, on the other; and a Republic—a government of the concurrent majority, in contradistinction to an absolute democracy—or a government of the numerical majority" (*Discourse*, 133). A "democratic, federal republic" expressed the Founders' vision for American politics as distilled by Calhoun. The government was democratic because popular participation was encouraged, although guided by concurrent provisions; it was federal implying a regime designed to incorporate "systems of governments" into a workable whole; and it was republican, suggesting that concurrent measures operated at all levels of governance.
27. "Letter to Congress," in *Jonathan Elliot's Debates in the Several State Conventions on the Adoption of the Federal Constitution: The Federal Convention of 1787*, ed. James McClellan and M. E. Bradford, 2:495–96 (hereafter cited as *Debates*).
28. According to Max Farrand's *Framing of the Constitution of the United States*, a draft of the document "is in the handwriting of Gouverneur Morris and presumably

simply providing a "different organization" of government from the
one prescribed under the Articles of Confederation. This "different
organization" implied neither a complete rejection of the unique role
for state responsibility under the Articles nor the acceptance of a "national," centrally administered entity.[29] Calhoun cited the document's
definition of this "different organization" as a "federal government of
these states" dedicated to preserving the paramount position of the
states in the overall configuration.[30] The "Letter" provided a summary
of the Constitutional Convention's insight regarding the fundamental
relationship of the states to the "general government of the Union"
and demonstrated the felicity and autonomy of state function that
were expected to contribute to the perseverance of the political order. In tracing the development of this original relationship and the
prospects for recovering it, Calhoun began with the Declaration of
Independence.

The Declaration initiated the legitimate delineation of state and
federal authority and a properly constituted mode of popular rule
through first articulating the primary nature of the union. Contrary to
the persistent habit of depicting the Declaration as part of American
hagiography unconnected to the more salient aspects of the American political tradition, and contrary to the obdurate notion that its
second paragraph supplied the philosophical core of the Founding,
Calhoun offered a more comprehensive and engaging defense of the
Declaration's insight regarding the foundational dispersion of political authority in American politics. In fact, these critical dimensions
obliged the assimilation of the Declaration's discernment within the
larger tradition, which Calhoun often articulated in an experiential
manner:

> The path of principle was clear. I had but to act consistently with
> myself—but to look back to the past to see what point I ought to

---

was composed by him," 183. Washington was entrusted with the responsibility "that
he retain the journal and other papers [from the Convention], subject to the order of the
Congress," which he presented to the Secretary of State in 1796 (624). Calhoun attempts
to offer his interpretation of the "Letter" at several junctures, including his "Speech in
Reply to Daniel Webster on the Force Bill," February 26, 1833, *Papers*, 12:123.

29. *Papers*, 11:624.

30. *Debates*, 495. The "Letter" also suggested the limits of the Articles and the need
for a "consolidation of the Union," defining consolidation, not as the establishment
of a national superstructure, but as a plea to the states for greater cooperation and
shared purpose, "to be less rigid, in points of inferior magnitude, than might have
been otherwise expected" (495).

go forward. If I be asked, in what those principles, which have heretofore governed me, consist?—my answer is, that they will be found in those that led to the war of the Revolution; that they are contained in the Declaration of Independence.[31]

For Calhoun, the Declaration illuminated and explained the foundations of the American republic as also resting upon a political compact. In contradistinction to a social compact, a political compact does not unite individuals or governments. Instead, such an agreement forms a republic "with the same equality of rights among the States composing the Union, as among the citizens composing the States themselves."[32] A federal republic, united by the political compact, evolved through the mutual interaction between the elements that unite to form a republic. As the levels of contact and cooperation increased, obstacles to greater integration could be overcome. The Declaration encouraged a political compact that developed with "time and experience" into a model of political and social stability, Calhoun argued. Instead of predicating the success of the compact upon a detailed or formulaic conclusion, with sovereignty or national security as prominent examples of such an end, a political compact resolved the problem of obligation by allowing the elements to retain a high degree of autonomy. Autonomy among the elements or states was ensured through "a firm reliance on the protection of divine Providence," and the shared obligation to "mutually pledge to each other our lives, our Fortunes and our sacred Honor."[33] Calhoun suggested that the sinew of mutual cooperation found in the Declaration provided "our peculiar system of governments" and the "embryo state of our political existence."[34] As the model for this "system of governments," the Declaration supplied a division of authority among the elements, with each state required to participate more thoroughly in the overall arrangement than was either allowed or anticipated under the previous colonial order, while also preserving the locus of authority within each individual state. For Calhoun, the Declaration expressed the foundation for popular rule and for a territorial republic that came to fruition in the Constitution:[35]

31. "Speech at Pendleton, S.C.," September 7, 1826, *Papers*, 10:202.
32. "Speech in Support of the Veto Power," February 28, 1842, *Papers*, 16:140.
33. *The Declaration of Independence* (hereafter cited as *Declaration*).
34. *Discourse*, 135.
35. See Orestes Brownson, *The American Republic;* and *Discourse*, 193.

> Thus, the region occupied by them, came to be divided into
> as many States as there were colonies, each independent of the
> others—as they were expressly declared to be; and only united to
> the extent necessary to defend their independence, and meet the
> exigencies of the occasion—and hence that great and, I might say,
> providential territorial division of the country, into independent
> and sovereign States, on which our entire system of govern-
> ment rests.[36]

This territorial model of republican government, as outlined in the
Declaration, presented the authoritative understanding of the original design for the Carolinian. The Articles of Confederation and
the Constitution assumed various modifications based upon this appreciation of the relationship of the states to each other and to the
"united" government, although these modifications "were not in the
foundation, but in the superstructure of the system."[37] To further
elucidate this insight, Calhoun again referred to Washington's "Letter
to Congress" and its description of a "different organization" in the
original Constitution. As a "different organization," the Constitution presented a continuation of the political insight found in the
Declaration. It was possible to revise certain arrangements while
maintaining the same basic structure and vision for the regime. The
Constitution provided a "different organization," while possessing
the Declaration's fundamental understanding of diffused authority.
The basic premise underlying the relationship between the states was
also reaffirmed: the parts had relative autonomy, with provisions for
a general government that was limited in scope and function. The
"baptismal name" ascribed to the regime was the "United States," a
term that embodied the overarching plurality that defined the states
and their interconnectivity, with each state maintaining the status of
a "free and independent" entity.[38]

    As the model of a political compact, Calhoun also considered the
Declaration to be a fundamentally conservative document, in contrast
to the perverse "revolution" in social and political thought that accompanied the aggrandizement of power on the behalf of the general
government during the first half of the nineteenth century.[39] The

36. *Discourse*, 135. For a contemporary statement of these principles see Russell
Kirk, "The Prospects for Territorial Democracy in America."
37. *Discourse*, 85.
38. Ibid., 84; *Declaration*.
39. *Discourse*, 89.

absorption of authority rightly reserved to the states was encouraged by a failure to recognize the primary distinction regarding the nature of the compact that Calhoun defended at the outset of the *Discourse:* the American political tradition proceeded from a political rather than a social compact. The rising influence of the general government was tied to the promotion of a social compact premised upon an understanding of the American people as a collective, undifferentiated mass. Calhoun pointed out that the conflation of the social with the political was never promulgated. Accordingly, the Declaration's "United States of America" was itself a political rather than a social or geographical formulation, according to Calhoun. The Declaration's "United Colonies," who joined ranks to confront England, presented their concerns as political protests towards the political goal of transitioning from a collection of protectorates to "Free and Independent" states.[40] Each colony (or state) possessed a "separate charter and government" indicating a fundamentally independent relationship among the constituent elements that also affirmed the primary disposition of sovereignty as residing within the individual states in the new configuration.[41] As "distinct communities" and not as a unified regime, these thirteen "United Colonies" declared their independence in the same manner in which the constituent parts had previously conducted all internal and external affairs.[42] In essence, the thirteen entities began moving from the status of colonial appendages to sovereign states through the combined political labors of the individual states as expressed by the Second Continental Congress's Declaration.[43]

While the Declaration appropriately described the status of "Free and Independent States" as intrinsic to the republic, the document clearly stated what would become the conceptional thesis of the *Discourse:* the states "ordained" or created the republic.[44] This ordaining and creating force of the states remained, according to Calhoun, the determining factor in all aspects of America's political development and a reminder of the continuation of the original political compact. In all matters, the states constituted the procreative elements within

40. *Declaration.*
41. *Discourse,* 89.
42. Ibid.
43. Virginia, for example, had already severed its tie to England on May 15, 1776, and on June 29, the state adopted a constitution ("Virginia Declaration of Rights and Constitution," June 12 and 29, 1776). Virginia was a "republic" before the Declaration of Independence.
44. *Discourse,* 94.

the political order, and they were naturally considered more integral and compelling than any other composite assemblage or "aggregate" institutional measures.[45] Without the indispensable contribution of the states as a source of restraint and innovation, the republic's prospects for survival were greatly diminished. It was precisely the degradation of the creative role assumed by the states and first represented in the Declaration that encouraged Calhoun's attempt to reclaim the Declaration's message for a new generation of Americans.

To recover the formative political qualities articulated in the Declaration—during an age in which a paradigmatic shift towards the centralization of authority had commenced—required a return to the "principles embodied by Jefferson in the Declaration of Independence," Calhoun argued.[46] As noted earlier in this chapter, the Declaration's most enduring contribution was its rudimentary expression of the original design. But the Declaration neither enunciated a new theory of politics nor provided for a revolutionary social and political order, despite frequent claims to the contrary. Against this commonplace presentation of the Declaration as holy writ or as a "preface" to the Constitution,[47] Calhoun suggested that the work deserved great prominence as an imperfect but vital representation of theoretical moderation against the potentially tyrannical extremes of a plebiscitarian social compact on one hand and despotic colonial rule on the other.[48] Calhoun also praised the work as a plan for securing liberty and the diffusion of political authority, although he admitted that the Declaration was an outgrowth of an earlier political culture that valued distinctiveness as a political and personal virtue. As Garry Wills notes, the American revolution and political tradition were "not born from a Pentecost of mutual understanding, but from a Babel."[49] The ensuing crisis forced the thirteen separate colonies to plead for

45. Ibid., 95.
46. Calhoun to James E. Scott and Others, August 11, 1840, *Papers,* 15:329.
47. Mortimer Adler, *We Hold These Truths,* 7.
48. *Discourse,* 89. Pauline Maier's recent *American Scripture: Making the Declaration of Independence* (hereafter cited as *Scripture*) agrees with our earlier effort to separate the Declaration from the hagiography that has clouded recent interpretative efforts. In Maier's attempt to provide a more accurate account, she unfortunately suggests an overly pedestrian reading of the Declaration as "a workaday document of the Second Continental Congress" (xviii). Conversely, some scholars continue to defend this hagiographic tradition; they include Carl L. Becker *(The Declaration of Independence),* Harry V. Jaffa *(How to Think about the American Revolution),* and Mortimer Adler *(We Hold These Truths).*
49. Garry Wills, *Inventing America: Jefferson's Declaration of Independence,* 47.

the "chartered rights of Englishmen," not issue a manifesto of creative nationalism or abstract natural right. In other words, Calhoun, perhaps more than any person of his generation, was cognizant of the limitations of viewing the Declaration as articulating a grand theory of politics. The "Free and Independent States" supported the Declaration as a political and legal instrument because it assumed the form of a statement of principles in accord with their republican worldview.

While clearly praising Jefferson's labors in composing and revising the Declaration, and noting the importance of the text to his own understanding of American political thought, Calhoun nevertheless criticized the Sage of Monticello for his extravagance of expression. For Calhoun, the Declaration served as a testimony against the "crimes" or abuses of "chartered rights" at the time of the Second Continental Congress.[50] The strength of the document was contained in its defense of diffused authority and its listing of offenses committed by the English Crown. As Calhoun often suggested, the Declaration was a statement of principle, but principle nourished by a legal and philosophical tradition grounded in practice. Besides reaffirming the self-contained status of the colonies qua states, the existing political bonds among the "United Colonies," and the need for relinquishing all ties with England, the Declaration was indistinguishable from other pronouncements against tyrannical rule in the seventeenth and eighteenth centuries. The Declaration was in every regard an address and a petition, not a formal treatise. Interestingly, some of Jefferson's most elaborate textual embellishments, especially the second paragraph, survived amidst numerous attempts at revision.[51] The historian Pauline Maier suggests that the actual purpose of the second paragraph was simply to declare the right to revolution, a concept that would have appealed to most colonists. Maier agrees with the conclusions of earlier studies that suggest Jefferson was not offering an elaborate theory of rights or a defense of natural right in any sense.[52] The Declaration merely "summarized succinctly" the prevailing notions of republican rule:

> By the time of the Revolution those ideas had become, in the generalized form captured by Jefferson, a political orthodoxy

50. *Discourse*, 193, 197; *Papers*, 11:267, 12:530.
51. See *The Papers of Thomas Jefferson*, vol. 1, ed. Julian P. Boyd, 315–19, 413–33; and Maier, appendix C, *Scripture*, 235–41.
52. Willmoore Kendall and George W. Carey, *The Basic Symbols of the American Political Tradition*; M. E. Bradford, *A Better Guide Than Reason*, 185–203.

whose basic principles colonists could pick up from sermons
or newspapers or even schoolbooks. . . . The sentiments Jefferson eloquently expressed were, in short, absolutely conventional
among Americans of his time.[53]

Calhoun both affirmed and endorsed the Declaration as a defense of
republican government and popular rule. As suggested in chapter 2,
Calhoun understood himself to be perpetuating many critical aspects
of Jefferson's interpretative and philosophical worldview for a new
and troubled political environment. His solitary reservation regarding
the Declaration concerned Jefferson's inclusion of the sentence "all
men are created equal." The endorsement of natural equality found
in the Declaration was "the most false and dangerous of all political
errors," Calhoun argued. Jefferson's affirmation of equality within the
Declaration was not only an aberration from the Sage of Monticello's
valued contribution to political thought, but, more important, it was
a theoretical and practical impossibility: "All men are not created
equal. . . . It was inserted in our Declaration of Independence without any necessity."[54] Following Calhoun's understanding of human
nature as outlined in chapter 3, any attempt to incorporate equality
within a theory of statecraft was "impossible."[55] The Declaration's
commitment to equality was also inconsistent with the patrimony of
American political thought as understood by Calhoun. The genesis of
the American Revolution was found, after all, in a conservative defense of the rights of Englishmen, not in an attempt to re-create society:

> Breach of our chartered privileges, and lawless encroachment
> on our acknowledged and well-established rights by the par-
> ent country, were the real causes,—and of themselves sufficient,
> without resorting to any other, to justify the step. Nor had it any
> weight in constructing the governments which were substituted
> in the place of the colonial. They were formed of the old materials
> and on practical and well-established principles, borrowed for the
> most part from our own experience and that of the country from
> which we sprang.[56]

Calhoun contended that the Declaration was, as a statement of American principles, primarily a bill of particulars addressed to the king.

53. Maier, *Scripture,* 135.
54. *Works,* 4:507, 508.
55. *Papers,* 13:64.
56. *Works,* 4:508–9.

Instead of providing a radical plan for redesigning government and civil society, the Declaration offered a critique and defense of political liberty that was articulated more completely by the Articles of Confederation and the Constitution. In providing an introduction to these seminal texts, the Declaration does not impinge upon the status of the Constitution as the primary blueprint for American government. Again, Calhoun argued for a continuity of vision among the principal works. Additional evidence for this theoretical consistency can be found in what M. E. Bradford described as the "antecedent integrity" that existed among the states throughout the various periods of their political development.[57] One is again forced to consider the ramifications of Calhoun's fundamental insight regarding origins: the states gave birth to the nation. States signed the Declaration, affirmed the Articles, and ratified the Constitution not as the aggregate of national interests or a collective citizenry, but as independent entities. While dismissing the possibility of equality among individuals, Calhoun allowed for a nuanced notion of equality of authority among the states that composed the nation. In fact, the diffusion of political control required the equality of "rights and privileges" among the states as the "deep and solid foundation of our political fabric; preserve that, and all is safe—destroy it, and the whole would rush headlong to the dust."[58] For Calhoun, the first concrete exemplar of this arrangement was found in the Articles of Confederation.

If the Declaration supplied the prologue to the original design for the republic, it was the Articles of Confederation, the first American embodiment of the design, that incorporated this insight into the fundamental law of the regime. For Calhoun, the provisions and language of the Articles served as an authentic precursor to the American Constitution. The Constitution of 1787 was incomprehensible without first having assimilated the political theory of the Articles. Drafted in stages from 1776 to 1777, the Articles extended and revised the Declaration's ennobling of diffused authority and its delineation of state autonomy, while establishing popular rule based upon the deliberative, decentralized, community-centered participation of the citizenry. In his assessment of the Articles, Calhoun also clearly contradicted the accepted interpretation of the initial American attempt

57. M. E. Bradford, *Original Intentions*, 68.
58. Calhoun to Richard J. Smith, et al., June 12, 1839, *Papers*, 14:620. Calhoun addressed the problem of equality in a variety of ways; see *Papers*, 10:392; 13:64, 397; 14:56; 15:585; 16:430; and *Works*, 4:344, 473, 507–9.

at composing a constitution as it has been described by historians and political theorists during the nineteenth and twentieth centuries. The accepted caricature of the Articles portrays the work as a dismal failure in all respects; the Articles could not provide for a system of popular rule or supply the young regime with the security measures that were needed to ensure its survival. The critics of the Articles usually cite the plan's inability to endow a national government with the power to levy taxes or regulate commerce, thereby discouraging all efforts at national cohesion. The authoritative scholarly commentary on the Articles succinctly describes this flawed, albeit normative interpretation: the Articles were "the product of ignorance and inexperience and the parent of chaos."[59] The Articles, in other words, embody the political weaknesses and failures associated with American politics during the interregnum between the Declaration and the Philadelphia Convention.

Calhoun's thorough effort at reclaiming the Articles concentrated upon appreciating the work as integral to a larger enterprise, initiated by the Declaration and brought to fruition in the Constitution, that was devoted to recovering the original design and encouraging a system of popular rule:

> The style of the present constitution and government is precisely the style by which the confederacy that existed when it was adopted, and which it superseded, was designated. The instrument that formed the latter was called—"Articles of Confederation and Perpetual Union." Its first article declares that the style of this confederacy shall be, "The United States of America;" and the second, in order to leave no doubt as to the relation in which the states should stand to each other in the confederacy about to be formed, declared—"Each state retains its sovereignty, freedom and independence; and every power, jurisdiction, and right, which is not, by this confederation, expressly delegated to the United States in Congress assembled." If we go one step further back, the style of the confederacy will be found to be the same with that of the revolutionary government, which existed when it was adopted, and which it superseded.[60]

The Articles possessed the means for affirming popular rule, diffusing political authority, and allowing the "governed" to govern. The Arti-

---

59. Merrill Jensen, *The Articles of Confederation,* 3.
60. *Discourse,* 83–84.

cles also encouraged genuine popular rule by defining the concept as active participation by the citizenry under self-imposed limitations, through the "organic arrangements" of the states. As in the case of the Declaration, the Articles perpetuated the original design for the "territorial division of the country, into independent and sovereign States, on which our entire system of government rests," according to Calhoun.[61]

By defining the status of the Articles within the American political tradition in the manner described, Calhoun might seem vulnerable to the criticism that he was merely offering another revisionist interpretation of the work, or molding the Articles' purpose and legacy to prop his understanding of popular rule. Such a judgment of Calhoun's interpretation would prove convincing, if he also denied the inefficacy of the Articles. In denying any limitations associated with the Articles as a guide for establishing a government for the newly independent colonies, Calhoun would have appeared to endorse the Articles' distribution of political authority and participation merely for the sake of expediency. In actuality, the antithesis is true: Calhoun appropriately detailed the limitations associated with the Articles with great regularity. According to Calhoun, the Articles' weaknesses resulted from a lack of precision regarding the text's central theoretical propositions, rather than the absence of specific programmatic proposals. While integral to the primary focus of the American political enterprise, the Articles could not serve their intended purpose: "[E]xperience soon proved that the confederacy was wholly inadequate to effect the objects for which it was formed." The Articles, according to Calhoun, were a "contract between agents [states]" that did not fully integrate the people as the ultimate sovereign voice into the decision making and affairs of state.[62]

Instead of placing genuine authority in the people as represented in the states, the Articles delineated sovereignty as residing in the states' representatives, which prohibited the fulfillment of a political compact among the people, who, after all, constituted the zenith of authentic sovereignty. The Articles merely formed "a league made by ambassadors," while the Constitution represented "a league made by sovereigns—the latter no more tending to unite the parties into a

---

61. Ibid., 136, 135.
62. Ibid., 137; "Speech in Reply to Daniel Webster on the Force Bill," February 26, 1833, *Papers*, 12:122.

single sovereignty than the former."[63] In other words, the original design remained intact, although incapable of providing anything more than a simplified confederacy, and offered a muted concurrent response to the political exigencies of the day. By not fully representing the sovereign voice of the people organized as states, or presenting a definite concurrent alternative to the joint agency of the Continental Congress, the Articles affirmed state distinctiveness at the expense of popular sovereignty.

Furthermore, if we refine Calhoun's insight regarding popular rule to imply that concurrent government is defined by its self-imposed limitations, it may be concluded that the Articles lacked the necessary moral discipline to facilitate an authentic dispersion of political authority. The absence of moral discipline prohibited the people of the states from responding to crises with the cohesion necessary to preserve the regime. Depending too heavily upon the appointed representatives of the state governments instead of authentic state sovereignty and popular rule, the "United States" under the Articles were unable to exert the moral discipline to fulfill the confederacy's stated purposes. The Articles had created "an assembly of diplomatists" unable to fully articulate this discipline, and a corrective was needed. For Calhoun the remedy was found in "substituting a government in place of the Congress of the confederation," and he believed this was "the great and essential change made by the [constitutional] convention."[64] It was precisely the path towards a "government" that produced the Constitution.

By strengthening the foundations laid by the Articles, the Constitution provided the final and most profound manifestation of the South Atlantic republican worldview's defense of popular rule and the diffusion of political authority. While the Declaration and the Articles contributed to this evolving discernment, the Constitution presented the definitive maturation from a confederacy to a federal government, and Calhoun again identified this movement as within "the character of the system":

> It involved, in the next place, an important change in the character of the system. It had previously been, in reality, a league between the governments of the several States; or to express it more fully

63. "Speech in Reply to Daniel Webster on the Force Bill," February 26, 1833, *Papers*, 12:122.

64. *Discourse*, 117.

and accurately, between the States, through the organs of their respective governments; but it became a union, in consequence of being ordained and established between the people of the several States, by themselves, and for themselves, in their character of sovereign and independent communities. It was this important change which (to use the language of the preamble of the constitution) "formed a more perfect union." It, in fact, perfected it. It could not be extended further, or be made more intimate. To have gone a step beyond, would have been to consolidate the States, and not the Union—and thereby to have destroyed the latter.[65]

The Constitution reaffirmed the Declaration's and the Articles' understanding of sovereignty as residing in the citizenry. The most authentic organic and delineatory manifestations of the people were the states, although the citizenry retained final and complete political authority. Such a Constitution, in Calhoun's view, was most appropriately identified as a concurrent constitution because it served primarily as an exemplification of the states' role in preserving the regime. The Constitution also provided a careful enumeration and specification of power consigned to the general government.[66] By replacing the Articles' restrictive mode of executing delegated authority, the Constitution allowed the general government (of the states) to assume a variety of distinctively blended functions based upon the delegation of political authority. Some powers were clearly delegated to the general government and were potentially subject to scrutiny from the states. In other words, Calhoun argued, since they formed a concurrent foundation for the political order, the states should, in times of crisis, exert their concurrent prerogative and repossess certain delegated power from the federal government if needed and in accord with the Constitution—especially in situations where the federal government had usurped power from the states. Through their adoption of the Constitution, the American people accepted a "joint supplemental government" that retained the states as the primary voice of the people.[67]

The Constitution also gave birth to a political order that allowed for a mode of popular rule constrained by the provisions of the fundamental law. Following the original design and incorporating the restraint necessary for popular rule to flourish encouraged a

65. Ibid., 118–19.
66. Ibid., 119.
67. Ibid., 142.

concurrent or truly "constitutional democracy"—as opposed to an absolute, or unrestricted, plebiscitarian system. The American political tradition, as the *Disquisition* and *Discourse* suggest, was premised upon concurrent majoritarianism, the "sense of all its parts," according to the Carolinian.[68] In surveying the political history of the republic, Calhoun observed that the deliberation on and eventual ratification of the Constitution itself were the result of concurrent measures. The success of the Convention and subsequent state ratifying conventions demonstrated the centrality of concurrent measures as a means of resolving the most troubling political dilemmas the country might encounter. A minority of the population (as estimated by the numerical majority) had established the "corporate character" of the Constitution by endorsing the fundamental law as separate entities who were defined by their representative function, and not merely by population. The states performed as "equals" in founding a government, which allowed a minority either to affirm or to reject changes in the structure of the regime.[69] But the Founders had also envisioned that concurrent measures, and ultimately popular rule, should be considered in reference to population. This nexus of state authority and "federal numbers" provided the prevailing and indispensable concurrent tension within the structure of the general government. It was formed by what Calhoun described as the "two majorities" of American politics:

> It thus appears, on a view of the whole, that it was the object of the framers of the constitution, in organizing the government, to give to the two elements, of which it is composed, separate, but concurrent action; and, consequently, a veto on each other, whenever the organization of the department, or the nature of power would admit. . . . That, in organizing a government with different departments, in each of which the States are represented in a twofold aspect, in the manner stated, it was the object of the framers of the constitution, to make it more, instead of less popular than it would have been as a government of the mere numerical majority—that is, as requiring a more numerous, instead of a less numerous constituency to carry its powers into execution—may be inferred from the fact, that such actually is the effect. Indeed, the necessary effect of the concurrent majority is, to make the government more popular—that is, to require more wills to put it

68. Ibid., 121.
69. Ibid., 124.

in action, than if any one of the majorities, of which it is composed, were its sole element.[70]

The two majorities affirmed Calhoun's fundamental premise regarding popular rule, and were confirmed by the Constitution: the citizenry participated in republican government by accepting certain self-limitations regarding their involvement, the scope and capacity of the regime, and the need to preserve liberty under law. As Calhoun had already proved in the *Disquisition*, these two competing majoritarian visions—the numerical, or absolute, majority and the concurrent, or constitutional, majority—could not simply be conflated into a single system. The numerical majority offered the possibility of assessing "federal numbers," or electoral votes, but could not penetrate the deeper social and political ramifications of political participation and republican government. The limitations associated with the numerical majority resulted from its radical majoritarian conception of popular rule, which reduced the necessarily varied framework of political participation to the solitary act of voting. As a response to this misunderstanding of the original design, the *Discourse* revised and clarified the earlier wisdom of the *Disquisition* by demonstrating that voting alone was incapable of resolving all conflict, especially in societies where strongly antagonistic forces attempt to control the government. To its credit, the numerical majority might compute "federal numbers," or the sum total of all voting, but this could not be assumed to represent the sense of the community.[71] Given its design, the numerical majority also possessed a troubling propensity for reporting cumulative electoral outcomes without regard for the natural divisions of political power.

The countervailing force against the numerical majority's influence upon the regime remained the concurrent majority, or "organism." It served to preserve and perpetuate the original design amidst disruptions in the social and political order by establishing a government with a more "numerous, instead of a less numerous constituency" of participation from the citizenry.[72] In chapter 3, we discussed many problems associated with the possibility of attaining a numerical majority, as well as the limitations associated with the concept from a theoretical perspective. The *Discourse* continued the earlier critique

70. Ibid., 129–30.
71. Ibid., 133.
72. Ibid., 129.

of the numerical majority presented in the *Disquisition*, but, more important, it affirmed the distinctiveness of the concurrent organism in practice within American politics. For Calhoun, the concurrent foundation of the American regime was distilled into four divisions, or characteristics: the sovereignty of the states; the division of constitutional powers into "constitution-making and law-making powers"; the proper assignment of delegated powers to the general government and reserved powers to the states; and the distribution of the power of the general government among the "several departments" that compose the regime.[73] These divisions equipped each section (or state) with the "power of self-protection" against potential encroachments upon their constitutionally apportioned power and duties. For such a system to function, each section or division needed a check of some variety, which usually assumed the form of a veto. In presenting the concurrent basis of American politics, Calhoun began with the Congress, "which, in all popular governments, must be the most prominent, and, at least in theory, the strongest."[74] Following the Constitution's design, Calhoun described the concurrent force at work in the legislature. Putting the legislature first among the branches in the Constitution suggested the primacy of the legislative branch, or what is often described as the theory of legislative supremacy. For Calhoun, the Congress was the most important popular division of government, possessing a vital concurrent quality:

> To it, all the functionaries of the other two departments are responsible, through the impeaching power; while its members are responsible only to the people of their respective States—those of the Senate to them in their corporate character as States; and those of the House of Representatives, in their individual character as citizens of the several states.[75]

In praising the legislative "department" as an example of the concurrent majority in action, Calhoun offered an appreciation for the merits of legislative supremacy, although he remained a devotee of the separation of powers. According to his interpretation, the Constitution provided the legislative branch with the same privileged position as that found in the Declaration and the Articles. Legislatures during this

73. Ibid., 153–60.
74. Ibid., 154.
75. Ibid.

period, according to historian Gordon Wood, "were no longer to be merely adjuncts or checks to magisterial power, but were in fact to be the government."[76] Calhoun clearly dismissed this view, and the other extreme cases made on the behalf of legislative supremacy. The legislature rightly deserved a special status, according to Calhoun, but one that was moderated internally by the concurrent interaction between the House and the Senate, and externally by its equal footing with the executive and judicial branches.[77] The Senate, of course, provided the most complete and acute witness to concurrentism as the result of its interspersing of political power among the states, which promoted a wider augmentation of participation. Greater involvement was a necessity because of the need to have "more wills to put it in action, than if any one of the majorities, of which it is composed, were its sole element."[78] The prospect of legislative supremacy also raised complications for a political order grounded in concurrent measures. Prominent among the difficulties resulting from elevating the position of the legislature above the other branches was the possibility that the House of Representatives and the Senate could overstep the already generous provisions for legislative authority outlined in the "necessary and proper" clause of the Constitution (art. 1, sec. 8). The clause, which provided the basis for the doctrine of implied powers, gave the legislature great discretion in its decision making. In approving legislative distinctiveness as a principle, Calhoun had nevertheless witnessed the abuse of the implied powers during his lifetime, and along with Jefferson he feared that the national government would assume questionable authority from time to time, ultimately limiting popular rule and prohibiting the states from checking the inordinate growth of the general government. Both Jefferson and Calhoun eventually argued for the use of the Constitution's amending power to allow states to protect their rightful authority.[79] In opposition to

76. Gordon S. Wood, *The Creation of the American Republic, 1776–1787,* 163.

77. Among the advocates for legislative supremacy during the Revolutionary Period, Thomas Paine offered an articulate case for the proposition. In this regard, Paine actually endorsed a view of representative government different from Calhoun's, defending the numerical majority as the primary means of communal assertion. Calhoun clearly rejected this notion. For a related criticism of Paine, see Michael P. Federici, *The Challenge of Populism,* 9–16.

78. *Discourse,* 130. Among the many examples within the Constitution of concurrent provisions for encouraging popular rule, none was more appealing to Calhoun than the Senate.

79. Homer Carey Hockett, *The Constitutional History of the United States, 1826–1876,* 81–91.

legislative hegemony, the executive and judicial branches possessed checks against its authority, as well as the authority of each other. The president, with the capacity to veto the legislature's proposals, to nominate officials to office, and to preside over the "administration of government," was an effective concurrent deterrent to the abuse of authority. The judicial branch was uniquely blessed with a "negative on the acts of the other departments—resulting from the nature of our system of government." But the protections offered by these divisions only partially aided the cause of promoting popular rule. The most substantive defense of the concept was found in the "reciprocal action and reaction" demanded by the Constitution for relations between the national and state governments.[80]

The general government could be maintained through the "divisions of power," but it was subject to the same inert weaknesses as were individuals. The limitations resulting from the "constitution or law of our nature," with the stronger elements coercing the weaker elements, would eventually enfeeble the divisions.[81] The only remedy, Calhoun surmised, was the original design. The general government stood in relation to state governments as "co-ordinate governments" that provided a "partition" of authority: "[T]he government of the United States is, in each State, the co-ordinate of its separate government; and taken together, the two make the entire government of each, and of all the States. On the preservation of this peculiar and important division of power, depend the preservation of all the others, and the equilibrium of the entire system."[82] If the numerical majority served as the only means of decision making within the regime, the result would be majority tyranny, or the dissolution of the regime, as suggested at earlier junctures. On the other hand, the original design provided a mutual negative from within the very nature of the states, beginning with the ratification process. As the repository of reserved power, the states were invested with an equal capacity to judge infractions against the general government. In situations where the general government and the states were in conflict, each possessed a "mutual negative" on the other's actions.[83] At this point, Calhoun cited the record of the Virginia ratifying convention and the Tenth Amendment to the Con-

80. *Discourse*, 156–57, 168.
81. John C. Calhoun, *A Disquisition on Government*, in *Union and Liberty: The Political Philosophy of John C. Calhoun*, ed. Ross M. Lence, 5 (hereafter cited as *Disquisition*).
82. *Discourse*, 160.
83. Ibid., 173.

stitution as primary evidence of the doctrine. The Virginia convention provided, along with its New York counterpart, the most erudite and complete commentary on the interpretation of the fundamental law besides the records of the Constitutional Convention itself. Of the many defenses of mutual checks, few resemble Calhoun's wisdom in the *Discourse* more than James Madison's speeches delivered before the Virginia convention in 1788. It was Madison, the political thinker Calhoun considered responsible "for the form of the government under which we live,"[84] whose defense of diffused authority prefigured the *Discourse:*

> [T]he powers granted by the proposed Constitution, are the gift of the people, and may be resumed by them when perverted to their oppression, and every power not granted thereby, remains with the people, and at their will. It adds likewise, that *no right of any denomination,* can be cancelled, abridged, restrained, or modified, by the General Government, of any of its officers, except in those instances in which power is given by the Constitution for these purposes. There cannot be a more positive and unequivocal declaration of the principles of the adoption—that every thing not granted, is reserved.[85]

Calhoun's own inherited vision of American politics was confirmed by Madison and the South Atlantic republican tradition's insight: in situations of disputed authority, the states possessed the right of self-protection. The Tenth Amendment, with its emphasis upon state authority, was more than a declaratory statement about the role of the states against encroachment from the general government. In the worldview of Calhoun and those who shared his understanding, the Tenth Amendment was not merely "a rule of interpreting the Constitution."[86] In fact, the Tenth Amendment was a guide for defining the theoretical core of the republic and an important premise of constitutional theory. Against the often condescending and disparaging expositions of the Tenth Amendment during Calhoun's lifetime

---

84. "Remarks on the Proposed Purchase of James Madison's Notes on the Philadelphia Convention," February 18, 1837, *Papers,* 13:444.

85. *The Documentary History of the Ratification of the Constitution,* vol. 10, *Ratification of the Constitution by the States, Virginia,* ed. John P. Kaminski, Gaspare J. Saladino, et al., 1501–2.

86. Walter Berns, "The Meaning of the Tenth Amendment." This effort to diminish the veracity of the Tenth Amendment is part of a prolonged attempt to promote the centralization of authority (see Berns, "The Constitution as Bill of Rights").

and in contemporary America, it is useful to consider that the Tenth
Amendment remains a part of the fundamental law and may be
invoked by the Supreme Court or lower court decisions. The Tenth
Amendment serves as a vital and beneficial aspect of the fundamental
law, according to the legal historian Raoul Berger, who identifies the
continued authentication of the Amendment's importance in the *Fry v.
United States* (1975) case. In *Fry*, the Supreme Court's decision affirmed
that "[t]he [Tenth] Amendment expressly declares the constitutional
policy that Congress may not exercise power in a fashion that impairs
the States' integrity or their ability to function effectively in a federal
system."[87] Twenty-two years later, in the *Printz v. United States* (1997)
decision, the High Court again forcefully affirmed the Tenth Amendment's approach to defining the fundamental diffusion of political
authority in America:

> Residual state sovereignty was also implicit, of course, in the
> Constitution's conferral upon Congress of not all governmental
> powers, but only discrete, enumerated ones, which implication
> was rendered express by the 10th Amendment's assertion that
> "the powers not delegated to the United States by the Constitu-
> tion, nor prohibited by it to the states, are reserved to the states
> respectively, or to the people."[88]

At the heart of the matter, Calhoun recognized that the Founders
intended for the Tenth Amendment to limit the general government's
sphere of influence while facilitating genuine popular rule. In its refining of the boundaries of governmental authority, Calhoun's interpretation closely resembled Justice Joseph Story's depiction of the Tenth
Amendment as excluding "any interpretation, by which other powers
should be assumed beyond those, which are granted."[89] Protecting
the reserved powers secured the regime while allowing for more
deliberation, Calhoun opined.[90]

The recovery of the concurrent voice in the "action of the government" was even more critical if the states—as the sovereign building
blocks of the republic—became over time the weaker parties to the

---

87. *Fry v. United States*, 421 U.S. 542, note 7 (1975), as quoted in Raoul Berger,
*Federalism: The Founders' Design*, 85.

88. Justice Antonin Scalia, "For the Majority," *Printz v. United States*, 521 U.S. 98
(1997).

89. Joseph Story, *Commentaries on the Constitution of the United States*, vol. 2, sec. 1808.

90. *Discourse*, 130.

Constitution.[91] The more numerous the concurrent provisions, especially between the states and the general government, the stronger the
regime. By referring to the ratification model of constitution making
once more, Calhoun presented the starkest defense of state authority, and ultimately popular authority, in the forming, shaping, and
reformation of the government:

> If proof be required, it will be found in the fact—which cannot
> be controverted, so far as the United States are concerned—that
> the people of the several states, acting in the same capacity and in
> the same way, in which they ordained and established the federal
> constitution, can, by their concurrent and united voice, change or
> abolish it, and establish another in its place; or dissolve the Union,
> and resolve themselves into separate and disconnected States.[92]

Of course, Calhoun acknowledged that any action of this sort should
not be taken lightly. The more dramatic the measure, the greater the
need for "prudence and propriety" and to act with "greatest caution
and forbearance." Working within a Jeffersonian and Madisonian
framework, as demonstrated in chapter 2, Calhoun could only ac-
quiesce to the use of state authority to "interpose" when the general
government had clearly abrogated the Constitution. And even under
these circumstances, a state (or states) could only assert its authority
if the violation was "a clear and palpable infraction of the instrument
[Constitution]" and only as a "last resort."[93] A state (or states) was
allowed to assume such a course of action only if the goal was to
protect the state's (or states') citizens and the Constitution. Recovering
this necessary responsibility of the states in relation to the general
government might make decision making less efficient, but it would
allow the regime to "gain vastly in moral power."[94] In Calhoun's
interpretation, the interposing and amending power of the states
implicit in the Constitution could only augment authentic popular
rule by allowing for a greater diffusion of authority. Calhoun's critics
have argued that restricting the ability of the general government to
act might in some fashion produce its own variety of hegemonic or
tyrannical rule.[95] But these assessments misrepresent Calhoun as a

91. Ibid., 188.
92. Ibid., 194.
93. Ibid., 197.
94. Ibid., 219.
95. For example, James S. Fishkin, an advocate of "deliberative democracy" and
one who is sympathetic to aspects of Calhoun's understanding of popular rule, never-

political thinker who sought to undermine the structure of the American regime. In actuality, Calhoun's purpose was the preservation of the original balance of authority and the fortification of the American political system against the obstacles it faced. The vindication of Calhoun's critique can be witnessed in the effects of the centralization of political power in America and throughout the world during the century and a half since his death, which has in most cases either limited or repealed long-standing modes of deliberation and popular rule.[96] For Calhoun, it was "indispensable that the government of the United States should be restored to its federal character" in theory and in practice.[97]

---

theless identifies the limitations of the concept: "Calhoun's proposal is vulnerable to several objections. One is that tyranny can be produced through omission as well as commission. Threats of a veto could prevent measures from passing that would relieve ongoing tyranny, while the effort to avoid anarchy could motivate acquiescence in an unjust status quo" (*Democracy and Deliberation: New Directions for Democratic Reform*, 40).

96. The *Discourse* included a remarkably cogent criticism of Section 25 of the Judiciary Act of 1789, which attempted to deny state supreme courts the right to question the validity of a federal statute.

97. *Discourse*, 267.

# 5

## Restoring the Concurrent Republic

The *Disquisition* and *Discourse* serve as Calhoun's most profound attempt to ensure a firmer grounding for popular rule through the recovery of a proper understanding of the interrelationship between liberty and authority. While maintaining a lifelong appreciation of voting and majority rule, Calhoun also acknowledged the limitations of these concepts. As he had noted years earlier to his friend Virgil Maxcy, "We have much to learn in political science. The rule of the majority & the right of suffrage are good things, but they alone are not sufficient to guard liberty, as experience will teach."[1] Instead of endorsing purely abstract notions of majority rule and voting, Calhoun preferred to define both within a historical context. His use of the historical should be appreciated as an attempt at refining and explaining the importance of the Founding principles within a distinctively nineteenth-century framework. Regardless of the political system, some restriction upon those who assumed control over the government was needed. In presenting his recapitulative theory of politics, Calhoun expanded upon his earlier work on the "organism" that promoted restraint within the polity. He also employed a myriad of titles to describe this quality of restraint: the concurrent voice, the sense of the community, and most prominently, the concurrent majority.

As both a theoretical and a practical means of encouraging consensus, securing liberty, promoting the diffusion of power, and ultimately ensuring the regime's survival, the concurrent majority was the preeminent American contribution to political thought, according

1. Calhoun to Virgil Maxcy, August 6, 1831, *Papers*, 11:451.

to Calhoun. But the concurrent majority had been supplanted by the hegemonic forces that controlled the general government. The Jacksonian democratic dream had become the American political nightmare. A steady concentration of political power in the general government, increasing social and regional hostilities resulting from the quest for control, and the debasement of popular rule were ominous signs to Calhoun of the future that awaited the country:

> As the Government approaches nearer and nearer to the one absolute and single power, the will of the greater number, its actions will become more and more disturbed and irregular; faction, corruption, and anarchy, will more and more abound; patriotism will daily decay, and affection and reverence for the Government grow weaker and weaker, until the final shock occurs, when the system will rush to ruin, and the sword take the place of the law and Constitution.[2]

Calhoun's efforts to recover the concurrent majority suggest a vigilant desire to return to the original understanding of liberty and authority within the American political tradition. Such a mission depended upon "dividing and distributing the powers of government" and supplying each "division" with "either a concurrent voice in making and executing the laws, or a veto in their execution."[3] Reviving the concurrent majority in American politics was (and remains) primarily an effort at restoration and preservation. Ironically, many proponents of the diffusion of authority, especially American conservatives, have failed to recognize the importance of Calhoun's insight for contemporary political science. In some cases, these critics have misrepresented Calhoun's valued contribution to the American political tradition for the purpose of temporal political gain.[4]

---

2. "Speech in Support of the Veto Power," February 28, 1842, *Papers,* 16:149.

3. John C. Calhoun, *A Disquisition on Government,* in *Union and Liberty: The Political Philosophy of John C. Calhoun,* ed. Ross M. Lence, 21 (hereafter cited as *Disquisition*).

4. John O'Sullivan, the former editor of the *National Review,* dismissed Calhoun indirectly as responsible for "the emergence of legal theories, in the writing of Lani Guinier et al., that would revive 'fancy franchises' and 'concurrent majorities' on the underlying assumption that minorities and majorities are not continually forming and reforming on different issues, but permanently frozen along ethnic and racial lines" ("Mistaken Identities," 56). Some reputedly conservative critics of Calhoun have argued that he derailed American political thought. In a published letter, Harry Jaffa suggested, "Do I not bring philosophy down from the heavens and into the city— making it practical and political—when I demonstrate by my critiques of Kendall,

By returning to the source, one discovers that the concurrent major-ity was neither an invention based upon Enlightenment notions nor a purely mechanistic "device" to protect Southern political and eco-nomic concerns.[5] The concurrent majority served as the most "repub-lican" element in the American constitutional and political tradition, establishing a system of government predicated upon popular rule rightly constituted.[6] It was also not a panacea for resolving America's political crises—instead, Calhoun consistently argued that the concur-rent majority was a stopgap measure, and was to be exercised only until a more substantial constitutional consensus of three-fourths of the states could be secured.

The combination of the concurrent majority (or voice) and voting produced genuine constitutional and popular rule; however, voting alone could never provide for a stable mode of popular rule. As the foundation of republican government, popular rule must acknowl-edge other means of recognizing preferences among the citizenry than voting by simple plebiscite. Appropriately, Calhoun argued that concurrent measures were already present in the American consti-tutional structure and clearly operative during the formative period of the political union. The original American Constitution abounds with examples of measures designed to counterbalance the perver-sion of republican government into plebiscitarianism, or a govern-ment of the "simple majority."[7] The *Discourse* presents these con-current features of the American Constitution—including the Sen-ate, the Electoral College, the Supreme Court, and the separation of powers, to a degree—as contributing to the original design for popular rule. In presenting this understanding of American politics,

---

Bradford, and Wills, that their doctrines are merely varieties of Confederate doctrine, and that the vital center for their beliefs is derived from John C. Calhoun? Do I not do that even more profoundly, when I show that the 'Marx of the Master Class' is not, in the crucial respect, so very different from Marx himself, since the proslavery attack on free society, and the Marxist critique of capitalism, closely coincide?" (*American Conservatism and the American Founding*, 136).

5. Wilson Carey McWilliams's description of Calhoun's work as "entirely based on Enlightenment concepts" (*The Idea of Fraternity in America*, 260) serves as a representa-tive example of the widespread failure to appreciate the depths of Calhoun's political thought. Several recent works present useful, although inadequate, challenges to pre-vious scholarship. See James D. Clarke, "Calhoun and the Concept of the 'Reactionary Enlightenment' "; and Lacy K. Ford, Jr., "Inventing the Concurrent Majority."

6. John C. Calhoun, *A Discourse on the Constitution and Government of the United States*, in *Union and Liberty: The Political Philosophy of John C. Calhoun*, ed. Ross M. Lence, 133 (hereafter cited as *Discourse*).

7. "Rough Draft of An Address to the People of South Carolina," *Papers*, 11:273.

Calhoun suggested that the numerical majority could not represent the full character of the republic. Participation was originally encouraged, nurtured, and protected in the political process through the implementation of the concurrent majority. The recovery of the concurrent majority could rejuvenate participation discouraged by decades of neglect and patronage. The concurrent majority would aid the unfolding and augmentation of participation and the interspersing of political power. More important, this amalgamation of voting and the concurrent majority would provide a basis for offsetting "the tendency of government to oppression and abuse of power; and to restrict it to the fulfillment of the great ends for which it is ordained."[8] For Calhoun, the disadvantages of limiting temporary majorities were outweighed by the benefits that accrued from allowing for thoughtful deliberation and authentic consensus building. Recovering the concurrent majority in union with a disciplined mode of true majoritarian participation offers the possibility of reclaiming popular rule.

Reiterating the centrality of popular rule, Calhoun argued that there are actually two competing majoritarian visions in American politics: that of the numerical or absolute majority, and that of the concurrent or constitutional majority. Without considering the diversity within the community itself, the numerical majority assesses overall electoral outcome as the only indicator of preference. Numerical majorities are based upon electoral "numbers," a radical majoritarian understanding of participation that eschews all considerations besides the act of voting itself.[9] Such a concept of popular government requires a unitary vision of politics and the state. It also supposes that the apparatus of voting can resolve all conflict, even in profound crises where no consensus of opinion exists. To its credit, the numerical majority can tabulate the "sense of the greater number; that is, of the stronger interests or combination of interests, and to assume this to be the sense of the community."[10] Resulting from its "simplicity and facility of construction," the numerical majority possesses a troubling propensity for reporting cumulative electoral outcomes without regard for the natural divisions of authority.[11]

---

8. *Disquisition*, 22.
9. Ibid., 24.
10. Ibid., 23.
11. Ibid., 57. For a more generous reading of the numerical majority's function, see August O. Spain, *The Political Theory of John. C. Calhoun*, 132–35.

The numerical-majoritarian concept of popular rule also presumes that humankind can participate in governing en masse, at every available opportunity, and with the necessary leverage to undertake any possible action. Calhoun's fundamental criticism of such an understanding of popular rule suggests that attaining a numerical majority under any circumstances is illusory at best, and utopian at worst. The numerical majority can only function effectively in a political world devoid of geographical and economic divisions and without competing claims upon authority. In fact, Calhoun argued that this "simple" numerical majority could not sustain authentic popular rule and was incompatible with a comprehensive appreciation of the concept. In addition, if popular rule is predicated upon providing the citizenry with an expedient option to initiate whatever they desire, then popular rule itself must no longer be claimed as the primary achievement of republican or democratic political theory. Individual and communal assertion and preference, after all, are often prominently associated with other political systems, especially modern authoritarian and totalitarian regimes that discourage true popular rule in any concrete form while professing to represent the actual sentiments of an oftentimes amorphous populace. More important, at the end of the twentieth century, Calhoun's insight provides a guide for understanding and responding to the crisis of a postmodern internationalism that promotes a vulgarized model of popular rule consisting merely of the collection of individual wills and sentiments without regard to the substantial and historical limitations of humankind.

By presenting the limitations of the numerical majority, Calhoun demonstrated that a more inclusive approach is necessary if the true preferences of the citizenry in any political system are to be ascertained. Voting alone cannot assimilate the level of insight necessary for governing, due to its inability to properly incorporate an understanding of the diverse interests that must be considered. Unfortunately, Calhoun's use of the term *interest* in explaining this aspect of his political thought has diverted scholarly attention from the author's purpose and encouraged numerous academic assessments that fail to appreciate the meticulousness of his thought. Most of these appraisals attempt to explain Calhoun's use of *interest* either as a means of defending the South and slavery or as the philosophical precursor to contemporary theories of interest group politics.[12] As a lot, these cri-

12. For the former, see Ralph Lerner, "Calhoun's New Science of Politics," 931; for the latter, see Peter F. Drucker, "A Key to American Politics: Calhoun's Pluralism"; Dar-

tiques evidence the influence of contemporary liberal political theory, especially the schema of "possessive individualism."[13] Viewing social and political life as obsessed with the acquisition of wealth and power, "possessive individualism" as a philosophical approach assumes that the desire for personal aggrandizement is primary among man's longings. With antecedents in the thought of Rousseau and Kant, *interest* is viewed as synonymous with human self-determination or the search for autonomy. Calhoun rejected all narrow views of the word and defended it as an intrinsic manifestation of the body politic, grounded in the community. The natural and evolutionary predilections of the regime ascertained through the most reliable units, the states, deserved protection from the arbitrary exertion of force by the general government against these elements. Viewing the diversity within the community as important to the survival of the country and as the only practical basis for embodying a totality of concerns, Calhoun mirrored Publius's earlier plea for "the regulation of these various and interfering interests" as a primary requirement for American politics.[14] But *interest*, Calhoun declared, should not be defined as purely individual assertion:

> It results, from what has been said, that there are two different modes in which the sense of the community may be taken: one, simply, by the right of suffrage, unaided; the other, by the right through a proper organism. Each collects the sense of the majority. But one regards numbers only, and considers the whole community as a unit having but one common interest throughout; and collects the sense of the greater number of the whole, as that of the community. The other, on the contrary, regards interests as well as numbers—considering the community as made up of different and conflicting interests, as far as the action of the government is concerned; and takes the sense of each, through its majority or appropriate organ, and the united sense of all, as the sense of the entire community. The former of these I shall call the numerical, or absolute majority; and the latter, the concurrent or constitutional majority.[15]

---

ryl Benny Baskin, "The Pluralist Vision of John C. Calhoun"; and Peter J. Steinberger, "Calhoun's Concept of the Public Interest."

13. C. B. MacPherson, *The Political Theory of Possessive Individualism*, 51–53.

14. *The Federalist*, ed. George W. Carey and James McClellan, No. 10 (Madison), 45 (hereafter cited as *The Federalist*).

15. *Disquisition*, 23–24.

In upholding such an understanding of *interest*, Calhoun more closely resembled Publius than contemporary theorists' ideas of "interest group" or pluralistic democracy.[16] Publius and Calhoun incorporated similar conceptions of human agency into their appreciation for the decision making of autonomous or semiautonomous communities, as well as for the interconnected roles these communities play in addressing the most profound social and political issues that a republic must confront. Instead of relying upon purely private economic and political preferences to synthesize community and regime responses into a composite whole, Publius and Calhoun insisted upon assimilating the deeper, more comprehensive needs of the whole by focusing upon the responses of the communities and the republic in their particularity. A consensus might be possible if the distinct preferences of all communities in a regime were considered, but only after much trial and error. An unrefined or less articulate majority serves only to discourage participation, and ultimately it undermines the regime's legitimacy.[17]

By merging the "sense" of the communities within a republic into a truer and inclusive majority, a republic could be sustained, urged Calhoun. Concentrating solely upon electoral success, the numerical (or absolute) majority cannot adequately provide such a foundation for popular rule. Instead of clarifying and collecting the "sense[s]" of the diverse communities that make up a regime, the numerical majority actually misrepresents and overrates the homogeneity of the

---

16. As a commentary on his earlier "Fort Hill Address" (1831) and a reminder of his consistency in this regard, Calhoun composed a public letter to South Carolina Governor Hamilton further clarifying his understanding of interests nearly two decades before writing the *Disquisition:* "When, then, it is said, that a majority has the right to govern, there are two modes of estimating the majority, to either of which, the expression is applicable. The one, in which the whole community is regarded in the aggregate, and the majority is estimated, in reference to the entire mass. This may be called the majority of the whole, or the absolute majority. The other, in which it is regarded, in reference to its different political *interests* [italics added], whether composed of different classes, of different communities, formed in one general confederated community, and in which the majority is estimated, not in reference to the whole, but to each class or community of which it is composed, the assent of each, taken separately, and the concurrence of all constituting the majority. A majority thus estimated may be called the concurring majority" (Calhoun to James Hamilton, Jr., August 28, 1832, *Papers,* 11:640). Whereas previous misconceptions regarding the role of interest in *The Federalist* have been challenged by recent scholarship, Calhoun's use of the concept has not experienced such a needed reevaluation. See George W. Carey, *The Federalist;* and David F. Epstein, *The Political Theory of The Federalist.*

17. While a political order based upon unanimity is appealing, Calhoun rejected such a possibility because it would prove "impracticable" (*Disquisition,* 24–25).

political environment. Although exhibiting many other debilitating characteristics, the numerical majority is most deficient in its inability to fully incorporate an understanding of the preferences and opinions of the populace into the practice of governing. If the numerical majority could function as claimed, it would be "a true and perfect model of a popular constitutional government; and every departure from it would detract from its excellence," declared Calhoun. However, the numerical majority fails to meet these expectations and should not be confused with the actual majority, or genuine popular rule. Calhoun argued that the numerical majority's propensity to consider an incomplete "sense" of the regime as authoritative, "a part over a part," was actually a dangerous perversion of true popular rule.[18] It may then be maintained that a government of the numerical majority has a predisposition towards diminishing the concurrent qualities integral to the survival of the regime. The numerical majority naturally benefits from a diminution of concurrent measures; from the perspective of numerical majoritarianism, concurrent elements are an imposition upon the will of the majority. In subjugating the entire republic to the dictates of a questionable collection of votes from elections not predicated upon appraising the regime's complex preferences, the numerical majority threatens to undermine the electoral and constitutional foundations of republican government. Accordingly, recent scholarship has confirmed that concurrent measures can actually advance the genuine participation and deliberation vital to popular rule. Roberta Herzberg, for example, argues that Calhoun's "design would result in a decision process more stable than that expected under simple majority rule. Moreover, each interest included in the decision-making process would be protected against any policy change that would make it worse off."[19] Against the dire claims of Calhoun's critics, Herzberg suggests that his understanding of popular rule and democratic theory merits reconsideration.

Herzberg's research and some of the studies assessed in chapter 1 affirm Calhoun's argument that the electoral and participatory attributes of popular rule suffer as the result of the numerical majority's tendency to identify the majority as whomever votes in a particular election while disregarding the range of responses necessary to adequately canvass the citizenry. On the other hand, confusing the

18. *Disquisition*, 25.
19. Roberta Herzberg, "An Analytic Choice Approach to Concurrent Majorities," 78.

governmental structure established by such a deficient majority with the more commodious "government of the whole" provided by the concurrent majority impairs the constitutional infrastructure in terms of its ability to facilitate popular rule. Finally, the spirit of restraint so essential to the American constitutional and political tradition suffers a devaluation.

Restraint—societal and personal—encourages a tenor of resiliency within the constitutional order by imposing some limitations upon a temporally elected majority's ability to assert sovereign authority. Envisioning restraint at the heart of republican government, Publius defined this centrality of purpose in terms of deliberativeness: the operation and power entrusted to government must be diffused or filtered "to refine and enlarge the public views, by passing them through the medium of a chosen body of citizens, whose wisdom may best discern the true interest of their country."[20] For Calhoun, this purpose was best fulfilled by a "simple government, instituted by the states, for their mutual security, and more perfect protection of their liberty and tranquillity."[21] Imbued with societal and personal restraint, this type of government also guards against the impulse of the moment controlling its decision making, while developing political institutions that mirror those qualities premised upon restraint. It is precisely the inculcation of these habits into social and political structures and the citizenry that defines the concurrent majority in action. Not bound by restraint like the concurrent majority, the numerical majority inadvertently encourages the rise of oligarchic rule. Offering an initially appealing and laudable strategy of providing for a more democratic regime, but without any mode of restraint or resistance, the numerical majority leads to a tyranny of the majority.

There are, of course, alternative measures capable of counteracting the numerical majority's influence besides the concurrent majority, even though these choices may function most effectively in tandem with the concurrent majority, to limit the intrusiveness of the general government. A formal, written constitution, establishing parameters for the scope and function of the general government, has always been viewed as a protection against disruptions to the political order. Calhoun maintained a great love for constitutions, especially the American version. The statesman described the Constitution as the

20. *The Federalist*, No. 10 (Madison), 47.
21. "Speech on the Bill to Prevent the Interference of Certain Federal Officers in Elections," February 22, 1839, *Papers*, 14:565.

greatest manifestation of the citizenry's understanding of political order.[22] A constitution functions as a major source of restraint against the excesses of flawed human reason and promotes liberty through its invocation and nurturing of this restraint among the citizenry.

Relying upon a constitution alone, though, would present a republic with an insurmountable problem: even though governmental authority would be formally restricted, the constitutive parts of the regime actually responsible for constraint would not have "the means of enforcing their observance."[23] In other words, the citizenry and the states would be presented with the theoretical tools to protect the regime but not with the necessary pragmatic power of enforcement to complete the task. Influenced by the sinful impulse discussed in chapter 3, the struggle for control would naturally result in a conflict between the dominant party in charge of government and the weaker party outside of it. Following the prescriptions of a numerical majority, the dominant party would contest any limits on its power. In response, the weaker or minority party's only recourse would be to seek rigid enforcement of all formal restrictions upon authority, resulting in a struggle between the "liberal" and the "strict" constructions or interpretations of the constitution. As a result of the numerical majority's inability to accept any authenticating standard for popular rule besides a concept of voting, the dominant party would always control such conflicts, perpetuating the denigration of the minority.

Calhoun's defense of the original constitutional design differed substantially from the current advocacy of "original intent." For Calhoun, the evocative power of the American Constitution was found in its ethical spirit. Simply recovering the "ideas" of the Framers would not suffice: only a determined effort to reclaim the ethical worldview and the authentic constitutional arrangements for the diffusion of political authority could restore genuine popular rule in America.

Calhoun's discussion of majority/minority tensions in the *Disquisition* is less an extended apology for his personal struggles than a recognition of the limits of rational discourse in politics. The success of the numerical majority also suggests a crisis of reason within the republic. Various political movements arose in the country during Calhoun's career as a statesman that refused any attempt to understand the na-

---

22. "Second Speech on Amendments to the Compensation Law," January 20, 1817, *Papers*, 1:393, 16:138.
23. *Disquisition*, 26.

ture of politics in a comprehensive manner.[24] As the American regime
approached the mid-nineteenth century, the increasingly ideological
nature of political debate, especially the concept of "immediatism"
articulated by the Abolitionists, suggested a refusal to depend upon
republican political theory, deliberation, and the interchange of ideas
to resolve the increasingly divisive political situation. For Calhoun,
this shift marked another attempt, both explicit and implicit, to ignore
the limitations of human nature.[25] Viewing these movements as potentially dangerous and philosophically untenable, Calhoun described
them as extremely misguided: "With more zeal than understanding,
it [Abolitionism] constantly misconceived the nature of the object
regardless of the means, by which it is to be effected."[26] In confronting
the political crisis encouraged by Abolitionism, Calhoun continued
to defend the standard of original restraint; he affirmed the providential character of social and political existence, as well as the vital
nexus between liberty and constitutionalism in American politics.
This interrelationship depended upon the Constitution to provide a
framework for liberty, but liberty was to be nourished by the diversity
of the "authority which created" it, the states, and protected against
the numerical majority's inevitable movement towards hegemony:

> To talk of liberty, without a Constitution, or, which is the same
> thing, an organic or fundamental system of legislation, by which
> the will of the Government may be effectually coerced or re-
> strained, is to utter ideas without meaning; and to suppose an
> ultimate power, on the part of the Government, to interpret the
> Constitution as it pleases, and to resort to force, to execute its in-
> terpretation, against the authority which created the Constitution
> itself, is to be guilty of the grossest political absurdity that can be
> imagined.[27]

Without the concurrent majority, the constitution was easily subverted
through the machinations of the dominant party. If combined with the
concurrent majority, the constitutional framework could be preserved

24. Aileen Kraditor, *Means and Ends in American Abolitionism,* 178–234; Eugene D.
Genovese, *A Consuming Fire,* 3–71.
25. Calhoun also criticized his fellow South Carolinians during the "Bluffton Movement" of 1844 for sacrificing principle for expediency. See *Papers,* 19:525.
26. "Report from the Select Committee on the Circulation of Incendiary Publications," February 4, 1836, *Papers,* 13:62.
27. Calhoun, "To a Committee in Columbia County, Georgia," September 9, 1833,
*Papers,* 12:170.

and prosper as the result of their intended union. Calhoun argued that
the reclamation of the American political tradition could come from
within: through the implementation of the concurrent majority, the
Constitution could provide for the greatest amount of liberty possible,
and be fortified against any impediments that the tradition might
encounter. The concurrent majority was, as we have suggested, part
of the Founders' design as seen in the ratification and amending processes. Against the many criticisms of the Constitution, including the
Abolitionists' steady vilification of it as a "pro-slavery compact,"[28] Calhoun defended the document as the greatest testament of the country's
achievement of freedom under law. Additional measures or devices
conceived outside of the same constitutional ethos and aimed at supporting or reforming the political and constitutional structures were
in his view superfluous and usually counterproductive. The most
useful correctives were of an iterative quality, according to Calhoun.[29]
For example, efforts at dividing the function of government into
departments (sometimes described as the "departmental theory" of
politics during the nineteenth century) for the purposes of improving
administration and discouraging the concentration of power could
never succeed. Unless the departments were distributed to the major
regions or "communities" of the nation, with each given a negative
check on the other, the dominant party would simply assume control
of the departments and the operation of government.[30] And Calhoun's
most famous and perhaps least significant proposal for amending the
Constitution, a dual presidency, was offered within the larger constitutional framework and not as a modification originating outside of
this realm.[31] In essence, Calhoun advocated a retrogressive theory of
constitutionalism, preferring to locate the restorative features of the
tradition within the original "purity" of the document.[32] In returning
to the Founding as a guide for facing America's future, Calhoun was
influenced neither by a romantic nostalgia for the Founding nor by a

28. This method of dismissing the Constitution was prominent during Calhoun's
lifetime and is present in contemporary political thought as well. See Wendell Phillips,
*The Constitution as a Pro-Slavery Compact.*

29. Frustrated by the perceived inadequacies of the American Constitution, many
scholars have proposed "extra-constitutional" measures designed to promote particular interpretations of popular rule, although most are of a plebiscitarian cast. See
Robert A. Dahl, *A Preface to Democratic Theory,* 134–35; Claude Lefort, *Democracy and
Political Theory,* 9–20; and Lani Guinier, *The Tyranny of the Majority.*

30. *Disquisition,* 27–28.

31. *Discourse,* 275–77.

32. *Papers,* 15:28, 354.

proceduralism founded upon a faith in measures beyond the Constitution. Instead, Calhoun was inspired by a genuine devotion to the republic. At some junctures Calhoun appeared to assume a pessimistic posture regarding the future of the Constitution and the American regime. His responses to these problems were most typically critiques of prominent efforts to separate the principles of popular rule under the fundamental law as he understood them—namely, the concurrent majority sustained by voting—from each other. If these elements were diminished in some fashion, leaving the numerical majority no longer restrained by constitutional and concurrent means, the Constitution would be reduced to a "dead letter."[33]

Amidst the possibility of disorder, with anarchy as the worst outcome, Calhoun reaffirmed the mutual compatibility of the concurrent majority and voting as forming the essence of genuine popular rule. To provide the most salutary foundation for popular rule, both positive and negative authority are needed. Positive authority is contributed through the process of participation. In regard to voting, the numerical majority might assist in a limited way in the process of gauging preferences, although its "simplicity and facility of construction" would eventually prove "incompetent" when required to provide for a complex republic. As a positive authority within the political system, voting allows for the establishment of a government by regularly and partially confirming preferences, electing officials, and responding to new circumstances within the country. This positive authority contributes substantially to the regime, supplying government with some of the "power of acting," or in other words, supplementing the original design for the public sphere with a spirit of animation.[34] As a contribution of positive authority, voting assumes special importance in a system guided by concurrent measures. Unlike the numerical majority, the concurrent majority depends upon the regular and sustained participation of the citizenry in decision making. Instead of concentrating upon simple electoral totals to dictate public policy, a concurrent system values the depth of participation as expressed within the communities forming the regime. Calhoun envisioned the concurrent majority as allowing for an extension of the voting "franchise" to a large portion of the citizenry. The numerical majority also encourages voting, although it makes no distinction between typologies of interest or communities as the natural subdivisions

33. *Papers*, 12:7, 86.
34. *Disquisition*, 57, 34–35.

of the republic. The lack of discrimination and restraint intrinsic to numerical majoritarianism could thwart popular rule. The advocates of the numerical majority are more likely to make way for demagogues or candidates who appeal to the capriciousness of the moment than for leaders with prudence and character. On the other hand, the concurrent majority gives countenance to the Founders' notion that those who are elected to office should be virtuous citizens capable of acting responsibly in all matters, as well as being amenable to the needs of the communities they represent. Calhoun anticipated that the concurrent majority would draw upon the preexisting personal restraint and discipline among the leaders in the various communities, molding people of insight and wisdom to guide the republic. Calhoun believed that some citizens possessed the capacity to lead:

> [I]n governments of the concurrent majority . . . mere numbers have not the absolute control; and the wealthy and intelligent being identified in interest with the poor and ignorant of their respective portions or interests of the community, become their leaders and protectors. And hence, as the latter would have neither hope nor inducement to rally the former in order to obtain the control, the right of suffrage, under such a government, may be safely enlarged to the extent stated, without incurring the hazard to which such enlargement would expose governments of the numerical majority.[35]

In this regard, the concurrent majority embodies a theory of aristocratic statesmanship. The statesmanship nurtured by the concurrent majority assumes that leaders will exhibit integrity and morality in their daily lives. A theory of concurrent statesmanship requires individual restraint and virtue that will nurture these same qualities in the government and the larger society. The citizenry's opinions and preferences can then be filtered through the leaders, communities, and representative institutions, so that the "sense" of the republic is ascertained.

Positive power can establish a government, but it cannot independently sustain the republic. The balance to positive power is the equally vital negative power: the concurrent force behind the constitution that serves as the most concrete form of restraint in the political order. The negative provides checks against the abuse and concentration of power, while at the same time containing a "mutual negative

35. Ibid., 36.

among its various conflicting interests, which invests each with the power of protecting itself—and places the rights and safety of each, where only they can be securely placed, under its own guardianship." If "negative power . . . makes the constitution," then government as the prudent amalgamation of concurrent measures and voting will provide the diffusion of power necessary to take "the sense of each, through its majority or appropriate organ, and the united sense of all, as the sense of the entire community." In "making" the constitution, the negative encourages government, society, communities, and individuals to exhibit the restraint necessary to resist the sinful impulse and the related quest for control of the public sphere. The negative aids the weaker, albeit important, human propensity to seek the good against the innate "constitution of man which leads those who govern to oppress the governed," eventually causing resistance on behalf of the oppressed.[36]

In providing this contribution, the negative or concurrent element also entails a more inclusive approach to resolving potential conflicts within the republic. Instead of yearning to dictate all decision making by controlling government, the concurrent majority recognizes and incorporates the natural divisions of authority into a coherent whole through a mode of deliberation premised upon compromise. With the numerical majority (and more absolutist forms of governing), the only path to power is found in the domination of the government. In an effort to avoid the oppression that must eventually result from such a struggle, the concurrent majority relies upon compromise among the constitutive parts of the republic to ameliorate tension and promote cooperation. Even though the process of compromise may suggest unanimity of opinion as an appealing goal, in reality, such a thorough consensus is improbable.[37] The concurrent majority, therefore, offers the best practicable indication and public confirmation of preferences. It contributes substantially to affirming popular rule by depending upon this exchange of ideas among the groups or divisions, furthering the peaceful resolution of conflict. Without such a diffusion of power and interactivity among the parts of the republic, decision making could lead to conflict and eventual despotism or anarchy. The alternative to the concurrent majority's reliance on compromise is force. Calhoun urged the avoidance of conflict whenever possible.

36. Ibid., 28, 23–24, 30.
37. Ibid., 50–53.

In presenting his understanding of positive and negative power, Calhoun explained how the concurrent majority served as the greatest theoretical and practical achievement of the American political experience: the government of the concurrent majority implied a sacred obligation to protect the country and to provide order. The "voice of the people," expressed most completely through concurrent means, and united against the sinful impulse, approximated the "voice of God" in this effort to preserve society.[38]

Relying upon a providential view of social and political life, Calhoun believed that republican government must consist of more than the flux of voting and interest coalitions, political parties struggling to possess the "honors and emoluments" associated with patronage, and the pursuit of power. The numerical majority naturally fosters the rise of two political parties determined to control government. It is guided by the desire to monopolize the perquisites that accompany majority status in the regime. The struggle for superiority between two political parties usually limits and confines participation in government to a portion of the majority party. The ensuing political struggles provoke a movement towards the inevitable "concentration of power" in the general government.[39] The only remedy against the maladies associated with republican government can be found in the concurrent majority. As Calhoun's tonic against the devolution of republics into "debased" forms of popular rule, the concurrent majority provides the theoretical and practical ingredients to ensure survival.

Perhaps the most neglected and important contribution of concurrent majoritarianism concerns the cultivation of moral habits and self-restraint among the citizenry. As we have argued, the concurrent majority assists a republic in resolving disputes, and this settlement of differences "tends to unite . . . and to blend the whole in one common attachment to the country." The spirit of compromise reduces tensions and encourages "each portion to conciliate and promote the interests of the others . . . towards purifying and elevating the character of the government and the people, morally, as well as politically."[40] This attribute becomes even clearer when viewed in light of the numerical

38. Ibid., 31.
39. Ibid., 33. Calhoun typically avoided associations with national parties during his lifetime, interpreting their function as self-preservation (*Discourse*, 218). The possibility of a party that would embody the agrarian concerns of a large portion of the nation, or at least the South, was occasionally appealing to the statesman (*Papers*, 15:172; *Works*, 4:394).
40. *Disquisition*, 37, 38–39.

majority's shallowness in relation to the complexities and profound dilemmas of politics. With its goal of controlling government at any cost, it must remain more devoted to political party than to any other objective, including the survival of the republic. In other words, political success becomes synonymous with electoral success. It follows that the numerical majority contains no impediment against the drive for control, or what might be described as political egotism. The numerical majority is further defined by the conflict and struggle for power it fosters. This egotism, or unbridled self-interest, is the predominant characteristic of the plebiscitarian or simple democratic variety of popular rule.[41] Against the egotistic urge, the concurrent majority's promotion of the diffusion of authority remains of vital importance, but its capacity for encouraging self-restraint is potentially even more significant. Predisposing individuals at home and in local associations to practice self-restraint and moral leadership benefits communities in general and society as a whole and eventually impacts the government.

Calhoun made a lasting contribution to American political theory. His affirmation of a South Atlantic republican inheritance during his lifetime encouraged a return to the original diffusion of political authority and authentic popular rule. His worldview serves as the philosophical foundation for a full-fledged theory of politics, and one that is of significance to a larger audience because it frames a notion of personal and societal restraint as an alternative to political partisanship and superficiality. For Calhoun, restraint and concern for the common good were more important than the perpetuation of any particular regime or political party.[42] In presenting his political philosophy in this fashion, we hope that Calhoun might be appreciated as a thinker of great importance for the modern world.

41. Egotism of this sort may also be associated with Thomas Hobbes, although recent studies have aptly presented him as a defender of both self-interest and the commonwealth in opposition to "political disintegration" (David Walsh, *The Growth of the Liberal Soul*, 114).

42. "I would do any thing for Union, except to surrender my principles," in letter to B[olling] Hall, February 13, 1831, *Papers*, 11:553.

# BIBLIOGRAPHY

## PRIMARY SOURCES

*Annals of Congress of the United States*. 42 vols. Washington, D.C.: Gales and Seaton, 1834–1856.

Brownson, Orestes. *The American Republic: Its Constitution, Tendencies, and Destiny*. New York: P. O. O'Shea, 1866.

Calhoun, John C. *Calhoun: Basic Documents*. Edited by John M. Anderson. State College, Pa.: Bald Eagle Press, 1952.

———. *Correspondence of John C. Calhoun*. Edited by J. Franklin Jameson. Washington, D.C.: Government Printing Office, 1900.

———. *A Disquisition on Government and Selections from the Discourse*. Edited with an introduction by C. Gordon Post. Indianapolis: Bobbs-Merrill Co., 1953; reprint, with a foreword and selected bibliography by Shannon C. Stimson, Indianapolis: Hackett Publishing Co., 1995.

———. *The Essential Calhoun*. Edited with an introduction by Clyde N. Wilson. New Brunswick, N.J.: Transaction, 1992; reprint, 2000.

———. *The Papers of John C. Calhoun*. 26 vols. to date. Edited by Clyde N. Wilson et al. Columbia: University of South Carolina Press, 1959–.

———. *Union and Liberty: The Political Philosophy of John C. Calhoun*. Edited by Ross M. Lence. Indianapolis: Liberty Fund, 1992. Includes complete texts of the *Disquisition* and *Discourse*.

———. *The Works of John C. Calhoun*. 6 vols. Edited by Richard K. Crallé. New York: D. Appleton and Co., 1853–1855.

Clay, Henry. *Life and Speeches of the Hon. Henry Clay, In Two Volumes*.

Compiled and edited by Daniel Mallory. New York: Van Am-
bringe and Bixby, 1844.

―――. *The Papers of Henry Clay*. 9 vols. to date. Lexington: University
Press of Kentucky, 1959–.

*The Documentary History of the Ratification of the Constitution*. Vol. 10,
*Ratification of the Constitution by the States, Virginia*. Edited by
John P. Kaminski, Gaspare J. Saladino, et al. Madison, Wis.: State
Historical Society of Wisconsin, 1993.

Farrand, Max, ed. *The Records of the Federal Convention of 1787*. 4 vols.
New Haven: Yale University Press, 1911; reprint, 1986.

Hamilton, James A. *Reminiscences of James A. Hamilton; or, Men and
Events, At Home and Abroad, During Three Quarters of a Century*.
New York: Charles Scribner and Co., 1869.

[Hunter, Robert M. T.] *Life of Calhoun. Presenting a Condensed History of
Political Events from 1811–1843*. New York: Harper and Brothers,
1843.

Jefferson, Thomas. *The Complete Jefferson*. Edited by Saul K. Padover.
Freeport, N.Y.: Books for Libraries Press, 1969.

―――. *Jefferson's Parliamentary Writing*. Edited by Wilbur Samuel
Howell. Princeton: Princeton University Press, 1988.

―――. *A Manual of Parliamentary Practice for the Use of the Senate of the
United States*. Georgetown: Joseph Milligan and William Cooper,
1812.

―――. *The Papers of Thomas Jefferson*. Edited by Julian P. Boyd et al.
Princeton: Princeton University Press, 1950–.

―――. *The Portable Thomas Jefferson*. Edited by Merrill Peterson. New
York: Penguin Books, 1977.

―――. *The Writings of Thomas Jefferson*. 10 vols. Edited by Paul L. Ford.
New York, 1892–1899.

―――. *The Writings of Thomas Jefferson*. 20 vols. Edited by Andrew
A. Lipscomb. Washington, D.C.: Thomas Jefferson Memorial
Association of the United States, 1904–1905.

*Jonathan Elliot's Debates in the Several State Conventions on the Adoption
of the Federal Constitution*. Vol. 2, *The Federal Convention of 1787*.
Edited by James McClellan and M. E. Bradford. Richmond: James
River Press, 1991.

Monroe, James. *The People, the Sovereign*. Philadelphia: J. B. Lippincott,
1867; reprint, Cumberland, Va.: James River Books, 1987.

―――. *The Writings of James Monroe*. 7 vols. Edited by Stanislaus M.
Hamilton. New York: G. P. Putman's Sons, 1898–1903.

Rawle, William. *A View of the Constitution of the United States of America.* Philadelphia: H. C. Carey and I. Lea, 1825.

Tazewell, Henry. Letter to James Madison, July 12, 1798. Unpublished, Rives Papers, Library of Congress, Washington, D.C.

Thornwell, James H. *The Collected Writings of James Henley Thornwell.* 4 vols. Edited by Benjamin M. Palmer. Richmond: Presbyterian Publications Committee, 1871–1873.

——. *Thoughts Suited to the Present Crisis, A Sermon, On Occasion of The Death of Honorable John C. Calhoun.* Columbia, S.C.: A. S. Johnson, 1850.

Tucker, St. George. *A Dissertation on Slavery With a Proposal for Gradual Abolition of It in the State of Virginia.* Philadelphia: Matthew Carey, 1796.

*The Virginia Report of 1799–1800 Touching the Alien and Sedition Laws; Together With the Virginia Resolutions of December 21, 1798, The Debate and Proceedings Thereon in the House of Delegates of Virginia, and Several Other Documents.* Richmond: J. W. Randolph, 1850.

SECONDARY SOURCES

Adler, Mortimer. *We Hold These Truths.* New York: Macmillan, 1987.

Ahlstrom, Sydney. *A Religious History of the American People.* New Haven: Yale University Press, 1972.

Allen, W. B., and Gordon Lloyd, eds. *The Essential Antifederalist.* Lanham, Md.: University of America Press, 1985.

Anderson, James L., and W. Edwin Hemphill. "The 1843 Biography of John C. Calhoun: Was R. M. T. Hunter Its Author?" *Journal of Southern History* 38 (August 1972): 469–74.

Andresen, Karl Adolf. "The Theory of State Interposition to Control Federal Action: A Study of the Kentucky and Virginia Resolutions of 1798, of Calhoun's Doctrine of Nullification, and the Contemporary Interposition Resolutions of Some Southern States." Ph.D. diss., University of Minnesota, 1960.

Appleby, Joyce. *Capitalism and a New Social Order.* New York: New York University Press, 1984.

——. "Republicanism in Old and New Contexts." *William and Mary Quarterly* 43 (January 1986): 20–34.

——. "Social Origins of American Revolutionary Ideology." *Journal of American History* 44 (1978): 935–58.

Aquinas, St. Thomas. *Saint Thomas Aquinas: On Law, Morality, and Politics.* Edited by William P. Baumgarth and Richard J. Regan. Indianapolis: Hackett Publishing, 1988.

———. *Treatise on the Virtues.* Translated by John A. Oesterle. Notre Dame, Ind.: University of Notre Dame Press, 1984.

Aristotle. *Nicomachean Ethics.* Translated by J. A. K. Thompson. London: Penguin Books, 1987.

Ashworth, John. *Slavery, Capitalism, and Politics in the Antebellum Republic.* New York: Cambridge University Press, 1995.

Atwell, Priscilla Ann. "Freedom and Diversity: Continuity in the Political Tradition of Thomas Jefferson and John C. Calhoun." Ph.D. diss., University of California, Los Angeles, 1967.

Augustine, Saint. *The Political Writings of St. Augustine.* Edited by Henry Paolucci. Chicago: Regnery Gateway, 1962.

Babbitt, Irving. *Democracy and Leadership.* Indianapolis: Liberty Classics, 1979.

———. *Rousseau and Romanticism.* With an introduction by Claes G. Ryn. New Brunswick, N.J.: Transaction, 1991.

Bailyn, Bernard. *The Ideological Origins of the American Revolution.* Cambridge, Mass.: The Belknap Press, 1967.

Banning, Lance. "Jeffersonian Ideology Revisited: Liberal and Classical Ideas in the New Republic." *William and Mary Quarterly* 43 (January 1986): 3–19.

———. *The Sacred Fire of Liberty: James Madison and the Founding of the Federal Republic.* Ithaca, N.Y.: Cornell University Press, 1995.

Bartlett, Irving H. *The American Mind in the Mid-Nineteenth Century.* New York: Thomas Y. Crowell, 1982.

———. *John C. Calhoun: A Biography.* New York: W. W. Norton and Co., 1993.

Baskin, Darryl. "The Pluralist Vision in American Political Thought: Adams, Madison, and Calhoun on Community, Citizenship, and the Public Interest." Ph.D. diss., University of California, Berkeley, 1966.

———. "The Pluralist Vision of John C. Calhoun." *Polity* 2 (fall 1969): 49–65.

Bassani, Luigi Marco. "Jefferson, Calhoun, and States' Rights: The Uneasy Europeanization of American Politics." *Telos* no. 114 (winter 1999): 132–54.

Becker, Carl L. *The Declaration of Independence: A Study in the History of Political Ideas.* New York: Vintage Books, 1962.

Beer, Samuel H. *To Make a Nation: The Rediscovery of American Federalism.* Cambridge, Mass.: Belknap Press, 1993.

Berger, Raoul. *Federalism: The Founders' Design.* Norman: University of Oklahoma Press, 1987.

———. *The Fourteenth Amendment and the Bill of Rights.* Norman: University of Oklahoma Press, 1989.

Berns, Walter. "The Constitution as Bill of Rights." In *How Does the Constitution Secure Rights?* edited by Robert A. Goldwin and William Schambra, 50–73. Washington, D.C.: American Enterprise Institute, 1985.

———. "The Meaning of the Tenth Amendment." In *A Nation of States,* edited by Robert A. Goldwin, 126–31. Chicago: Rand McNally and Co., 1963.

Berthoff, Rowland. "Peasants and Artisans, Puritans and Republicans: Personal Liberty and Communal Equality in American History." *Journal of American History* 69 (December 1982): 579–98.

Bessette, Joseph M. *The Mild Voice of Reason: Deliberative Democracy and American National Government.* Chicago: University of Chicago Press, 1997.

Bestor, Arthur. "State Sovereignty and Slavery: A Reinterpretation of Proslavery Constitutional Doctrine, 1846–1860." *Journal of the Illinois State Historical Society* 54 (summer 1961): 117–80.

Bishirjian, Richard. *The Development of Political Theory: A Critical Analysis.* Dallas: The Society for the Study of Traditional Culture, 1978.

Blum, Carol. *Rousseau and the Republic of Virtue.* Ithaca, N.Y.: Cornell University Press, 1986.

Boorstin, Daniel J. *The Genius of American Politics.* Chicago: University of Chicago Press, 1953.

Bradford, M. E. *Against the Barbarians, and Other Reflections on Familiar Themes.* Columbia: University of Missouri Press, 1992.

———. *A Better Guide Than Reason: Studies in the American Revolution.* Peru, Ill.: Sherwood Sugden and Co., 1979.

———. *Original Intentions: On the Making and Ratification of the United States Constitution.* Athens: University of Georgia Press, 1993.

———. *The Reactionary Imperative: Essays Literary and Political.* Peru, Ill.: Sherwood Sugden and Co., 1990.

Brown, Chandos M. *Benjamin Silliman: A Life in the Young Republic.* Princeton: Princeton University Press, 1989.

Brown, George Tindall. *America: A Narrative History.* Vol. 1. 2d ed. New York: W. W. Norton and Co., 1988.

Brown, Guy Story. *Calhoun's Philosophy of Politics*. Macon, Ga.: Mercer University Press, 2000.

Buchanan, Allen. *Secession*. Boulder: Westview Press, 1991.

Buckley, Thomas E. *Church and State in Revolutionary Virginia*. Charlottesville: University of Virginia Press, 1977.

Bundy, Judy. "John C. Calhoun's Reflections on 'Federalist' Number Ten: The Concurrent Majority as a Foundation for American Pluralist Theory." Ph.D. diss., University of Houston, 1987.

Busby, Michael Vardaman. "The Political Philosophy of John C. Calhoun." Ph.D. diss., Stephen F. Austin State University, 1978.

Butler, Gregory S. *In Search of the American Spirit: The Political Thought of Orestes Brownson*. Carbondale: Southern Illinois University Press, 1992.

Calhoon, Robert M. *Evangelicals and Conservatives in the Early South, 1740–1861*. Columbia: University of South Carolina Press, 1988.

Capers, Gerald M. *John C. Calhoun, Opportunist*. Gainesville: University of Florida Press, 1960.

Carey, George W. *The Federalist: Design for a Constitutional Republic*. Urbana: University of Illinois Press, 1989.

———. *In Defense of the Constitution*. Indianapolis: Liberty Fund, 1995.

———. "James Madison on Federalism: The Search for Abiding Principles." *Benchmark* 3 (January–April 1987): 27–57.

———. "Restoring Popular Self-Government." *Modern Age* 40 (winter 1998): 44–52.

Carpenter, Jesse T. *The South as a Conscious Minority, 1789–1861*. New York: New York University Press, 1930; reprint, Columbia: University of South Carolina Press, 1990.

Carr, Craig L., and Michael J. Seidler. "Pufendorf, Sociality, and the Modern State." *History of Political Thought* 17 (autumn 1996): 354–78.

Carwardine, Richard J. *Evangelicals and Politics in Antebellum America*. New Haven: Yale University Press, 1993.

Ceaser, James W. *Liberal Democracy and Political Science*. Baltimore: Johns Hopkins University Press, 1990.

———. *Reconstructing Democracy: The Symbol of America in Modern Thought*. New Haven: Yale University Press, 1997.

Clarke, Erskine. *Our Southern Zion: A History of Calvinism in the South Carolina Low Country, 1690–1990*. Tuscaloosa: University of Alabama Press, 1996.

Clarke, James D. "Calhoun and the Concept of the 'Reactionary En-

lightenment': An Examination of the Disquisition on Government." Ph.D. diss., University of Keele, England, 1982.

Cochran, Clarke E. *Character, Community, and Politics.* Tuscaloosa: University of Alabama Press, 1982.

Coit, Margaret L. *John C. Calhoun: American Portrait.* Boston: Houghton
Mifflin Co., 1950.

————, ed. *Great Lives Observed: John C. Calhoun.* Englewood Cliffs,
N.J.: Prentice-Hall, 1970.

Coleman, Frank M. *Hobbes and America: Exploring the Constitutional
Foundations.* Toronto: University of Toronto Press, 1977.

Combee, Jerry. *Democracy at Risk: The Rising Tide of Political Illiteracy and
Ignorance of the Constitution.* Cumberland, Va.: Center for Judicial
Studies, 1984.

Commager, Henry Steele, ed. *Documents of American History.* 4th ed.
New York: Appleton-Century-Crofts, 1948.

Coulanges, Numa Denis Fustel de. *The Ancient City.* Baltimore: Johns
Hopkins University Press, 1980.

Craven, Wesley F. *The Southern Colonies in the Seventeenth Century.*
Baton Rouge: Louisiana State University Press, 1949.

Croce, Benedetto. *Philosophy of the Practical.* Translated by Douglas
Ainslie. New York: Biblo and Tannen, 1969.

Cunningham, Noble E., Jr. *The Presidency of James Monroe.* Lawrence:
University Press of Kansas, 1996.

Current, Richard. *John C. Calhoun.* New York: Washington Square
Press, 1963.

————. "John C. Calhoun, Philosopher of Reaction." *Antioch Review* 3
(1943): 223–34.

Curry, J. L. M. *The Southern States of the American Union.* New York: G.
P. Putnam's Sons, 1894.

Curti, Merle. *The Growth of American Thought.* New York: Harper and
Brothers, 1943.

Dahl, Robert A. *A Preface to Democratic Theory.* Chicago: University of
Chicago Press, 1956.

Davidson, Donald. *The Attack on Leviathan.* Chapel Hill: University
of North Carolina Press, 1938; reprint, Gloucester, Mass.: Peter
Smith, 1962.

————. *Still Rebels, Still Yankees.* Baton Rouge: Louisiana State University Press, 1972.

Davis, Jefferson. "Life and Character of the Hon. John Caldwell Calhoun." *North American Review* 145 (September 1887): 246–60.

Dawidoff, Robert. *The Education of John Randolph.* New York: W. W. Norton and Co., 1979.

DeRosa, Marshall L. *The Confederate Constitution of 1861: An Inquiry into American Constitutionalism.* Columbia: University of Missouri Press, 1991.

———. *The Ninth Amendment and the Politics of Creative Jurisprudence: Disparaging the Fundamental Right of Popular Control.* New Brunswick, N.J.: Transaction, 1996.

Diamond, Martin. *The Founding of the Democratic Republic.* Itasca, Ill.: F. E. Peacock Publishers, 1981.

Dietze, Gottfried. *American Democracy: Aspects of Practical Liberalism.* Baltimore: Johns Hopkins University Press, 1993.

———. *The Federalist: A Classic of Federalism and Free Government.* Baltimore: Johns Hopkins University Press, 1965.

Dillenbeck, Bruce L. "The Decade after Moses: The Legacy of John C. Calhoun (South Carolina)." Ph.D. diss., Florida State University, 1990.

Dodd, William E. *Statesmen of the Old South.* New York: Book League of America, 1929.

Donoghue, Francis John. "The Economic and Social Policies of John C. Calhoun." Ph.D. diss., Columbia University, 1969.

Dreisbach, Daniel L. *Real Threat and Mere Shadow: Religious Liberty and the First Amendment.* Westchester, Ill.: Crossway Books, 1987.

Drucker, Peter F. "A Key to American Politics: Calhoun's Pluralism." *Review of Politics* 10 (October 1948): 412–26.

Duncan, Christopher M. *The Anti-Federalists and Early American Political Thought.* DeKalb: Northern Illinois University Press, 1995.

Dwortz, Steven. *The Unvarnished Doctrine: Locke, Liberalism, and the American Revolution.* Durham, N.C.: Duke University Press, 1990.

Earle, Timothy. *How Chiefs Come to Power: The Political Economy in Prehistory.* Stanford: Stanford University Press, 1997.

Eaton, Clement. *The Growth of Southern Civilization, 1790–1860.* New York: Harper and Row, 1961.

Ellis, Richard F. *The Union: Jacksonian Democracy, States' Rights, and the Nullification Crisis.* New York: Oxford University Press, 1987.

Elwell, Margaret Coit. "The Continuing Relevance of John C. Calhoun." *Continuity: A Journal of History* 9 (fall 1984): 73–85.

Ely, John Hart. *Democracy and Distrust.* Cambridge: Harvard University Press, 1980.

Engeman, Thomas S., Edward J. Erler, and Thomas B. Hofeller, eds.

*The Federalist Concordance.* Chicago: University of Chicago Press, 1988.

Engler, John. "The Michigan Miracle: A Model for the Twenty-first Century." In *The Future of American Business,* edited by Richard M. Ebeling. Hillsdale, Mich.: Hillsdale College Press, 1996.

Epstein, David F. *The Political Theory of The Federalist.* Chicago: University of Chicago Press, 1986.

Ericson, David F. "The Nullification Crisis, American Republicanism, and the Force Bill Debate." *Journal of Southern History* 61 (May 1995): 249–70.

———. *The Shaping of American Liberalism: The Debates over Ratification, Nullification, and Slavery.* Chicago: University of Chicago Press, 1993.

Farrand, Max. *The Framing of the Constitution of the United States.* New Haven: Yale University Press, 1962.

Faulkner, Ronnie W. "Taking John C. Calhoun to the United Nations." *Polity* 15 (summer 1983): 473–91.

Fears, J. Rufus, ed. *Selected Writings of Lord Acton.* Vol. 1. Indianapolis: Liberty Classics, 1986.

Federici, Michael P. *The Challenge of Populism: The Rise of Right-Wing Democratism in Postwar America.* New York: Praeger, 1991.

Feller, Daniel. *The Jacksonian Promise: America, 1815–1840.* Baltimore: Johns Hopkins University Press, 1995.

Ferenbacher, Don E., ed. *Abraham Lincoln: A Documentary Portrait through His Speeches and Writings.* Stanford: Stanford University Press, 1964.

Filmer, Sir Robert. *Patriarcha and Other Political Works.* Edited by Peter Laslett. Oxford: Basil and Blackwell, 1949.

Finnis, John. *Natural Law and Natural Rights.* Oxford: Clarendon Press, 1988.

Fishkin, James S. *Democracy and Deliberation: New Directions for Democratic Reform.* New Haven: Yale University Press, 1991.

Fitzgerald, Michael Stuart. "Europe and the United States Defense Establishment: American Military Policy and Strategy, 1815–1821." Ph.D. diss., Purdue University, 1990.

Fleming, Thomas. *The Politics of Human Nature.* New Brunswick, N.J.: Transaction, 1988.

Ford, Lacy K., Jr. "Inventing the Concurrent Majority: Madison, Calhoun, and the Problem of Majoritarianism in American Political Thought." *Journal of Southern History* 60 (February 1994): 19–58.

———. *Origins of Southern Radicalism: The South Carolina Upcountry, 1800–1860*. New York: Oxford University Press, 1988.

———. "Recovering the Republic: Calhoun, South Carolina, and the Concurrent Majority." *South Carolina Historical Magazine* 89 (July 1988): 146–59.

———. "Republican Ideology in a Slave Society: The Political Economy of John C. Calhoun." *Journal of Southern History* 54 (August 1988): 405–24.

Fowler, Robert Booth. *The Dance with Community: The Contemporary Debate in American Political Thought*. Lawrence: University Press of Kansas, 1991.

Freehling, William W. *Prelude to Civil War: The Nullification Controversy in South Carolina, 1816–1836*. New York: Harper and Row, 1965.

———. "Spoilsmen and Interests in the Thought and Career of John C. Calhoun." *Journal of American History* 52 (June 1965): 25–42.

Frohnen, Bruce. *The New Communitarians and the Crisis of Modern Liberalism*. Lawrence: University Press of Kansas, 1996.

———. *Virtue and the Promise of Conservatism: The Legacy of Burke and Tocqueville*. Lawrence: University Press of Kansas, 1993.

Gabriel, Ralph Henry. *The Course of American Democratic Thought: An Intellectual History Since 1815*. New York: The Ronald Press, 1940.

Garson, Robert A. "Proslavery as Political Theory: The Examples of John C. Calhoun and George Fitzhugh." *South Atlantic Quarterly* 84 (spring 1985): 197–212.

Gebhardt, Jürgen. *Americanism: Revolutionary Order and Societal Self-Interpretation in the American Republic*. Baton Rouge: Louisiana State University Press, 1993.

Genovese, Eugene D. *A Consuming Fire: The Fall of the Confederacy in the Mind of the White Christian South*. Athens: University of Georgia Press, 1998.

———. *The Slaveholders' Dilemma: Freedom and Progress in Southern Conservative Thought, 1820–1860*. Columbia: University of South Carolina Press, 1992.

———. *The Southern Front: History and Politics in the Cultural War*. Columbia: University of Missouri Press, 1995.

———. *The Southern Tradition: The Achievement and Limitations of American Conservatism*. Cambridge: Harvard University Press, 1994.

Gentz, Friedrich. *The French and American Revolutions Compared*. Translated by John Quincy Adams. Chicago: Henry Regnery Co., 1955.

Gillman, Howard. "The Collapse of Constitutional Originalism and the Rise of the Notion of the 'Living Constitution' in the Course of American State-Building." *Studies in American Political Development* (fall 1997): 191–247.

Glendon, Mary Ann. *Rights Talk: The Impoverishment of Political Discourse.* New York: The Free Press, 1991.

Goldwin, Robert A., and William A. Schambra, eds. *How Federal Is the Constitution?* Washington, D.C.: American Enterprise Institute, 1987.

Goodwin, Charles Stewart. *A Resurrection of the Republican Ideal.* Lanham, Md.: University Press of America, 1995.

Graham, George J., and Scarlet G. Graham, eds. *Founding Principles of American Government: Two Hundred Years of Democracy on Trial.* Chatham, N.J.: Chatham House Publishers, 1984.

Grant, Ruth. *John Locke's Liberalism.* Chicago: University of Chicago Press, 1987.

Green, Fletcher. *Constitutional Development in the South Atlantic States, 1776–1860.* Chapel Hill: University of North Carolina Press, 1930.

Grimes, Alan. *American Political Thought.* New York: Holt, Rinehart and Winston, 1960.

Guinier, Lani. *The Tyranny of the Majority: Fundamental Fairness in Representative Democracy.* New York: The Free Press, 1994.

Gutzman, K. R. Constantine. "The Virginia and Kentucky Resolutions Reconsidered: 'An Appeal to the *Real Laws* of Our Country.'" *Journal of Southern History* 66 (August 2000): 473–96.

Gutzman, Kevin R. "Preserving the Patrimony: William Branch Giles and Virginia versus the Federal Tariff." *Virginia Magazine of History and Biography* 104 (summer 1996): 341–72.

———. "A Troublesome Legacy: James Madison and 'the Principles of '98.'" *Journal of the Early Republic* 15 (winter 1995): 569–89.

Hallowell, John H. *The Moral Foundation of Democracy.* Chicago: University of Chicago Press, 1958.

Hamilton, Alexander, James Madison, and John Jay. *The Federalist.* Edited by George W. Carey and James McClellan. Dubuque, Iowa: Kendall-Hunt, 1990.

Hamowy, Ronald. "Cato's Letters, John Locke, and the Republican Paradigm." *History of Political Thought* 11 (summer 1990): 273–94.

Hanson, Russell L. *The Democratic Imagination in America.* Princeton: Princeton University Press, 1985.

Harp, Gillis J. "Taylor, Calhoun, and the Decline of a Theory of Political Disharmony." *Journal of the History of Ideas* 46 (January–March 1985): 107–20.

Harris, J. William. "Last of the Classical Republicans: An Interpretation of John C. Calhoun." *Civil War History* 30 (1984): 255–67.

Harris, Robert J. "States' Rights and Vested Interests." *Journal of Politics* 15 (November 1953): 457–71.

Hartz, Louis. *The Liberal Tradition in America.* New York: Harvest Books, 1955.

Harvard, William C., and Joseph L. Bernd, eds. *200 Years of the Republic in Retrospect.* Charlottesville: University of Virginia Press, 1987.

Hatsell, John. *Precedents of Proceedings in the House of Commons.* Vol. 2. London: Payne, Cadell, and Davies, 1796.

Heidler, David, and Jeanne Heidler. *Old Hickory's War: Andrew Jackson and the Quest for Empire.* Mechanicsburg, Pa.: Stackpole Books, 1996.

Hernon, Joseph Martin. *Profiles in Character: Hubris and Heroism in the U.S. Senate, 1789–1990.* New York: M. E. Sharp, 1997.

Herzberg, Roberta. "An Analytic Choice Approach to Concurrent Majorities: The Relevance of John C. Calhoun's Theory of Institutional Design." *Journal of Politics* 54 (February 1992): 54–81.

Hobbes, Thomas. *Leviathan.* Edited by Michael Oakeshott. Oxford: Blackwell, 1947.

Hobson, Charles F. *The Great Chief Justice: John Marshall and the Rule of Law.* Lawrence: University Press of Kansas, 1996.

Hockett, Homer Carey. *The Constitutional History of the United States, 1826–1876.* New York: Macmillan, 1939.

Hoffert, Robert W. *A Politics of Tension: The Articles of Confederation and American Political Ideas.* Boulder: University Press of Colorado, 1991.

Hofstadter, Richard. *The American Political Tradition and the Men Who Made It.* New York: Vintage Books, 1948.

Holifield, E. Brooks. *The Gentlemen Theologians: American Theology in Southern Culture, 1795–1860.* Durham, N.C.: Duke University Press, 1978.

Holst, Hermann von. *John C. Calhoun.* Boston: Houghton, Mifflin, and Co., 1882.

Holt, Michael F. *The Rise and Fall of the Whig Party.* New York: Oxford University Press, 1999.

Horowitz, Robert H., ed. *The Moral Foundations of the American Republic.* Charlottesville: University of Virginia Press, 1987.

Horton, Thomas Bruce. "Moses Waddel: Nineteenth Century South Carolina Educator." Ed.D. diss., University of South Carolina, 1993.

Hummel, Jeffrey Rogers. *Emancipating Slaves, Enslaving Free Men: A History of the American Civil War.* Chicago and La Salle, Ill.: Open Court, 1996.

Humphrey, Carol Sue. *The Press of the Young Republic, 1783–1833.* Westport, Conn.: Greenwood Press, 1996.

Hunt, Gaillard. *John C. Calhoun.* Philadelphia: George W. Jacobs and Co., 1907.

Hyneman, Charles S., and George W. Carey, eds. *A Second Federalist: Congress Creates a Government.* Columbia: University of South Carolina Press, 1967.

Jaffa, Harry V. *American Conservatism and the American Founding.* Durham, N.C.: Carolina Academic Press, 1984.

———. *Defenders of the Constitution: Calhoun versus Madison, A Bicentennial Celebration.* Dallas: University of Dallas, 1987.

———. *How to Think about the American Revolution.* Durham, N.C.: Carolina Academic Press, 1978.

———. *A New Birth of Freedom: Abraham Lincoln and the Coming of the Civil War.* Lanham, Md.: Rowman and Littlefield, 2000.

———. *Original Intent and the Framers of the Constitution.* Washington, D.C.: Regnery, 1994.

Jaki, Stanley L. *The Road of Science and the Ways to God.* Chicago: University of Chicago Press, 1978.

Jeffrey, Robert Campbell, Jr. "The Thought of John C. Calhoun: The Key to the Liberal Critique of American Politics." Ph.D. diss., University of Dallas, 1985.

Jenkins, John S. *The Life of John C. Calhoun.* Auburn, Ala.: James M. Alden, 1850.

Jensen, Merrill. *The Articles of Confederation.* Madison: University of Wisconsin Press, 1948.

Kaminski, John P., and Richard Leffler, eds. *Federalists and Antifederalists.* Madison, Wis.: Madison House, 1987.

Kammen, Michael. *Spheres of Liberty: Changing Perceptions of Liberty in American Culture.* Ithaca, N.Y.: Cornell University Press, 1986.

Kateb, George. "The Majority Principle: Calhoun and His Antecedents." *Political Science Quarterly* 83 (December 1969): 583–605.

Kendall, Willmoore. *The Conservative Affirmation in America.* Chicago: Gateway Editions, 1985.

———. *Willmoore Kendall contra Mundum.* Edited by Nellie D. Kendall. New Rochelle, N.Y.: Arlington House, 1971.

Kendall, Willmoore, and George W. Carey. *The Basic Symbols of the*

*American Political Tradition*. Baton Rouge: Louisiana State University Press, 1970.

Kesler, Charles R., ed. *Saving the Revolution: The Federalist Papers and the American Founding*. New York: The Free Press, 1987.

Ketcham, Ralph. *Presidents above Party: The First American Presidency, 1789–1829*. Chapel Hill: University of North Carolina Press, 1987.

Kilpatrick, James Jackson. *The Sovereign States: Notes of a Citizen of Virginia*. Chicago: Henry Regnery Co., 1957.

Kirk, Russell. *America's British Culture*. New Brunswick, N.J.: Transaction, 1994.

———. *The Conservative Mind: From Burke to Eliot*. 7th rev. ed. Chicago: Regnery Books, 1987.

———. "The Prospects for Territorial Democracy in America." In *A Nation of States*, edited by Robert A. Goldwin, 42–64. Chicago: Rand McNally and Co., 1963.

———. *The Roots of American Order*. Malibu, Calif.: Pepperdine University Press, 1974.

Klein, Rachel N. *Unification of a Slave State: The Rise of the Planter Class in the South Carolina Backcountry, 1760–1808*. Chapel Hill: University of North Carolina Press, 1990.

Knupfer, Peter B. *The Union as It Is: Constitutional Unionism and Sectional Conflict, 1787–1861*. Chapel Hill: University of North Carolina Press, 1991.

Koch, Adrienne, and Harry Ammon. "The Virginia and Kentucky Resolutions: An Episode in Jefferson's and Madison's Defense of Civil Liberties." *William and Mary Quarterly* (3d series) 5 (April 1948): 147–76.

Kraditor, Aileen. *Means and Ends in American Abolitionism*. New York: Pantheon Books, 1967.

Kuehnelt-Leddihn, Erik von. *Liberty or Equality: The Challenge of Our Time*. Caldwell, Idaho: Claxton Printers, 1952; reprint, Front Royal, Va.: Christendom Press, 1993.

Kyvig, David E. *Explicit and Authentic Acts: Amending the U.S. Constitution, 1776–1995*. Lawrence: University Press of Kansas, 1996.

Lander, Ernest McPherson. *Reluctant Imperialists: Calhoun, the South Carolinians, and the Mexican War*. Baton Rouge: Louisiana State University Press, 1980.

Leander, Folke. *The Inner Check*. London: Edward Wright, 1974.

Lefort, Claude. *Democracy and Political Theory*. Translated by David Macey. Minneapolis: University of Minnesota Press, 1988.

Lerner, Ralph. "Calhoun's New Science of Politics." *American Political Science Review* 57 (December 1963): 918–32.

———. *The Thinking Revolutionary: Principle and Practice in the New Republic.* Ithaca: Cornell University Press, 1987.

Levy, Michael B., ed. *Political Thought in America: An Anthology.* Chicago: The Dorsey Press, 1988.

Lewis, C. S. *The Abolition of Man.* New York: Macmillan, 1947.

Lienesch, Michael. *New Order of the Ages: Time, the Constitution, and the Making of Modern American Political Thought.* Princeton: Princeton University Press, 1988.

Lijphart, Arend. *Democracy in Plural Societies: A Comparative Exploration.* New Haven: Yale University Press, 1977.

———. "Majority Rule versus Democracy in Deeply Divided Societies." *Politikon* 4 (December 1977): 113–26.

———. "Unequal Participation: Democracy's Unresolved Dilemma." *American Political Science Review* 91 (March 1997): 1–14.

Lindsey, David. *Andrew Jackson and John C. Calhoun.* Woodbury, N.Y.: Barron's Educational Series, 1973.

Locke, John. *An Essay Concerning Human Understanding.* Vol. 1. Edited by Alexander C. Fraser. New York: Dover Publications, 1959.

———. *A Letter Concerning Toleration.* Indianapolis: Bobbs-Merrill Co., 1975.

Lutz, Donald S. *The Origins of American Constitutionalism.* Baton Rouge: Louisiana State University Press, 1988.

———. *Popular Consent and Popular Control: Whig Political Theory in the Early State Constitutions.* Baton Rouge: Louisiana State University Press, 1980.

———. *A Preface to American Political Theory.* Lawrence: University Press of Kansas, 1992.

Lytle, Andrew Nelson. *From Eden to Babylon: The Social and Political Essays of Andrew Nelson Lytle.* Edited by M. E. Bradford. Washington, D.C.: Regnery Gateway, 1990.

MacPherson, C. B. *The Political Theory of Possessive Individualism.* London: Oxford University Press, 1962.

Madison, G. B. *The Logic of Liberty.* New York: Greenwood Press, 1986.

Maier, Pauline. *American Scripture: Making the Declaration of Independence.* New York: Alfred A. Knopf, 1997.

———. "The Road Not Taken: Nullification, John C. Calhoun, and the Revolutionary Tradition in South Carolina." *South Carolina Historical Magazine* 28 (January 1981): 1–19.

Marmor, Theodore R. *The Career of John C. Calhoun*. New York: Garland Publishing, 1988.

Mathews, Donald G. *Religion in the Old South*. Chicago: University of Chicago Press, 1977.

Mattern, David B., ed. *The Papers of James Madison*. Vol. 17. Charlottesville: University Press of Virginia, 1991.

Matthews, Merrill, Jr. "Robert Lewis Dabney and Conservative Thought in the Nineteenth Century: A Study in the History of Ideas." Ph.D. diss., University of Texas at Dallas, 1989.

McClay, Wilfred M. *The Masterless: Self and Society in Modern America*. Chapel Hill: University of North Carolina Press, 1994.

McClellan, James. *Joseph Story and the American Constitution*. Norman: University of Oklahoma Press, 1971.

McCuen, Winston Leigh. "The Constitution of Man: John C. Calhoun and a Solid Foundation for Political Science." Ph.D. diss., Emory University, 1999.

McDonald, Forrest. *Novus Ordo Seclorum: The Intellectual Origins of the Constitution*. Lawrence: University Press of Kansas, 1985.

McGee, Charles M., Jr., and Ernest M. Lander, Jr. *A Rebel Came Home: The Diary and Letters of Floride Clemson, 1863–1866*. Columbia: University of South Carolina Press, 1989.

McGuigan, Patrick B., and Jeffrey P. O'Connell, eds. *The Judges War: The Senate, Legal Culture, Political Ideology, and Judicial Confirmation*. Washington, D.C.: Free Congress Research and Education Foundation, 1987.

McIlwain, Charles Howard. *The Growth of Political Thought in the West: From the Greeks to the End of the Middle Ages*. New York: Macmillan, 1932.

McWilliams, Wilson Carey. *The Idea of Fraternity in America*. Berkeley: University of California Press, 1973.

Meigs, William M. *The Life of John Caldwell Calhoun*. 2 vols. New York: Neale Publishing Co., 1917.

Merriam, Charles. *American Political Ideas, 1865–1917*. New York: Macmillan, 1929.

———. *A History of American Political Theories*. New York: Macmillan, 1928.

———. "The Political Philosophy of John C. Calhoun." In *Studies in Southern History and Politics*, 319–38. New York: Columbia University Press, 1914.

Mill, John Stuart. *Considerations on Representative Government*. Indianapolis: Bobbs-Merrill, 1958.

Miller, Joshua. *The Rise and Fall of Democracy in Early America, 1630–1789.* University Park: Pennsylvania State University Press, 1991.

Morley, Felix. *Freedom and Federalism.* Indianapolis: Liberty Fund, 1981.

Niven, John. *John C. Calhoun and the Price of Union.* Baton Rouge: Louisiana State University Press, 1988.

Noll, Mark A. *A History of Christianity in the United States and Canada.* Grand Rapids, Mich.: Eerdmans, 1992.

Noll, Mark A., Nathan Hatch, and George Marsden. *The Search for Christian America.* Colorado Springs, Colo.: Helmers and Howard, 1989.

O'Brien, Conor Cruise. *The Long Affair: Thomas Jefferson and the French Revolution, 1785–1800.* Chicago: University of Chicago Press, 1996.

O'Sullivan, John. "Mistaken Identities." *National Review,* November 25, 1996, 50–56.

Pangle, Thomas. *The Spirit of Modern Republicanism.* Chicago: University of Chicago Press, 1988.

Parrington, Vernon Louis. *Main Currents in American Thought.* Vol. 2, *The Romantic Revolution in America, 1800–1860.* Norman: University of Oklahoma Press, 1987.

Peterson, Merrill D. *The Great Triumvirate: Webster, Clay, and Calhoun.* New York: Oxford University Press, 1987.

———. *The Jefferson Image in the American Mind.* New York: Oxford University Press, 1960.

Phillips, Wendell. *The Constitution as a Pro-Slavery Compact.* New York, 1856.

Pinckney, Gustavus M. *Life of John C. Calhoun.* Charleston: Walker, Evans and Cogswell, Publishers, 1903.

Pocock, J. G. A. *The Machiavellian Moment: Florentine Political Thought and the Atlantic Republican Tradition.* Princeton: Princeton University Press, 1975.

———. *Virtue, Commerce, and History.* New York: Cambridge University Press, 1986.

Powell, H. Jefferson. *Languages of Power: A Source Book of Early American Constitutional History.* Durham, N.C.: Carolina Academic Press, 1991.

———. *The Moral Tradition of American Constitutionalism: A Theological Interpretation.* Durham, N.C.: Duke University Press, 1993.

Preyer, Norris W. "Southern Support of the Tariff of 1816—A Reappraisal." *Journal of Southern History* 25 (August 1959): 306–22.

Purcell, Edward A., Jr. *The Crisis of Democratic Theory: Scientific Naturalism and the Problem of Value.* Lexington: University Press of Kentucky, 1973.

Putterman, Theodore L. "Calhoun's Realism?" *History of Political Thought* 12 (spring 1991): 107–24.

Rahe, Paul A. *Republics Ancient and Modern.* Chapel Hill: University of North Carolina Press, 1992.

Randolph, John. *Collected Letters of John Randolph of Roanoke to Dr. John Brockenbrough, 1812–1833.* Edited by Kenneth Shorey. New Brunswick, N.J.: Transaction, 1988.

Ravitch, Diana, and Chester E. Finn. *What Do Our 17-Year-Olds Know?* New York: Harper and Row, 1987.

Rice, Daryl H. "John C. Calhoun." *History of Political Thought* 12 (summer 1991): 317–28.

Richard, Carl J. *The Founders and the Classics: Greece, Rome, and the American Enlightenment.* Cambridge: Harvard University Press, 1994.

Ritchie, David G. *Natural Rights: A Criticism of Some Political and Ethical Conceptions.* New York: Macmillan, 1895.

Ritz, Wilfred J. *Rewriting the History of the Judiciary Act of 1789: Exposing Myths, Challenging Premises, and Using New Evidence.* Edited by Wythe Holt and L. H. LaRue. Norman: University of Oklahoma Press, 1990.

Roberts, J. M. *The Pelican History of the World.* Rev. ed. London: Penguin Books, 1987.

Roche, John P., ed. *American Political Thought.* New York: Harper and Row, 1967.

Röpke, Wilhelm. *The Social Crisis of Our Time.* Translated by Annette and Peter Schiffer Jacobsohn. Chicago: University of Chicago Press, 1950.

Rousseau, Jean Jacques. *The Basic Political Writings.* Translated by Donald Cress. Indianapolis: Hackett Publishing Co., 1988.

———. *The Government of Poland.* Translated by Willmoore Kendall. Indianapolis: Hackett Publishing Co., 1985.

Rushdoony, R. J. "The Disastrous War." *Chalcedon Report,* no. 369 (April 1996): 2–3.

Ryn, Claes G. *Democracy and the Ethical Life: A Philosophy of Politics and Community.* 2d ed., expanded. Washington, D.C.: The Catholic University of America Press, 1990.

———. *The New Jacobinism: Can Democracy Survive?* Washington, D.C.: National Humanities Institute, 1991.

————. "Universality and History: The Concrete as Normative." *Humanitas* 6 (fall 1992/winter 1993): 10–39.

————. "Virtue: Real and Imagined." In *The Unbought Grace of Life: Essays in Honor of Russell Kirk,* edited by James E. Person. La Salle, Ill.: Sherwood Sugden, 1994.

————. *Will, Imagination, and Reason: Irving Babbitt and the Problem of Reality.* New Brunswick, N.J.: Transaction, 1997.

Sabine, George H. *A History of Political Theory.* New York: Henry Holt and Co., 1937.

Sandel, Michael J. *Liberalism and the Limits of Justice.* New York: Cambridge University Press, 1989.

Sandoz, Ellis. "Foundations of American Liberty and Rule of Law." *Presidential Studies Quarterly* 24 (summer 1994): 605–17.

————. *A Government of Laws: Political Theory, Religion, and the American Founding.* Baton Rouge: Louisiana State University Press, 1990.

Sangster, W. E. *The Path to Perfection.* London: Epworth Press, 1943; reprint, 1984.

Scalia, Justice Antonin. "For the Majority," *Printz v. United States,* 521 U.S. 98 (1997).

Schambra, William A., ed. *As Far as Republican Principles Will Admit: Essays by Martin Diamond.* Washington, D.C.: American Enterprise Institute Press, 1992.

Schneck, Stephen F. "Habits of the Head: Tocqueville's America and Jazz." *Political Theory* 17 (November 1989): 638–62.

Seller, Charles. *The Market Revolution: Jacksonian America, 1815–1846.* New York: Oxford University Press, 1991.

Shain, Barry Alan. *The Myth of American Individualism: The Protestant Origins of American Political Thought.* Princeton: Princeton University Press, 1994.

Shalhope, Robert E. "Republicanism and Early American Historiography." *William and Mary Quarterly* 39 (April 1982): 334–56.

————. "Thomas Jefferson's Republicanism and Antebellum Southern Thought." *Journal of Southern History* 42 (November 1976): 529–56.

————. "Toward a Republican Synthesis: The Emergence of an Understanding of Republicanism in American Historiography." *William and Mary Quarterly* 39 (January 1972): 49–80.

Sharp, James Roger. *American Politics in the Early Republic: The New Nation in Crisis.* New Haven: Yale University Press, 1993.

Sheldon, Garrett Ward. *The Political Philosophy of Thomas Jefferson.* Baltimore: Johns Hopkins University Press, 1993.

Shklar, Judith. "Redeeming American Political Theory." *American Political Science Review* 85 (March 1991): 3–15; reprinted as chapter in *Redeeming American Political Thought*, by Judith Shklar. Chicago: University of Chicago Press, 1998.

Simkins, Francis Butler. *A History of the South.* New York: Alfred A. Knopf, 1967.

Simon, Yves R. *Nature and Functions of Authority.* Milwaukee: Marquette University Press, 1940.

———. *Philosophy of Democratic Government.* Chicago: University of Chicago Press, 1951.

Sinclair, Barbara. *The Transformation of the U.S. Senate.* Baltimore: Johns Hopkins University Press, 1990.

Smith, J. Allen. *The Spirit of American Government.* Cambridge, Mass.: The Belknap Press, 1965.

Smith, Raymond Elroy. "The Political Mind-Set of the Antebellum South." Ph.D. diss., California State University, Fresno, 1989.

Snay, Mitchell. *Gospel of Disunion: Religion and Separatism in the Antebellum South.* New York: Cambridge University Press, 1993.

Snow, Dean R. "Hiawatha: Constitution-Maker." In *New York Notes.* Albany: New York State Bicentennial Commission, 1987.

Spain, August O. *The Political Theory of John C. Calhoun.* New York: Bookman Associates, 1951.

Spiller, Roger Joseph. "John C. Calhoun as Secretary of War, 1817–1825." Ph.D. diss., Louisiana State University, 1977.

Steinberger, Peter J. "Calhoun's Concept of the Public Interest: A Clarification." *Polity* 13 (spring 1981): 410–24.

Storing, Herbert J. *What the Anti-Federalists Were For.* Chicago: University of Chicago Press, 1981.

———, ed. *The Anti-Federalist.* Chicago: University of Chicago Press, 1985.

———, ed. *The Complete Anti-Federalist.* 7 vols. Chicago: University of Chicago Press, 1981.

Story, Joseph. *Commentaries on the Constitution of the United States.* Vol. 1, edited by Thomas M. Cooley. Boston: Little, Brown, and Co., 1873.

———. *Commentaries on the Constitution of the United States.* Vol. 2. Boston: C. C. Little and J. Brown, 1833.

Styron, Arthur. *The Cast-Iron Man: John C. Calhoun and American Democracy.* New York: Longmans, Green and Co., 1935.

Tabarrok, Alexander, and Tyler Cowen. "The Public Choice Theory of

John C. Calhoun." *Journal of Institutional and Theoretical Economics* 148 (December 1992): 655–74.

Taylor, John. *Tyranny Unmasked*. Edited by F. Thornton Miller. Indianapolis: Liberty Fund, 1992.

Thakur, Anirudh. *The Political Behavior of John C.Calhoun and Mohammad Ali Jinnah*. New Delhi: Classical Publishing Co., 1996.

Thomas, John L., ed. *John C. Calhoun: A Profile*. New York: Hill and Wang, 1968.

Thompson, C. Bradley. *John Adams and the Spirit of Liberty*. Lawrence: University Press of Kansas, 1998.

Thompson, Kenneth W., ed. *Statesmen Who Were Never President*. Lanham, Md.: University Press of America, 1996.

Tocqueville, Alexis de. *Democracy in America*. Vols. 1 and 2. Translated by Henry Reeve. New York: Schocken Books, 1974.

Tooker, E. "The League of the Iroquois: Its History, Politics, and Ritual." In *Handbook of North American Indians*, vol. 15, edited by B. G. Trigger, 418–41. Washington, D.C.: Smithsonian Institution, 1978.

Tourtellott, Marcia Ann. "Off Her Pedestal and Up a Head: John C. Calhoun and Gender Ideology." M.A. thesis, Clemson University, 1995.

Tucker, Beverley D. *Nathaniel Beverley Tucker: Prophet of the Confederacy, 1784–1851*. Tokyo: Nan'Un-Do, 1979.

Twelve Southerners. *I'll Take My Stand: The South and the Agrarian Tradition*. New York: Harper and Brothers, 1930; reprint, Baton Rouge: Louisiana State University Press, 1983.

Voegelin, Eric. *Anamnesis*. Translated by Gerhart Niemeyer. Columbia: University of Missouri Press, 1989.

———. "Equivalences of Experience and Symbolization in History." In *The Collected Works of Eric Voegelin*, vol. 12, edited by Ellis Sandoz. Baton Rouge: Louisiana State University Press, 1990.

———. *The New Science of Politics*. Chicago: University of Chicago Press, 1952.

———. *Order and History*. Vol. 4, *The Ecumenic Age*. Baton Rouge: Louisiana State University Press, 1974.

Wade, John Donald. *Augustus Baldwin Longstreet: A Study of the Development of Culture in the South*. New York: Macmillan, 1924.

Wakeman, Frederic, Jr. *History and Will: Philosophical Perspectives on Mao Tse-tung's Thought*. Berkeley: University of California Press, 1973.

Walker, Mary Meade. "Problems of Majority Rule in the Political

Thought of James Madison and John C. Calhoun." Ph.D. diss., Indiana University, 1971.

Walsh, David. *After Ideology: Recovering the Spiritual Foundations of Freedom.* New York: HarperCollins Publishers, 1990.

———. *The Growth of the Liberal Soul.* Columbia: University of Missouri Press, 1997.

Walsh, Michael, and Brian Davies, eds. *Proclaiming Justice and Peace.* Mystic, Conn.: Twenty-Third Publications, 1991.

Weaver, Richard M. *Ideas Have Consequences.* Chicago: University of Chicago Press, 1948.

Wills, Garry. *Inventing America: Jefferson's Declaration of Independence.* Garden City, N.Y.: Doubleday, 1978.

Wilson, Carson. "John C. Calhoun and the American Political Tradition." Paper presented at the annual meeting of the Southern Political Science Association, Tampa, Fla., November 1991.

Wilson, Clyde N. "Calhoun and Community." *Chronicles* (July 1985): 17–20.

———. *John C. Calhoun: A Bibliography.* Westport, Conn.: Meckler, 1990.

———. "John Caldwell Calhoun." In *Dictionary of Literary Biography,* vol. 3, edited by Joel Myerson, 44–54. Detroit: Gale Research Co., 1979.

Wilson, Francis Graham. *The American Political Mind.* New York: McGraw-Hill Book Co., 1949.

———. *The Case for Conservatism.* New Brunswick, N.J.: Transaction, 1990.

———. *The Elements of Modern Politics: An Introduction to Political Science.* New York: McGraw-Hill Book Co., 1936.

Wiltse, Charles M. "Calhoun's Democracy." *Journal of Politics* 3 (May 1941): 210–23.

———. *Jeffersonian Tradition in American Democracy.* Chapel Hill: University of North Carolina Press, 1935.

———. *John C. Calhoun: Nationalist, 1782–1828.* Indianapolis: Bobbs-Merrill Co., 1944.

———. *John C. Calhoun: Nullifier, 1829–1839.* Indianapolis: Bobbs-Merrill Co., 1949.

———. *John C. Calhoun: Sectionalist, 1840–1850.* Indianapolis: Bobbs-Merrill Co., 1951.

———. *The New Nation, 1800–1845.* New York: Hill and Wang, 1961.

Wish, Harvey, ed. *Ante-Bellum: The Writings of George Fitzhugh and Hinton Rowan Hepler on Slavery.* New York: Capricorn Books, 1960.

Wood, Gordon S. *The Creation of the American Republic, 1776–1787*. Chapel Hill: University of North Carolina Press, 1969.

———. *The Radicalism of the American Revolution*. New York: Alfred A. Knopf, 1992.

Woods, John A. "The Political Philosophy of John C. Calhoun." Ph.D. diss., University of Rochester, 1953.

Yarbrough, Jean M. *American Virtues: Thomas Jefferson on the Character of a Free People*. Lawrence: University Press of Kansas, 1998.

Zeigel, Elizabeth. "The Political Philosophy of John C. Calhoun." Ph.D. diss., Vanderbilt University, 1932.

Zvesper, John. "The American Founders and Classical Political Thought." *History of Political Thought* 10 (winter 1989): 701–18.

# INDEX

Abolitionism: as "immediatism," 164
Acton, Lord: on Calhoun, 32–33, 33n71
Adams, John: as anti-romanticist,
20; mutual trust of states, 45, 46;
mentioned, 38, 67
Adams, John Quincy: in Election of
1824, 66; Calhoun on, 66–68; on "pure
democracy," 67; as "divided self,"
67, 67n74; as "Patrick Henry," 68–76;
"Patrick Henry"–"Onslow" debate,
68–76; identity of "Patrick Henry," 69;
mentioned, 70, 74
Adler, Mortimer: on Declaration, 138n47,
138n48
Ahlstrom, Sydney: on New England, 3;
mentioned, 3n4
Alien and Sedition Acts, 28, 38, 41, 42,
43, 44, 45, 49, 52, 53, 126
*American Farmer:* Calhoun's article in,
85, 85n22; editor praises Calhoun,
85–86n22
American Political Science Association, 1
Antifederalism: and Calhoun, 8;
Lienesch on, 8, 9n16; as political
theory, 8–9; George Mason and, 8–9;
and ratification, 9; Storing on, 9; as
"weaker argument," 9n17
Appleby, Joyce: on "liberal
republicanism," 37, 37n5
Aquinas, St. Thomas: and Calhoun, 101,
101n60, 105, 105n74, 106n79; *Summa
Theologiae,* 101, 106n79; on habit,
105
Aristotle: shares "mean" with Calhoun,
11, 107, 107n83; on practicality, 81;
*Ethics,* 81n9; Filmer on, 97; on habit,

105; mentioned, 90, 91, 92n37, 93, 105,
105n74
Articles of Confederation: Madison on,
52; explicated, 142–45; mentioned, 128,
131, 134, 134n30, 148
Atwell, Priscilla Ann: on Calhoun and
Jefferson, 38n7
Ashworth, John: on Calhoun, 32, 32n67
Augustine, St.: and Calhoun, 100, 100n57,
103, 103n67

Babbitt, Irving, 20n37
Bailyn, Bernard: on republicanism, 36,
36n3; mentioned, 10
Banning, Lance, 49n33
Baptists, 3n4
Bartlett, Irving H.: on Calhoun, 33,
mentioned, 2n3, 127n7, 128, 128n11
Baskin, Daryl, 32n68, 159–60n12
Beard, Charles, 16
Becker, Carl L.: on Declaration, 80n5,
138n48
Berger, Raoul: on Tenth Amendment,
152, 152n87
Berns, Walter: on Tenth Amendment,
151, 151n86
Berthoff, Rowland: on "liberal
republicanism," 37, 37n6
Bill of Rights: mentioned, 4, 43
Blackstone, Sir William: and Tucker, 30;
*Commentaries,* 30n63
Bluffton Movement, 31, 165n25
Boyd, Julian P., 139n51
Bradford, M. E.: on republicanism, 6,
6n12; on Madison as "comic," 49,
49n33; on British influence, 123n126;

extended republic as error, 115;
mentioned, 20, 23n46, 28, 28n58, 38–39,
40–49 passim, 42n14, 66, 77, 89n30, 151
Maier, Pauline: on Declaration, 81n6,
138n48, 139n51, 140n53
Mao Tse-tung, 21n39
Marmor, Theodore, 33, 34n73, 66n72
Marsden, George, 7n13
Marshall, John, 56
*Martin v. Hunter's Lessee* (1816), 56, 56n49
Marx, Karl, 18, 157n4
Mason, George: as constitutional critic,
8–9; mentioned, 9n16
Massachusetts, 43
Massachusetts Bay settlement: political
development in, 2–4; compared with
Jamestown, 4–8
Massachusetts Body of Liberties (1641), 4
Mathews, Donald G.: mentioned, 5n8,
6n10
Maxcy, Virgil: and Calhoun, 155, 155n1
Mayflower Compact (1620), 3
McClay, Wilfred M., 119n114
McClellan, James, 23n46, 56n49, 89n30;
mentioned, 133n27, 160n14
McCuen, Winston Leigh, 33, 34n73
McDonald, Forrest, 9n17, 10n18
McLean, John, 66n73
McWilliams, Wilson Carey, 157n5
Meigs, William M., 127n7
Merriam, Charles: on Calhoun, 30–31;
misunderstanding of Tucker, 30n63;
mentioned, 16, 30n62, 30n63
Methodism: and Founding, 3n4;
Arminianism in, 5
Mill, John Stuart: on Calhoun, 32–33,
33n69, 33n70
Miller, Joshua: on Antifederalism, 9, 9n17
Monroe, James: on Calhoun, 65, 65n71
Montesquieu, 88
Morris, Gouverneur, 133n28

Native Americans, 23n45, 65, 121–22
Newton, Sir Isaac, 23
Niebuhr, Barthold, 123n125
Niemeyer, Gerhart, 6n12
Niven, John: on Calhoun, 29; mentioned,
28n57, 29n60
Noll, Mark, 3n4, 7n13
Nullification: as introduced by Jefferson,
47–49 passim; Calhoun on, 48–49
Numerical Majority: in American
politics, 118, 118n112, 146–50; limits of,
157–62

Oakeshott, Michael: on Hobbes, 103,
103n67, 103n68

Onslow, Sir Arthur. *See* "Patrick
Henry"–"Onslow" debate
Orders of Connecticut (1639), 4
O'Sullivan, John: misunderstanding of,
156n4

Packenham, Richard: exchanges with
Calhoun, 11n21
Padover, Saul K., 48n30
Paine, Thomas, 149n77
Pangle, Thomas, 37n6
Parrington, Vernon: on Calhoun, 30–31;
mentioned, 16, 30n62, 31n64
"Patrick Henry"–"Onslow" debate:
identity of "Patrick Henry," 69, 69n77;
analysis of, 68–76; mentioned, 125
Perdicaris, Gregory: and Calhoun, 88,
88n28
Phillips, Wendell, 166n28
Pickens, Andrew, 62n63
Plato: myth of metals, 119; *Republic*,
119n117
Pocock, J. G. A.: on republicanism, 10, 36;
mentioned, 36n3
Popular rule: on the recovery of, 11, 13,
32–43 passim; Jefferson's influence
on, 45; and nullification, 48–49; and
interposition, 51–60 passim; Patrick
Calhoun on, 60–61; and the federative
principle, 62–63, 78–79, 80; origins in
society, 107–8; and republicanism, 111–
19; as concurrent majority in practice,
117–24, 151–54, 155–71; in Poland,
121; in Iroquois Confederacy, 121–22;
in Rome, 122–23; and the British
Constitution, 123–24; in Declaration,
134–42; as "territorial democracy,"
135–36, 136n36, 143; in Articles,
142–45; in Constitution, 144–54; "two
majorities" theory, 146–47, 157–62; in
contemporary America, 154, 155–71;
numerical majority limits, 157–62
Post, C. Gordon, 80n4
Presidency (Executive Branch):
equilibrium with, 33; Madison on,
58–59; Calhoun as vice president,
66–69
*Printz v. United States* (1997): on state
authority, 152, 152n88
Publius. See *Federalist, The*
Pufendorf, 88
Purcell, Edward A., 101n61
Putterman, Theodore L.: on Calhoun and
science, 82, 82n11, 101, 101n61

Quasi-War, 41